the
_____

ART & MUSIC OF
JOHN LENNON

. . . .

the
ART & MUSIC OF
John Lennon

by
JOHN ROBERTSON

A Birch Lane Press Book
Published by Carol Publishing Group

First Carol Publishing Group Edition 1991

Copyright © 1990 by Omnibus Press

A Birch Lane Press Book
Published by Carol Publishing Group
Birch Lane Press is a registered trademark of
Carol Communications, Inc.

Editorial Offices	Sales & Distribution Offices
600 Madison Avenue	120 Enterprise Avenue
New York, NY 10022	Secaucus, NJ 07094

In Canada: Musson Book Company
A division of General Publishing Co. Limited
Don Mills, Ontario

Published by arrangement with Omnibus Press.

Queries regarding rights and permissions
should be addressed to: Carol Publishing Group,
600 Madison Avenue, New York, NY 10022

Manufactured in the United States of America

10 9 8 7 6 5 4 3 2 1

Carol Publishing Group books are available at special discounts
for bulk purchases, for sales promotions, fund raising, or
educational purposes. Special editions can also be created to
specifications. For details contact: Special Sales Department,
Carol Publishing Group, 120 Enterprise Ave., Secaucus, NJ 07094

Library of Congress Cataloging-in-Publication Data

Robertson, John
   The art & music of John Lennon / by John Robertson
   p.   cm.
   "A Birch Lane Press book."
   Includes discography and index.
   ISBN 1-55972-076-X
   1. Lennon, John, 1940-1980. 2. Rock musicians--Biography.
   3. Artists--Biography. I. Title. II. Title: Art and music of John
Lennon.
   ML420.L38R6   1991
   782.42166'092--dc20
   [B]   90-28953
                                           CIP
                                           MN

Contents

. . . .

Acknowledgements

. . . .

A book of this nature is necessarily a collaborative effort. I would like to thank everyone who has lent their time, enthusiasm and tape collections to the project—notably Peter Doggett and Mark Lewisohn for their source material and advice, Johnny Rogan, Louise Cripps, Mark Paytress, John Platt, Chris Charlesworth and many others. Thanks also to May Pang and Yoko Ono for each taking the trouble to answer my questions in brief conversations in recent years. The staff of the British Film Institute library, the National Sound Archive and the Riverside Studios in Hammersmith were also very helpful. The Westwood One radio series *The Lost Lennon Tapes* proved an invaluable fund of information, as did back copies of *New Musical Express*, *Melody Maker*, *Record Collector*, *Rolling Stone*, and *Beatles Monthly*.

John Lennon's music has been a source of inspiration for two decades or more: researching this book often led me to question the character of the man, but never the stature of his work. Finally, my biggest thanks must go to *National Lampoon*, for the most brilliant portrayal of John Lennon and his art, *Magical Misery Tour*, which is warmly recommended to anyone who is in danger of taking all this too seriously.

Introduction

Relax: this isn't another Beatles book. You won't have to read about the sweaty nights on stage in Hamburg, or the Marcos furore in the Philippines, or those witty press conferences that charmed America at the start of 1964, or the possibility that Brian Epstein might have been assassinated by jealous managerial rivals. The bones of The Beatles' story have been stripped bare over the last 25 years–particularly since the murder of John Lennon gave commentators the ideal opportunity to write an elegy for the group, and their generation.

Lennon has been dragged through the biographical mincer as well. Contemporary events receive minute examination in the media, but history depends on caricature. And the modern media thrive on instant history, leaving participants in the recent past to be caricatured and pigeonholed in their own lifetimes.

Caricaturists exaggerate; it's in the nature of the art. And so history rarely leaves us with complications: men of the past are either heroic or villainous. John Lennon's death on December 8, 1980, has evoked both responses. To Beatles fans, former wives, anyone who has been touched by his imagination and spirit of optimism, the deceased Lennon has become little short of a saint–a martyr sacrificed on the twin altars of peace and love, who had already foretold his own doom in his autobiographical song, 'The Ballad Of John And Yoko! Even at the time, it was difficult to know whether Lennon meant his reference there to Christ's crucifixion as ironic or sincere; a decade after his death, Lennon hagiographers can scarcely tell one from the other.

In the official histories, Lennon's tempestuous private life is ignored–

or at any rate forgiven, as the inevitable residue of major art. But what does that art consist of? Sometimes it seems that the whole of Lennon's career has been conveniently sieved into one song—Lennon's naïve statement of universal optimism, 'Imagine'.

At the other extreme, everyone from literary professors to tarot card readers has spotted the commercial potential of iconoclasm—pulling the giant statue at the heart of the Lennon myth to the ground, like the images of Stalin which once stood guard over the squares of a thousand Russian cities. In these unofficial accounts, Lennon is a bigot, a bastard, a cruel wretch whose private life acted as some kind of obscene parody of the ideals he expressed in his work. Drugs, rape, murder, kicking the baby around the room, attempting to burn his wife on the stove—all in a day's work for the overgrown child who had come to rule the world.

And again, the work is forgotten—or belittled as the drunken ravings of a man who enjoyed brief moments of glory with his Liverpool buddies in the sixties, but who then repeated ever more foolish slogans until even he couldn't hide the barrenness.

John Lennon—angel or devil? Well, that's a subject for another day, and another book. What both approaches ignore is the urge to create—and to perform—that pushed Lennon from Liverpool to Hamburg, to London, and then to New York in the company of a radical Japanese artist who was anathema to Lennon's followers and friends.

It's that urge, and the dazzling variety of art which it produced, that is the subject of this book. Yes, Lennon was a Beatle; he also wrote 'Imagine' and a clutch of other counter-culture anthems. But though these are the works for which he is most often remembered, they scarcely scratch the surface of his total output between the mid-fifties and the end of 1980.

Besides records, Lennon made home recordings—try-outs for new songs, rough and ready romps though favourite oldies, and sound collages that were as outlandish as anything rock has produced. He published two books at the height of his fame, and left sufficient material for a third to be compiled after his death. With his second wife, Yoko Ono, he spent three years pushing at the barriers of rock stardom, creating a series of avant-garde, bewildering and often plain aggravating films, staging exhibitions, planning events, and dedicating their lives to the twin aims of world peace and artistic fulfilment. Along the way, they lived up to one of the more extreme suggestions in Yoko's book, *Grapefruit*: the suggestion in *Shi (From The Cradle To The Grave Of Mr So)*, that the artist should capture their entire life on film. In their certainty that, as artists, everything they did was in some way a reflection of their art, John and Yoko came close to putting this ideal into practice, with the result that the initial years of their marriage are recorded in more detail than the lives of any other public figures.

Every previous study of Lennon's work has either ignored his non-musical activities, or else given them a token status as the bored ramblings of a self-indulgent rock star. What soon becomes obvious, though, as you examine the life and music of Lennon, is that the art, the films, the books and the music are the product of the same imagination.

Lennon wasn't, in his own eyes, a rock star who suddenly felt like making a film: both endeavours were personal statements. It may be true that his efforts in one medium were far more professional and innovative than in another; but that doesn't make them any the less revealing.

That was the impulse which launched this book, then: the realisation that you either take Lennon's art (he would have given it a capital A, of course) as a whole, or you misunderstand it. If nothing else, I hope that the following pages will ensure that you can never again consider his contributions to The Beatles' 'White Album' without remembering that at the same time he was recording the 'Two Virgins' album with Yoko, chopping his furniture in half for a public exhibition, filming the slow rise and fall of his semi-erect penis, and launching balloons into the air in the quest for international harmony. The 'White Album' was what sold, but the films, the abstract noise records and the art exhibitions were equally important to Lennon.

Why has this work been ignored? Because it doesn't fit the myth—or myths, in fact: one for The Beatles, one for John and Yoko. The Lennons were as guilty as anyone in perpetuating myths, as we'll see along the way. The Beatles' myth was created for them, though, as soon as the media latched onto the four-headed hydra from Liverpool with the matching haircuts and quick line in repartee. The group tried to puncture the media balloon early on—to say, as Lennon put it in a memorable phrase, "This is us with our trousers down,"—but it took John's relationship with Yoko, the failure of the *Magical Mystery Tour* movie in 1967, and the Lennon/Harrison drug busts for the 'boys' to return to mortality.

Lennon effectively capsized The Beatles' myth in 1970, with his searing attack on his former colleagues in the *Lennon Remembers* interview with *Rolling Stone*'s Jann Wenner. In its place he erected 'The Ballad Of John and Yoko'—eventually idealized as one of the century's great love stories, to be celebrated in films, a proposed Broadway musical, and a host of 1980 interviews. The Lennons, by this account, were examples to us all: they were human, and they had fought their battles along the way, but love and destiny had eventually conquered all. They had a baby, as ideal couples will, and then Lennon retired from his work to concentrate on house-husbandry, not touching the guitar pinned symbolically over his bed for nigh on five years, and re-emerging only to produce that 'Double Fantasy' of hope for the over-40s in 1980. Lennon's almost immediate death gave the whole tale a Shakespearian air of romance, which even the most bitter tales of drug addiction and antagonism which have emerged since have done little to tarnish.

Except: the myth of John and Yoko, polished to finesse in interviews given around the time that 'Double Fantasy' was released, and supposedly the latest instalment of the Lennons' totally honest and public uncovering of their trials and tribulations, wasn't strictly honest after all. As the American radio series *The Lost Lennon Tapes* has demonstrated, Lennon certainly didn't abandon music for five years in 1975; the songs on 'Double Fantasy' weren't the overnight product of an idyllic holiday in Bermuda in 1980; and, if certain biographers are to be believed, the

Lennons didn't spend their final years together ingesting nothing more toxic than French cigarettes.

Like the media freaks they were, John and Yoko were simply selling a story in 1980–or using a story to sell an album. But the discovery that they had lied about something as trivial as the date that Lennon composed his 'Double Fantasy' songs does suggest that their interviews should be treated as creative works of art more than expressions of absolute honesty.

Honesty was a Lennon watchword; it was a concept which he used to judge his own work and career. So The Beatles were honest in Hamburg, swearing on stage and pissing on nuns out of windows; dishonest when they wore suits, bowed and scraped before royalty and the establishment, and acted like trained poodles in their early movies. Lennon reasserted his honesty when he met Yoko in 1966, began writing about personal feelings rather than romantic clichés, and then clinched the victory of truth over falsehood when he split The Beatles and asserted that he believed only in "Yoko and me, and that's reality." From then on, he equated honesty with Yoko, dishonesty with separation. More to the point, the Lennons' relationship seems to have become alarmingly lopsided: regardless of what he produced without her, their separation induced a state of panic. His celebrated 'lost weekend' of 18 months between late 1973 and early 1975 actually saw him record more music than the 18 months before and after combined; but in the Lennons' myth it was a barren period of depression and loneliness. Forget the fact that his reunion with Yoko coincided with his creativity being stymied: Lennon felt safe, and–if the evidence of much of his songwriting in the last 10 years of his life is to be believed–perpetually guilty, and in her debt.

So I make no apology (he said, apologising) for the fact that much of this book is concerned with 'Johnandyoko' rather than John. Lennon always needed cohorts and partners; maybe we all do. At school there was fellow loudmouth Pete Shotton; at art college the talented and doomed Stuart Sutcliffe. In The Beatles, Lennon found a soulmate in Paul McCartney. And then, after 1966, there was Yoko.

What makes this relationship the most important of his life is not just its length: Lennon spent almost as long with McCartney. For Lennon, Yoko represented freedom from the past: her art didn't belong to the popular traditions in which John had always worked, but struck out for the margins of culture which he had merely imagined in his dreams. And, for the first time, Lennon found a partner who was stronger than him: not as mercurial or brilliant, but with a unified vision of the world that didn't allow for criticism or restraint. Plus, she was a woman, and John found her irresistible.

So when John became Johnandyoko, it was on Yoko's terms. It was her concepts, not his, that fuelled their bed-ins for peace, their films, their avant-garde recordings. But the collision between cultures and souls also allowed Lennon the freedom to dig deep into his own psyche, and strip bare the hurt and pain which his troubled childhood and fishbowl existence as a Beatle had lodged there. What resulted, in records like

'John Lennon Plastic Ono Band', 'Cold Turkey,' and 'Instant Karma', was the finest work of his career—maybe the finest work ever produced in rock. Without Yoko, it would never have been possible.

That brings us back to honesty, and deceit. What Yoko unleashed in Lennon was a ferocious spirit of self-examination, which would allow no pretence or fantasy. (In that light, the title of their 1980 comeback album takes on a new significance.) Having flung himself at the world naked, however, Lennon had to rebuild, which is why little of his later work has quite the same passion or conviction.

So maybe it's possible to see Lennon's entire artistic career as a process of concealment and uncovering, a continual battle between honesty and self-deceit which powered his songwriting from the moment in 1963 when he realised that he could be the subject of his own songs, through to the final confessional works in progress in late 1980. Maybe the Primal Therapy he underwent in the summer of 1970, which inspired the 'John Lennon Plastic Ono Band' album, actually did more than help John deal with his neurosis, and finally destroy his faith in father-figures: maybe it also dampened down the creative fire that had dragged him from 'Please Please Me' to 'Cold Turkey' in six short years.

That's something to ponder while you read, or dip into, this text; in a way, it's the hidden theme. But it's not the reason you're here. Function number one of the book is to drag all Lennon's work together, and try to pin down the creative urges which produced it. Function number two is more prosaic, perhaps, but none the less necessary: simply to catalogue the work, to place it chronologically in the context of Lennon's life and career, and to trace its evolution, through all the blind alleys into which he was led along the way.

Here you'll find full details of all his studio recordings; a survey of those of his home recordings and rehearsals which are known to have survived; details of all his prose writings, from the *Daily Howl* in the mid-fifties to the unfinished *Skywriting By Word Of Mouth* and the enigmatic programme notes for the unfinished musical, *The Ballad Of John And Yoko*; a summary of his film work, from *A Hard Day's Night* to the controversial promo clips which he was preparing for the 'Double Fantasy' album; and an insight into his visual art, from boyhood paintings through the infamous *Bag One* lithographs to his final self-caricatures.

It's a long and winding trip, and the danger is that the major works of art—'Strawberry Fields Forever,' 'John Lennon Plastic Ono Band', 'Imagine'—will be overshadowed by the discovery of a rehearsal tape of 'The Luck Of The Irish', or an uncollected book review in the *New York Times*. The case for the defence is that Lennon scarcely did anything half-heartedly: the same spirit invests his work on 'Sgt. Pepper' and his avant-garde ramblings with Yoko. In this theory, his drunken original take of 'Just Because' from the 1973 'Rock 'n' Roll' sessions tells us as much about the man as his finest creations—though *they* are the reason why we are here in the first place.

Although Lennon worked by himself, on songs, stories and drawings, from the mid-fifties until his death, he also spent nearly a decade with a rock band called The Beatles. Their career has been examined elsewhere in enormous detail; we know exactly what time of day they recorded 'Twist And Shout,' where they were on the evening of July 2, 1963, what colour jackets they wore for which live show in Tokyo in 1966. My initial impulse was not to write about The Beatles at all, but simply to concentrate on Lennon's solo career–beginning, perhaps, with his first collaborations with Yoko in 1968.

Then I realised how ridiculous it would be to write a book about the creativity of an ex-Beatle, without mentioning anything he did while he was in the group. I'm assuming, however, that anyone keen enough on Lennon to read this book is also a fan of The Beatles; and that they will at least know about, and in all probability have bought, some of the major reference works on The Beatles which have been published in recent years. Simply to repeat, verbatim, the information contained in Mark Lewisohn's books, *The Complete Beatles Recording Sessions* and *The Beatles Live!*, would be an insult to you (and to Mark Lewisohn). So you'll have to look elsewhere for the complete Beatles studio log, and the complete Beatles gig list. Here I've chosen to concentrate on significant stages in The Beatles' career, with obvious reference to Lennon's contributions rather than those of the rest of the group. I'm mindful of the bad example of Chet Flippo's biography *McCartney*, which might more accurately have been entitled *Beatles*.

As a recording band, of course, The Beatles survived for around seven years; Lennon was self-consciously creating art for 23. Here, for the first time, is the complete story of that strange and hazardous journey towards a destination that Lennon never reached–and which in all probability he had never quite managed to pin down.

Chapter 1

THE FIFTIES TO DECEMBER 1961

. . . .

Children create stories as a landscape for their play; and they love to express themselves visually on paper. Schooling turns these natural functions into adjuncts of the education system, and ensures that no one creates 'art' thereafter without being conscious of what they are doing. So the birth of an artistic career has to be dated from the day when a child becomes aware of himself as an artist. John Lennon wrote stories and poems, and painted pictures, both at home and at school. But it was only in adolescence that he began to differentiate between what came instinctively, and what was the product of his unique vision.

The earliest examples of Lennon's 'art' which have been exhibited in public are the school paintings which he used on the sleeve and booklet of the 'Walls And Bridges' album. Competent though they are, they tell us nothing about John Lennon the individual. To find him, we would have to look at the handwritten pages of *The Daily Howl*—the cod newspaper which Lennon circulated among friends at school and then at college.

This was not John's first pretence at being a journalist: like many another budding author, he had sketched out a magazine called *Sport, Speed And Illustrated* while he was still at primary school. But *The Daily Howl*, with its mix of word-play, scurrilous invention and lightning pencil caricature, was the clearest ancestor of *In His Own Write* and *A Spaniard In The Works*.

Only fragments of Lennon's teenage scribblings have survived, though it's possible that some of the pieces in *In His Own Write* date back to the mid-fifties. The very fact that Lennon chose to indulge himself in *The Daily Howl* was proof of a lively, restless imagination, however. The decision to prolong the indulgence into his twenties was either a sign of profound immaturity, or else a recognition that within him burned a view of the world which didn't conform to the models that society had on offer. Eventually, music allowed him the option of twisting the world into his way of thinking.

Little of Lennon's literary imagination surfaced in his music until The Beatles had already become established as the most successful pop band in Britain. Playing music was a form of self-expression, and an even more basic need—a method of peer group identification as much as it was a burning desire to perform, and to be seen performing.

The cultural influences on alert Liverpool teenagers in the mid-fifties have been the stuff of legend since the Merseybeat boom of a decade later. Liverpool was a sea port, a regular landing place for transatlantic crossings from New York. Sailors would return to Liverpool with new records they'd heard in the States, thus giving exposure to a type of music which would otherwise not only remain unheard but be almost unimaginable. Britain in 1955 was dominated by light popular music, much of it a watered-down replica of American idols like Frank Sinatra, Johnnie Ray and Frankie Laine. The British equivalents—Dickie Valentine and his ilk—had the sound but not the rhythm, or the sex appeal. The BBC Light Programme was the sole source of recorded music on the airwaves; it housed gentle dance-bands, crooners, novelty tunes and music hall routines, occasionally infiltrated by an invader from another planet, when a visiting American serviceman would request a tune by Hank Williams or Fats Domino.

Liverpool took the invasion in its stride; almost nowhere else in Britain was it possible to hear hillbilly music or rhythm and blues on pub jukeboxes, themselves a fresh innovation alongside the 45 rpm single in 1955. "There is the biggest country and western following in England in Liverpool, besides London," Lennon remembered in 1970. "I heard country and western music in Liverpool before I heard rock and roll. There were established folk, blues and country and western clubs in Liverpool before rock and roll."

Folk—songs of the working man, the miner, the labourer; blues—the cry of the black man on a plantation, or stuck in an urban ghetto; country—the white man's blues: these were influences which Lennon and his contemporaries took on board. They provided a stern antidote to the optimistic, naïve popular music which was otherwise the British staple diet. But as yet there were few musicologists to draw distinctions, and Lennon accepted both as music, nothing else. Elements of the blues, and of Disney tunes or show songs, permeated The Beatles' music to the end.

For Lennon, as for teenagers across the world, Bill Haley's 'Rock Around The Clock' marked a turning point; besides anything else, it introduced the world to the backbeat. No matter that Haley himself was a hillbilly at heart, performing music with a Negro flavour under duress; the song hinted at a more primitive excitement than anything Lennon had heard before.

But it was 1956 that introduced teenage music to Britain. Elvis

Presley's 'Heartbreak Hotel'–an echo-laden, almost incoherent mumble of despair–appalled traditional music lovers; but Lennon and many others recognised that Presley was speaking their language. Nearer to home, Scottish-born jazz musician Lonnie Donegan was putting a backbeat behind the classic folk tunes of Leadbelly and Woody Guthrie, and inventing skiffle. At its strongest, on 'Rock Island Line' and 'Cumberland Gap', skiffle came close to pure rock 'n' roll; and as far as Lennon was concerned, it had the advantage that anyone could play it. Across the country, teenagers founded skiffle bands, learning three or four simple guitar chords, and dragooned non-musicians to play the washboard or beat a dustbin for accompaniment. It was rough, raw and ready, and it appalled the hell out of your elders and betters. For Lennon, whose scholastic career seemed to be leading nowhere, skiffle equalled salvation. And so were born The Quarry Men–named after the Quarry Bank school Lennon and his friends attended.

- ## 1957: *THE QUARRY MEN*

When Lennon founded his skiffle group in March 1957, he briefly named them The Black Jacks; but The Quarry Men was the name under which they played their first known public engagement, at a 'Starmaker' audition in Liverpool on June 9, 1957. A month later, on July 6, to be exact, The Quarry Men appeared at a church fete in Woolton, performing Donegan's favourites 'Cumberland Gap' and 'Railroad Bill', plus a rocked-up adaptation of a Liverpool folk song, 'Maggie May.' According to legend, Lennon also bulldozed his way through Gene Vincent's 1956 rock hit 'Be-Bop-A-Lula'–while other likely inclusions in The Quarry Men's repertoire would have been The Dell-Vikings' 'Come Go With Me', and Presley hits like 'Hound Dog' and 'Blue Suede Shoes'. Whatever the songs were, they impressed 15-year-old audience-member Paul McCartney, who introduced himself to Lennon, and offered to join the band. After a brief run through 'Be-Bop-A-Lula' and 'Twenty Flight Rock' had convinced Lennon that McCartney could not only sing, but also knew the words to songs he himself had never managed to decipher, McCartney was in.

- ## 1958 TO 1962: *LENNON/McCARTNEY ORIGINALS*

By the time that The Beatles issued 'Love Me Do' in 1962, press agent Tony Barrow was able to declare that Lennon and McCartney had composed more than 100 original songs. McCartney would skip school in the afternoons, while Lennon missed another art college class, and the pair would sit hunched over their acoustic guitars in the McCartneys' sitting-room reworking their favourite rock songs.

Of the legendary 100 songs, few were ever recorded. During the 'Get Back' sessions in January 1969, Lennon and McCartney busked their way through otherwise unheard originals like 'Too Bad About Sorrows', 'I Lost My Little Girl', 'Just Fun', 'Thinking Of Linking', 'If Tomorrow Ever Comes', 'Wake Up In The Morning' and 'Won't You Please Say Goodbye'.

These 1969 renditions were humorous and nostalgic, and their composers made little effort to do their early compositions justice. Internal evidence suggests, however, that almost all of these songs were primarily McCartney compositions. It was Paul who immediately mastered song structure, and then married it to lyrics borrowed freely from the Tin Pan Alley clichés of the day. Lennon's forte at this point was lyrical improvisation, adding endless extempore verses to 'Ain't That A Shame' or 'Rock Island Line'. It is significant, meanwhile, that when The Quarry Men made their first recording, it was McCartney who contributed the only original song.

SUMMER 1958: *THE QUARRY MEN* '*That'll Be The Day*'/'*In Spite Of All The Danger.*'

In a home studio run by Percy Phillips in Liverpool, Quarry Men Lennon, McCartney, George Harrison, Colin Hanton and John Lowe recorded two songs on tape, which were transferred on to five acetate discs—only one of which remains, and is now in the possession of Paul McCartney. 'In Spite Of All The Danger,' in Paul's recollection, was one of his compositions, with Harrison given co-credit for his guitar solo. Lennon took lead vocals on the cover of Buddy Holly's hit with The Crickets, 'That'll Be The Day.' The scratchy, tinny evidence of this first Lennon recording is unrevealing; The Quarry Men sound like any enthusiastic bunch of amateurs, while Lennon does his best to ape Holly's vocal mannerisms, without ever managing to conceal his Liverpool rasp.

1958/1959: *COMPOSING* '*Hello Little Girl;*' '*The One After 909;*' '*Winston's Walk;*' possibly also '*I Call Your Name;*' '*What Goes On;*' and '*Long Black Train.*'

Of the Lennon/McCartney songs written during the fifties, these are the only survivors in which it is possible to see Lennon's hand at work. Lennon himself described 'Hello Little Girl' as "my first song," tracing its evolution back to the standard tune 'Delightful, Delicious, De-Lovely.' The more obvious influence is Buddy Holly, however; in fact, as it was originally written, it had a middle eight that borrowed clearly from Holly's 1958 hit, 'Maybe Baby.' Lennon was still performing the song as late as 1962, albeit in rewritten form; then he gave it to Liverpool band The Fourmost as their début single.

'The One After 909' is the best-known Lennon/McCartney song from this period, simply because it was revived in the *Let It Be* movie and soundtrack album. The 1969 Beatles were, for once, faithful to the spirit of the original, which was a simple 12-bar rocker with a stop-start chorus and a wonderfully naïve rhyming scheme (station/location is a highlight), and a line in American railroad clichés which must have entranced these English teenagers.

'Winston's Walk' was an instrumental, one of many in The Quarry Men's repertoire in the late fifties. Unlike McCartney's 'Catswalk,' however, it was never recorded, and all that remains today is the title. Likewise, 'Long Black Train', supposedly a Lennon original from 1959. Conway Twitty performed a song of the same name, however, and the phrase also crops up in the lyrics of the Junior Parker song 'Mystery Train' which Elvis Presley recorded at his final session for Sun Records in 1955. It's likely Lennon was rewriting one of these to fill out time at a Quarry Men gig. Of 'I Call Your Name', Lennon recalled: "That was my song, when there was no Beatles and no group—I just had it around. It was my effort as a kind of blues, originally, and then I wrote the middle eight when it came out years later. The first part had been written before Hamburg, even," i.e. before August 1960. 'What Goes On' was another attempt at an R&B song, which hung around until Ringo needed something to sing on 'Rubber Soul' at the end of 1965.

- **CIRCA MARCH 1960: *THE QUARRY MEN* rehearsing *'Hallelujah I Love Her So'/'I'll Follow The Sun'/'Hello Little Girl'/'The One After 909' (two versions)/'Wildcat'/'Movin' 'n' Groovin''/'I Will Always Be In Love With You'/ 'Matchbox'/'That's When Your Heartaches Begin'/plus various unidentified original songs and instrumental jams.*

The first suggestion that pre-Hamburg recordings of The Beatles had survived came with the publication of Philip Norman's 1981 biography, *Shout! The True Story Of The Beatles*. He described having heard an hour or so of roughly recorded bedroom jam sessions, through which it was apparently possible to catch the first stirrings of The Beatles magic.

Six years later, what appeared to be the same recordings finally emerged on bootleg albums. Advance reports of the sound quality were well founded; and the musical stature of these rehearsals, recorded apparently by Lennon, McCartney, Harrison and new bassist Stu Sutcliffe, is little more impressive, making these by far the most amateurish recordings ever to have been issued on bootleg. But their historical importance is undeniable—our first glimpse of The Beatles at play.

Exact dating of the recordings—even assuming they all come from the same day—is impossible, but the presence of three cover versions (Eddie Cochran's 'Hallelujah I Love Her So', Duane Eddy's 'Movin' 'n' Groovin'' and Gene Vincent's 'Wildcat') all issued in Britain in the early weeks of 1960 suggest that March that year is the most likely source.

Disappointingly, these tapes tell us much more about Messrs Sutcliffe, McCartney and Harrison than they do about Lennon. This was supposed to be Lennon's band, but it is McCartney who takes the lead vocals on everything apart from 'The One After 909', 'Hello Little Girl', Presley's B-side 'That's When Your Heartaches Begin' and a presumed cover version called 'You'll Be Mine'. Only on the last of these does any flash of the latter-day Lennon emerge, with a fleeting monologue reference to a "National Health eyeball." Four years later, it was National Health cows which inspired one of the contributions to Lennon's first book.

Instrumentally, it is impossible to make out Lennon's contribution to these tapes. Harrison takes most of the honours here, on almost endless blues instrumentals designed to show off his less-than-sparkling lead work. And with the exception of 'Hello Little Girl' and McCartney's surprisingly ambitious 'I'll Follow The Sun', all of the songs which sound like original compositions follow standard R&B structures.

· · ·   **1961: COMPOSING** *'Cry For A Shadow.'*

Recognisable new McCartney compositions surface throughout the early years of The Quarry Men and then The Beatles; Lennon's are far less obvious until the eve of their commercial success. From 1961, for example, the only known Lennon song introduced into The Beatles' repertoire was this instrumental–inspired, as its title suggests, by Cliff Richard's backing group, The Shadows, who were the forerunners of a stream of tidy non-vocal groups in Britain during the early sixties, stemmed only by The Beatles themselves.

'Cry For A Shadow' was actually a co-composition with George Harrison, the pair's only known collaboration. It's a safe assumption that Harrison 'wrote' the melody on his guitar, while Lennon supplied the chord changes and the churning rhythm guitar accompaniment.

· · ·   **MAY/JUNE 1961: *THE BEATLES (with Tony Sheridan)*** *recording 'Ain't She Sweet'/'Cry For A Shadow'/'Why'/'My Bonnie'/'The Saints'/'Nobody's Child'/'If You Love Me Baby.'*

By early 1961, John Lennon, Paul McCartney, George Harrison and Pete Best had settled on the name of Beatles for their group—coined by Lennon as a play upon 'beat' music and an oblique tribute to Buddy Holly And The Crickets. As part of their musical education, they won a four-month residency at first the Indra Club, and then the Kaiserkeller, in Hamburg, Germany during the last four months of 1960. They left as a group of unschooled teenagers; when they returned, they had been hardened by booze, pep pills and a gruelling work schedule into a fully-fledged rock 'n' roll band.

They went back to Hamburg at the end of March 1961, to perform nightly at the Top Ten Club—besides occasionally backing up London-born rocker Tony Sheridan, one of the legends of the pre-Beatles rock scene in Britain. Sheridan moved and sang like Elvis, but never scored a hit in his homeland—mostly because he was always working overseas. He had a record contract with Polydor in Germany, however, and when he was called in for a session in the early summer of 1961, he requested The Beatles as his backing band. Further sessions appear to have followed the next year, though at this stage no one is too sure of the exact chronology.

Most sources agree, however, that at least four songs came from these début sessions—The Beatles' second in a professional studio (if that's the correct way to describe the hall of a local infants' school, adapted for the occasion). Their first, the previous September, had seen Lennon, McCartney, Harrison, Sutcliffe and the drummer from Rory Storm's Hurricanes, one Ringo Starr, backing another Hurricane, Wally, on an impromptu version of 'Summertime! One copy of the acetate disc cut at the Akustic Studios in Hamburg on October 15, 1960 survives, but it has never been heard publicly.

The Sheridan recordings did surface, however, and have been reissued at regular intervals ever since. The Beatles backed him up on two rocked-up standards, 'My Bonnie' and 'The Saints;' neither bears any Beatles trademarks beyond an occasional backing vocal. Likewise Sheridan's own rockaballad, 'Why;' while 'Nobody's Child' might just as easily be The Shadows behind Sheridan's mournful lead vocal.

Listen to 'Ain't She Sweet', however, and you'll hear the unmistakable tones of the 20-year-old John Lennon as lead vocalist–a little short on vocal range, perhaps, and overplaying his stylistic touches in his excitement at being recorded, but recognisably the same voice which would emerge on *bona fide* Beatles records a year later. Also cut during the same sessions was 'Cry For A Shadow'–itself stunning proof of the distance The Beatles had covered since their Liverpool rehearsals a little over a year earlier.

- **JULY 6, 1961: *MERSEY BEAT* publishes 'Being A Short Diversion On The Dubious Origins Of Beatles!**

John's first appearance in print came in the début issue of a new fortnightly paper, edited by his college friend Bill Harry–who had met Lennon through their mutual confidant, Stuart Sutcliffe. Looking to capitalise on the burgeoning beat club scene in Liverpool, Harry planned a regular magazine which would feature articles about–and by–the local stars, plus photos, details of forthcoming concerts, and record reviews (soon contributed by future Beatles manager Brian Epstein).

For issue one, Harry approached the acknowledged leader of the city's foremost beat band–The Beatles–for an account of the group's history to date. He expected to receive a straightforward account of names and places, but instead Lennon sheepishly turned in a goonish, pun-laden treatise which was the first outside evidence that the Liverpool rocker was also a notable wit. Like any comic writing, it loses all its humour in translation; best read the piece for yourselves, as it was republished in Bill Harry's anthology *Mersey Beat* in 1978. Cast as a mock fairy-tale, it unleashed Lennon's child-like delight in word-play, and revealed a sense of fun that owed more to the spoken word than to what was normally accepted as written humour.

Besides references to major events in The Beatles' career–the trip round Scottish ballrooms backing Johnny Gentle, the clashes with German police which halted their first Hamburg residency–the piece also introduced a line in self-mythology which the group repeated for several years to come: 'Many people ask what are Beatles? Why Beatles? Ugh, Beatles, how did the name arrive? So we will tell you. It came in a vision–

a man appeared on a flaming pie and said unto them, "From this day on you are Beatles with an A." Thank you Mister Man, they said, thanking him.

- - - **AUGUST 17, 1961: *MERSEY BEAT* publishes *'I Remember Arnold.'***

Lennon quickly realised that *Mersey Beat* might prove to be an outlet—maybe the only possible outlet—for the bizarre poems and stories which he still occasionally committed to scraps of paper torn out of old school exercise books. Luckily, Bill Harry was intrigued by what Lennon had already shown him, and continued to publish Lennon compositions at irregular intervals over the next three years. Lennon appears to have given Harry a selection of pieces for safe keeping; but almost all of these, presumably what John considered to be the best of his writing since the days of the *Daily Howl* in the mid-fifties, were lost when the magazine moved to a new office sometime during 1962.

By then, Harry had already published this Lennon poem, later to appear as the final piece in Lennon's *In His Own Write*. This time it was the epitaph which was the literary form in the firing line of Lennon's zany humour, with a subject who not only changes name but also sex, and then meets a sticky end under a train. Like much of Lennon's early written work, the precursors are easy to spot—the word-play of Lewis Carroll, the inventiveness of Edward Lear, the anarchy of Spike Milligan; what was essentially Lennon was the cruelty, the matter-of-fact attitude to death and destruction, and the quick descent from bathos into gibberish which brings the poem to a kind of conclusion. And like the well brought-up Beatle he was, Lennon remembered his manners: the final lines read:
'Bumbleydy Hubledy Humbley
Bumdley Tum (Thank you).'

In that same issue of *Mersey Beat*, Lennon contributed the first of a series of parody classified ads—in a weird form of vanity publishing, he paid fourpence a word to see his jokes in print. The one-liners, sprinkled through a column of 'Musicians Wanted' ads and fan club announcements, tell their own story:
'HOT LIPS, missed you Friday, RED NOSE.'
'RED NOSE, missed you Friday, HOT LIPS.'
'ACCRINGTON welcomes HOT LIPS AND RED NOSE.'
'Whistling Jock Lennon wishes to contact HOT NOSE.'
'RED SCUNTHORPE wishes to jock HOT ACCRINGTON.'

- - - **SEPTEMBER 14, 1961: *MERSEY BEAT* publishes *'Around And About.'***

Like his dissertation on The Beatles' history, this comic travelogue through Liverpool's beat clubs and other notable landmarks was written to order. It inaugurated what editor Bill Harry no doubt intended as a regular column, for which he gave Lennon the honorary title of 'Beatcomber'—after J.B. Morton's essayist alter ego, Beachcomber.

Despite references to the 'Casbin' and 'Jackarandy' clubs, Lennon's account was strictly a vehicle for another round of anarchic puns and non-sequiturs. Both the club-by-club guide, and one particularly enigmatic sequence of sentences thereafter, were omitted when the piece was reprinted in *In His Own Write* under the title *Liddypool*.

The offending paragraph satirised the agony columns found in the popular press: 'We've been engaged for 43 years and he still smokes. I am an unmurdered mother of 19 years, am I pensionable? My dog bites me when I bite it.'

- **DECEMBER 14, 1961:** *MERSEY BEAT publishes more of Lennon's Classified Ads.*

With The Beatles performing either in Hamburg or on Merseyside almost every night—and many lunchtimes as well—Lennon had more profitable matters to hand than writing Beatcomber articles. But he still found time to visit Bill Harry's offices and waste a few more fourpences on cod classifieds—in this issue wishing an offbeat new year to The Beatles' Hamburg friend (and photographer) Jurgen Vollmer.

Chapter 2

JANUARY 1962 TO
FEBRUARY 1963

. . . .

. . . **1962: *SONGWRITING*** '*Please Please Me*'/'*Ask Me Why*'/'*I Saw Her Standing There.*'

McCartney continued to dominate The Beatles' songbook during 1962; 'I Saw Her Standing There' was basically his song, though he remembers Lennon altering 'She was just 17/never been a beauty queen' to the rather less precise 'She was just 17/you know what I mean.'

Aside from 'The One After 909' and 'Hello Little Girl', the only Lennon composition which The Beatles performed regularly during 1962 was 'Ask Me Why.' Like many of his pre-1964 originals, it boasted a rather uncomfortable melodic structure, hooked to a Latin rhythm no doubt inspired by the band's cheery rendition of The Coasters' single, 'Besame Mucho.' The lyrics were as contrived as ever, though it's hard not to believe that Lennon took some sly pleasure from singing 'I can't conceive' to audiences of pubescent Cavern-goers...

As for 'Please Please Me,' that was "My attempt at writing a Roy Orbison song." A year before The Beatles first supported, and then topped the bill over the Big O on a British tour, Lennon had been inspired by hits like 'In Dreams' and 'Only The Lonely' to write a song in the same dramatic vein. In its original arrangement, 'Please Please Me' had none of the zest of the eventual Beatles recording, though Lennon still had high hopes of its commercial appeal. Lyrically, the song went back to an even earlier influence, connected with Lennon's mother: one of the Bing Crosby numbers she had sung to her son had the memorable chorus line, 'Please lend your ears to my pleas.' The word-play struck a chord, as ever, and the double 'please' duly turned up in a Lennon composition as well.

• **JANUARY 1, 1962: *THE BEATLES* Decca auditions 'Like Dreamers Do'/ 'Money'/'Till There Was You'/'The Sheik Of Araby'/'To Know Her Is To Love Her'/'Take Good Care Of My Baby'/'Memphis'/'Sure To Fall'/'Hello Little Girl'/'Three Cool Cats'/'Crying, Waiting, Hoping'/'Love Of The Loved'/ 'September In The Rain'/'Besame Mucho'/'Searchin'.'**

During late 1961, newly-appointed Beatles manager Brian Epstein took a hand-held recorder into the Cavern Club in Liverpool, and taped a selection of songs as a demonstration of the group's abilities. The resulting tape was played to Liverpool record reviewer, and Decca Records sleeve-notes writer, Tony Barrow. He declined to mention the recordings in print; he later described the sound quality of the tape as 'abominable'. But as a favour to Epstein, he put the manager in touch with his employer in London.

And so it was that on New Year's Day 1962, The Beatles found themselves at the Decca Records studios in West Hampstead, attempting to impress A&R assistant Mike Smith into giving them a record contract. Unbeknown to them, Smith had also arranged to audition a more local band, Brian Poole And The Tremeloes, the same afternoon; and his boss, A&R man Dick Rowe, allowed Smith to sign one band or the other. On the basis of their auditions, and the fact that The Tremeloes would be easier to drag into the studio at short notice, Smith went with Poole's band—thus winning for the luckless Rowe the undeserved title of 'The Man Who Turned Down The Beatles', a tag that followed him to his grave.

The important question is whether Rowe and Smith were right not to sign The Beatles. On the evidence of the legendary audition tape, the answer is probably yes. As on the 1960 rehearsal tape by The Quarry Men, John Lennon takes a surprising backseat; George Harrison was the featured lead vocalist on 'Three Cool Cats', 'Crying, Waiting, Hoping', 'The Sheik Of Araby' and 'Take Good Care Of My Baby,' while an appallingly over-dramatic Paul McCartney held the limelight on 'Love Of The Loved', 'September In The Rain', 'Besame Mucho', 'Searchin',' 'Like Dreamers Do', 'Sure To Fall' and 'Till There Was You'.

That left Lennon with four contributions—one of which was the revamped 'Hello Little Girl'. Gone was the 'Maybe Baby' middle eight, and Holly-ish guitar intro; in its place was a bridge which any professional tunesmith could have written, with all the lack of imagination that that suggests. The whole song was taken at a much jauntier tempo; this had the dual effect of taking away The Everly Brothers feel of the original arrangement, and substituting the first true stirrings of what became known as Merseybeat.

With no suitable pop material to hand—Brian Epstein having vetoed raunchier material like 'The One After 909'—Lennon was forced to rely on covers for the rest of his contributions to the morning's events. Strangely tired versions of The Teddy Bears' 'To Know Her Is To Love Her' and Chuck Berry's 'Memphis' gave no hint of Lennon's vocal potential; only

Barrett Strong's 'Money,' built around guitars playing the same riff in tandem, without any of the stop-start rhythms The Beatles gave the tune later, represented anything like Lennon in full voice, and even then his nervousness was apparent. If Decca had signed The Beatles in January 1962, might Lennon have been consigned to history as The Beatles' third-string vocalist?

• • • MARCH/JUNE 1962: *BBC RECORDING SESSIONS*

Between March 1962 and June 1965, The Beatles made regular recordings for the BBC Light Programme radio service. Complex agreements with the Musicians' Union over the number of records which could be broadcast each day—needle time, as it was known—meant that the BBC relied heavily on specially recorded or even live material to fill out their pop programmes. As a result, it was not uncommon for even the most major stars to report to a small studio at Broadcasting House so they could tape special inserts for shows like *Saturday Club* and *Easy Beat*.

The Beatles were no exception, and their BBC recordings represent a goldmine for the band's archivists. Almost all of their session appearances have survived on tape, though often only in lo-fi quality. Two shows in March and June 1962 require special mention, as they were the only BBC sessions to feature The Beatles with Pete Best, rather than Ringo Starr. Their *Teenager's Turn* appearance on March 3 saw Lennon taking the lead vocal on 'Memphis' and The Marvelettes' 'Please Mr Postman', while McCartney was spotlighted on Roy Orbison's 'Dream Baby.'

An appearance on the live show *Here We Go* on June 15 had George Harrison singing Joe Brown's hit 'A Picture Of You', McCartney reprising his Decca audition track 'Besame Mucho', and Lennon providing a national première of his own 'Ask Me Why.'

• • • APRIL 1962: *RECORDING WITH TONY SHERIDAN* 'Sweet Georgia Brown'/'Swanee River.'

The Beatles definitely cut a second session with Tony Sheridan around this time, though exact details are vague. Some sources say that 'Swanee River' was actually recorded by Sheridan's regular backing crew, The Beat Brothers, and that 'Skinny Minnie' was The Beatles' back-up contribution. Either way, there is nothing to identify any of The Beatles on these three recordings. Sheridan subsequently recut his lead vocal on 'Sweet Georgia Brown' in 1963 to include new lyrics about The Beatles' success.

• • • JUNE 6, 1962: *EMI AUDITION* 'Ask Me Why'/'P.S. I Love You'/'Love Me Do'/ 'Besame Mucho.'

EMI's major labels had already turned down The Beatles when Brian

Epstein secured them one last chance—a hearing from Parlophone A&R chief, George Martin. In fact, it was his assistant, Ron Richards, who originally took charge of the session; only when he and engineer Norman Smith realised that The Beatles might be worth further investigation was Martin dragged out of the EMI canteen.

The evergreen McCartney showcase 'Besame Mucho' aside, the band chose to demonstrate their own material. 'Ask Me Why' was once again Lennon's solo turn, while The Beatles also played two recent McCartney compositions, 'Love Me Do' and 'P.S. I Love You.' 'Love Me Do' had yet to receive its trademark harmonica opening, so Lennon was restricted to harmony vocals on both tunes.

Around the same time, The Beatles made two sets of recordings at the Cavern Club in Liverpool. An afternoon session behind locked doors saw them tape reference versions of Lennon's 'The One After 909'—effectively unchanged since the 1960 rehearsal take—and McCartney's jaunty instrumental, 'Catswalk.'

A month or so later, an entire Beatles lunchtime session from the Cavern was also recorded; it is not certain whether this was at the behest of the group, or simply an enthusiastic fan. The tape featured just one Lennon/McCartney original, 'Ask Me Why,' plus versions of covers familiar to us from other sets of Beatles recordings, like 'Please Mr Postman,' 'Words Of Love,' 'Dizzy Miss Lizzy' and 'Matchbox,' all with Lennon on lead vocals; 'I Wish I Could Shimmy Like My Sister Kate,' 'Hippy Hippy Shake,' 'Your Feet's Too Big,' 'Till There Was You,' and 'Dream Baby' (all with McCartney taking the lead); and 'Roll Over Beethoven,' featuring George.

Less familiar additions to the group's repertoire included Tommy Roe's hit 'Sharing You,' also sung by George, as was the old Elvis Presley country song, 'I Forgot To Remember To Forget' and The Coasters' 'Young Blood;' and Paul singing James Ray's hit 'If You Gotta Make A Fool Of Somebody' and—ironically, in light of the fact that Lennon stole its harmonica sound for 'Love Me Do'—Bruce Channel's 'Hey Baby.'

• **AUGUST 22, 1962: *THE BEATLES* recording *'Some Other Guy'* and *'Kansas City; Hey Hey Hey Hey' (Granada TV)*.**

Though the clip wasn't aired until October, Granada visited the Cavern on this date to take note of what was fast becoming a local Liverpudlian phenomenon—the fact that the city's most popular beat group were virtually unknown outside of the Merseyside area. Granada's cameras captured one of the band's first gigs with their new drummer, Ringo Starr, who had just replaced the hapless Pete Best. A hint of the protests that followed can be heard in Granada's film of Lennon performing Barrett Strong's 'Some Other Guy'—not only a favourite Beatles cover of the period, and more evidence of Lennon's natural empathy with American R&B, but also worth noting because the simple two-note piano intro of Strong's record cropped up almost eight years later as the start of The Plastic Ono Band's 'Instant Karma.'

1 3

Granada never broadcast their film of 'Kansas City,' and the footage no longer exists with sound. Other performances of 'Some Other Guy' were taped around the same time, however, and persistent rumours suggest that manager Brian Epstein pressed up a small quantity of acetates of one such recording, for sale solely in his Liverpool music store.

· · ·   AUGUST 23, 1962: *MERSEY BEAT* publishes 'Small Sam.'

Far removed from the dramas of The Beatles' line-up changes, and after a hiatus of almost a year, Lennon–alias 'Beatcomber'–returned to writing for *Mersey Beat*, rather than filling its editorial pages with his beat group exploits. 'Small Sam' was not included in any of Lennon's books, though in late 1964 he did request a copy of this issue of *Mersey Beat* from Bill Harry so that he could revise the piece for *A Spaniard In The Works*. He evidently decided that this extended joke wasn't worth reprinting, though its humour–based around Small Sam's possession of a club foot–would not have been out of place alongside the numerous cripples who litter the pages of both Lennon's early prose collections.

· · ·   SEPTEMBER 4 AND 11, 1962: *THE BEATLES* recording 'How Do You Do It'/'Love Me Do'/'P.S. I Love You'/'Please Please Me.'

When Parlophone's producer George Martin sent The Beatles word of their first official EMI recording session, he enclosed a demo tape of a Mitch Murray composition he felt they should record as their début single. Lennon took the lead vocal on 'How Do You Do It', and turned in an appropriately lightweight performance on a catchy but insubstantial pop song. The track was eventually considered less suitable than McCartney's 'Love Me Do' and 'P.S. I Love You', and was never released.

The Beatles also had a stab at recording the Orbison-styled 'Please Please Me' during their second session; George Martin rejected their arrangement, and sent them away to prepare a more upbeat version.

· · ·   SEPTEMBER 6, 1962: *MERSEY BEAT* publishes 'On Safairy With Whide Hunter.'

Literary parody was still Lennon's inspiration in this brief 'story,' which according to the credits in *In His Own Write* was written 'in conjugal with Paul'–though in *Mersey Beat* it appeared under the regular 'Beatcomber' byline. The McCartney involvement suggests that this was a fairly recent composition, a theory backed up by the opening lines, which are based on the lyrics to The Tokens' early 1962 hit, 'The Lion Sleeps Tonight' (also known as 'Wimoweh').

The piece is full of obvious puns–with characters like 'Elepoon Bill' and 'Jumble Jim', Bungalow Bill doesn't seem too far away. And the references to 'rhinostrills and hippoposthumous' show both where literary critics thought they caught the inspiration of James Joyce, and more pertinently what Lennon was borrowing from the language of Lewis

Carroll. The parody, and the word-play, are their own ends here; there is none of the social satire found in Lennon's slightly later work.

On Safairy was reprinted in *In His Own Write* in 1964: just to prove that Lennon did more than simply reproduce his early writings verbatim, he added one explanatory sentence to the 'narrative', and also simplified some of the puns.

NOVEMBER 26, 1962: *THE BEATLES* recording *'Please Please Me'/'Ask Me Why'/'The Tip Of My Tongue'*

'Love Me Do' was duly issued as The Beatles' first single on October 5, 1962. Its mild chart success prompted a swift follow-up, and between September and November Lennon and McCartney had effectively spruced up the arrangement of 'Please Please Me' to the point where it was the obvious choice as their second single (issued on January 11, 1963).

The surge in confidence between this recording and the far more tentative 'Love Me Do' is remarkable, as is Lennon's assured lead vocal—most noticeable in the 'Come on' passages leading up to the chorus, when the sexual nature of his invitation is made obvious.

Little of that assurance carried over into Lennon's 'Ask Me Why;' even less into the Lennon/McCartney collaboration 'The Tip Of My Tongue', a true dog of a song which they later passed on to the luckless Tommy Quickly. The final verse included the mawkish lines: 'Soon enough my time will come/And after all is said and done/I'll marry you and we will live as one'. And the tune was no more memorable.

DECEMBER 31, 1962: *THE BEATLES* live in Hamburg 'I Saw Her Standing There'/'Nothin' Shakin''/'Twist And Shout'/'Falling In Love Again'/'Ask Me Why'/'Sheila'/'To Know Her Is To Love Her'/'Little Queenie'/ 'Red Sails In The Sunset'/'Reminiscing'/'Matchbox'/'I'm Talkin' 'Bout You'/'Long Tall Sally'/'I Wish I Could Shimmy Like My Sister Kate'/'Roll Over Beethoven'/'Your Feet's Too Big'/'Hippy Hippy Shake'/'I'm Gonna Sit Right Down And Cry'/'Sweet Little Sixteen'/'Lend Me Your Comb'/'Mr Moonlight'/'I Remember You'/'A Taste Of Honey'/'Everybody's Trying To Be My Baby'/'Besame Mucho'/'Where Have You Been All My Life'/'Till There Was You'/'Kansas City; Hey Hey Hey Hey'/'Red Hot;' (they also provide backing for an unknown vocalist on 'Be-Bop-A-Lula' and 'Hallelujah I Love Her So').

Although 'Love Me Do' was already showing in the British charts, The Beatles were under contract for one more residency at the Star Club in Hamburg, from December 18 to 31. On the final night of their engagement, the group were recorded on amateur equipment by Ted Taylor, the leader of another Liverpool band with a Hamburg residency, Kingsize Taylor And The Dominos. The tapes passed into the hands of former Beatles manager Allan Williams, who in turn offered them to current Beatles boss Brian Epstein. Epstein took a brief listen to these noisy, muddy tapes and turned them down. They then lay in the bottom of a cupboard for almost a decade, until Williams rediscovered them, and began negotiating for an official release.

Williams played the tapes to selected journalists in the mid-seventies, building up a modest media buzz. After undergoing remixing and cleaning up as far as late seventies technology would allow, 26 songs were issued on a German double album, then later in Britain, in that summer. A further four recordings surfaced soon afterwards on the equivalent American release.

In fact, it appears that Williams had access to more than one Beatles show from the Hamburg stint; or at least more than one set from that night. Alternative versions of some songs have since appeared on bootleg, together with Harrison's cover of Billy Lee Riley's rockabilly classic, 'Red Hot.' A version of 'Hully Gully' included on an American release of the tapes is not by The Beatles, however, but by another British band, Cliff Bennett And The Rebel Rousers.

"In Liverpool, Hamburg and other dance halls...what we generated was fantastic; we played straight rock, and there was nobody to touch us in Britain," Lennon recalled in 1970. "We always missed the club dates because that's when we were playing music."

By the end of December 1962, The Beatles were outgrowing the Hamburg beat clubs, and little of that excitement was captured on the Star Club tape. As a document, however, the recording does suggest what The Beatles must have been like before Brian Epstein smartened them up and put them in suits. Lennon baits the drunken club audience throughout the set, and the group show their contempt for the occasion with appropriate lyrical changes, turning 'A Taste Of Honey' into 'A Waste Of Money' and 'Shimmy Shimmy' into 'Shitty Shitty.'

The band deigned to perform only two original songs for the clubgoers— 'I Saw Her Standing There' and 'Ask Me Why.' The rest of the tape charts their taste in covers, with Lennon in charge on 'To Know Her Is To Love Her,' Chuck Berry's 'Little Queenie,' 'I'm Talkin' 'Bout You' and 'Sweet Little Sixteen,' 'I'm Gonna Sit Right Down And Cry' (as recorded by Elvis Presley on his 1956 début album), 'Mr Moonlight,' Arthur Alexander's favourite 'Where Have You Been All My Life,' and a brief version of the Bert Berns song trademarked by The Isley Brothers, 'Twist And Shout.'

• • •   **JANUARY 26, 1963: *THE BEATLES* recording 'Keep Your Hands Off My Baby'/'Some Other Guy' for the BBC.**

As we'll see shortly, The Beatles performed many more songs on radio in 1963 than they recorded for EMI; and one of them was Lennon's rendition of the Little Eva hit, 'Keep Your Hands Off My Baby.' Its title alone marked it out as a likely Lennon vehicle, though the song wasn't as vicious as its moniker suggested. It warrants mention here as one of the few non-originals that The Beatles played on tour early in 1963; and because constant rumour (and apparent confirmation in the pages of the British music press) suggested that the group recorded the song for the first album. It doesn't show up in the EMI logs of the band's studio sessions, but a reviewer for *Beat Monthly* actually described the track when he first heard an acetate of 'Please Please Me', which hints that there might be some truth in the tale after all.

• **FEBRUARY 1, 1963: *THE BEATLES*** recording *'I Saw Her Standing There'*/ *'Misery'*/*'Anna'*/*'Chains'*/*'Boys'*/*'Baby It's You'*/*'Do You Want To Know A Secret'*/*'A Taste Of Honey'*/*'There's A Place'*/*'Hold Me Tight'*/*'Twist And Shout.'*

The single-day session which produced the bulk of The Beatles' 'Please Please Me' album, plus an early rejected cut of McCartney's 'Hold Me Tight', has become the stuff of legend. The finished record has plenty of raw edges; listen to the songs in the order in which they were recorded, and you can hear their voices fray, until the climactic first take of 'Twist And Shout' which would have assured Lennon of minor league immortality if he had never recorded another note. The Beatles took that song, like most white group R&B, at full volume; as early as February 1963, Lennon was translating his emotions into vocal noise, producing as frenzied a piece of pop music as anything cut outside Memphis.

Lennon's other covers that day have their moments, as well: the arrangement of Arthur Alexander's 'Anna' dragged, but not Lennon's vocal, which set the scene for his own efforts in a similar vein later in the year. Likewise The Shirelles' 'Baby It's You', where after some initial nervousness Lennon relaxed into the song, and produced another smooth vocal that bit if you came too close.

The important news here, though, was the sudden emergence of a batch of new Lennon/McCartney compositions. All three were primarily Lennon songs, which hadn't so far surfaced in their live shows. 'Do You Want To Know A Secret' said least of the three, though it was also the most commercial, as fellow Liverpudlian Billy J. Kramer proved a little later in the year. Lennon thought little enough of the song, which was inspired by another Walt Disney film tune he remembered his mother singing, to give it to George to sing: "I thought it would be a good vehicle for him because it only had three notes and he wasn't the best singer in the world," he explained shortly before his death.

'Misery' was another attempted giveaway; he and Paul wrote it for Helen Shapiro at the start of 1963, but eventually had to rely on Kenny Lynch's cover. The first line of his version went 'You've been treating me bad', which is how it appeared on the sheet music; but Lennon and McCartney turned it into a chip-on-my-shoulder piece of romantic paranoia, with 'The world is treating me bad.' What's remarkable is not the simplicity of the song structure, or its admission that even big Lennons cry, but the sheer fact that a song about misery can sound so damn optimistic. In fact, like his 1974 version of Fats Domino's 'Ain't That A Shame', the whole piece had a swagger that suggested you shouldn't believe a single word.

'There's A Place' proved to be the landmark song, however. It had another unorthodox melodic opening, like 'Ask Me Why'—a hesitation before the action began. But it was the words which counted: Lennon's first real piece of introspection. 'There's a place where I can go/when I feel low/when I feel blue/and it's my mind/and there's no time when I'm alone.' Married to a joyous burst of harmonies, these simple lines escaped most people's attention; but this was Lennon's first admission that the external Beatle didn't tell the whole story. In times of trouble, he might escape inside—perhaps into the same pool of imagination that was already producing the stories, poems and conceits which would shortly be anthologised in *In His Own Write*.

Chapter 3

MARCH 1963 TO MARCH 1964

. . . .

MARCH 5, 1963: ***THE BEATLES*** *recording 'From Me To You'/'Thank You Girl'/'The One After 909.'*

This was the era of true Lennon/McCartney collaboration, and 'From Me To You' was composed on February 27, between shows in York and Shrewsbury on their first national tour. The recording session was already booked, and both songs which eventually made up their third single show signs of having been written to order. 'From Me To You' was perfectly commercial for the time, even a little simplistic; although its one-syllable lyrics could be adopted by any lovesick teenager as their own, the song was early proof that The Beatles could be as calculating as any professional songsmiths. It was an art which came under increasing demand over the next 12 months—not so much for The Beatles' own records, as for their gifts to fellow artists in the Brian Epstein management stable.

'Thank You Girl' was, as Lennon admitted in 1980, composed during the same quest for an A-side. Its ingredients were appealing enough—the rough Merseyside harmonies, the 'oh oh' hook, Lennon's raucous harmonica—but the entire performance never gelled. Not that the song was under any great competition as the next B-side: the band also attempted Lennon's 'The One After 909' during the same session, and in the effort to make it sound like R&B rather than the straight rock 'n' roll it patently was, they lost all the innocent enthusiasm which makes their 1969 revival of the piece so attractive. The importance of the occasion also drove George Harrison into one of his least impressive guitar solos.

· · · · **MARCH 16, 1963:** *THE BEATLES* recording 'Too Much Monkey Business' and 'I'm Talkin' 'Bout You' for the BBC.

As their record sales advanced, so the art of promotion became ever more important. During 1962, The Beatles' live shows had featured songs they felt like playing; now material they had issued on record, or were about to, took pride of place. Partly that was down to a natural pride in their achievements; partly it was sheer business sense.

But the Beatles retained enough enthusiasm for the music to dip into their past repertoire for their BBC radio performances, and this live recording for the BBC's pop flagship, *Saturday Club*, saw Lennon unveiling fiery renditions of two Chuck Berry sgons, 'Too Much Monkey Business' and 'I'm Talkin' 'Bout You'. The latter had already cropped up on the Hamburg tapes from the end of the previous year, but this remains the earliest extant Beatles take of 'Monkey Business'—unless you count the guitar intro that The Quarry Men superimposed onto Duane Eddy's 'Movin' And Groovin'' during their spring 1960 rehearsal session.

· · · · **MAY 1963:** *COMPOSING* 'Bad To Me.'

At the end of April, Lennon went on holiday to Spain with Beatles manager Brian Epstein—less than three weeks after the birth of his first son, Julian, in Liverpool. Almost as soon as the couple returned, Epstein's homosexuality had led Cavern DJ Bob Wooler to insinuate that the manager had had an affair with the Beatle: Lennon promptly beat Wooler up, which rather begged the question.

Whether the Lennon/Epstein flirtation was even consummated or not has little relevance to the other, less often reported fact about the holiday: Epstein used the break to persuade Lennon, and through him McCartney, that they should be writing more material for Epstein's other protégés—particularly Billy J. Kramer, who had already issued John and Paul's 'Do You Want To Know A Secret' as his début single, with McCartney's 'I'll Be On My Way' on the flipside. Epstein's interest was two-fold: The Beatles' talent might aid some of his lesser artists, and in the process Lennon and McCartney's reputations would benefit. Both expectations were happily and speedily fulfilled.

The majority of these giveaway songs were actually fashioned by McCartney—including 'A World Without Love,' 'Nobody I Know,' 'I Don't Want To See You Again' and 'Woman' for Peter and Gordon: 'One And One is Two,' originally offered to Kramer, who turned it down—"Billy J. is finished when he gets this song,' Lennon muttered as he watched McCartney cut his original demo—and then gifted to the luckless Mike Shannon; and 'It's For You' for Cilla Black.

But it was Lennon who provided the initial example, composing 'Bad To Me' specifically for Billy J. Kramer during the Spanish vacation. Back in London, he recorded a double-tracked acoustic demo as a blueprint for producer George Martin to follow, leaving Kramer with a melodic, optimistic piece of romanticism that showed no signs of any emotional attachment at all. Around the same period, Lennon also completed 'I Call Your Name', a song which he'd begun at the end of the fifties but never honed into shape. Kramer duly recorded it as the flipside of 'Bad To Me', before going on to record two further McCartney giveaways, 'I'll Keep You Satisfied' and 'From A Window,' over the next year.

• **MAY/SEPTEMBER: *THE BEATLES* recording** '*Money*'/'*You Really Got A Hold On Me*'/'*Too Much Monkey Business*'/'*Got To Find My Baby*'/'*A Shot Of Rhythm And Blues*'/'*Memphis*'/'*Some Other Guy*'/'*Too Much Monkey Business*'/'*Sure To Fall*'/'*Young Blood*'/'*Till There Was You*'/'*Long Tall Sally*'/'*Everybody's Trying To Be My Baby*'/'*Roll Over Beethoven*'/'*Sure To Fall*'/'*Side By Side*'/'*Pop Go The Beatles*'/'*That's All Right (Mama)*'/'*Carol*'/ '*Soldier Of Love*'/'*Lend Me Your Comb*'/'*Clarabella*'/'*Sweet Little Sixteen*'/ '*Lonesome Tears In My Eyes*'/'*So How Come*'/'*Nothin' Shakin*''/'*Matchbox*'/ '*Please Mr Postman*'/'*I'm Gonna Sit Right Down And Cry Over You*'/'*Crying, Waiting, Hoping*'/'*To Know Her Is To Love Her*'/'*The Honeymoon Song*'/'*I Got A Woman*'/'*Words Of Love*'/'*Glad All Over*'/'*I Just Don't Understand*'/ '*Devil In Her Heart*'/'*Slow Down*'/'*Ooh! My Soul*'/'*Don't Ever Change*'/ '*Lucille*'.

Take a breath for a second. During the summer of 1963, The Beatles hosted their own weekly BBC radio show—a regular chance for the band to indulge in some of the songs which weren't featured in their live sets any more, and which they hadn't so far committed to vinyl. The *Pop Go The Beatles* series ran for 13 weeks from June to September, and The Beatles also contributed regularly to shows like *Side By Side* (for which they recorded a jolly version of the title tune with The Terry Young Six), *Saturday Club* and *Easy Beat*. The tunes listed above were the goodies—the tracks that wouldn't have been familiar to anyone who knew The Beatles solely through their records. Those aside, the band also cut numerous alternative versions of their hits, plus little-aired original material like 'I'll Be On My Way' and 'I'll Get You'.

The BBC renditions of their own songs kept strictly to the framework of the originals; they might just as well have played the records instead. To judge from the intensity of the performances, it was the covers which interested The Beatles the most, and the parade of rock and R&B songs they toyed with is an accurate summary of where each of The Beatles was at in 1963.

On his rare solo excursions, George Harrison voted for the rockabilly of Carl Perkins; Lennon reflected the same interest, loping through the country ballad 'Sure To Fall' in tandem with McCartney, and teaming up with his partner again on the Perkins hit 'Lend Me Your Comb'. And whereas McCartney settled for straight rock 'n' roll, in the shape of 'Lucille', 'Clarabella', 'Hippy Hippy Shake' and the rest, Lennon preferred something a little more subtle—which is how he came to deliver sly, knowing takes on semi-rock songs like Johnny Burnette's 'Lonesome Tears In My Eyes' and Presley's 'I'm Gonna Sit Right Down and Cry Over You'.

As ever, though, two strands of American music tantalised Lennon during these sessions. The first was Chuck Berry, represented here by sterling versions of 'Carol', 'Got To Find My Baby,' 'Sweet Little Sixteen', 'Memphis' and 'Too Much Monkey Business'—all delivered with as much guts as the primitive BBC recording techniques would allow. The second? American rhythm and blues, then on the edge of transmuting into soul through the efforts of Solomon Burke and Sam Cooke. Arthur Alexander was a constant Lennon influence—witness 'Anna' on the 'Please Please Me' album. From the same source came that Merseybeat favourite, 'A Shot Of Rhythm And Blues', and—much more to the point—'Soldier Of Love'.

Many aficionados rate 'Soldier' as one of The Beatles' finest moments in a recording studio, and it's hard to disagree. The band turned their usual trick when it came to a cover: they hardened the edges of the song, and tightened the arrangements with their foolproof vocal harmonies. But it was Lennon's calm assurance and utter conviction that turned a rather weak romantic metaphor—the doomed soldier on the emotional battlefield—into a piece of poetry. History's irony ensured that Lennon's subsequent peace campaigns, and violent death, gave this once-only performance a piquancy unnoticed at the time.

'Soldier Of Love' was the pinnacle of these sessions, but there were many other highlights—Lennon's wailing blues harp on 'Got To Find My Baby,' for instance, or his tough rockabilly rendition of Ray Charles' 'I Got A Woman', arranged identically to Elvis Presley's 1956 version. And Lennon also threw in a future titbit for Beatles historians by delivering Carl Perkins' 'Honey Don't' in fluent style, a song that was subsequently tossed to Ringo Starr as his token contribution to the band's fourth album, 'Beatles For Sale'.

• • •   **JULY 1963: THE BEATLES** recording 'She Loves You'/'I'll Get You'/'You Really Got A Hold On Me'/'Money'/'Devil In Her Heart'/'Till There Was You'/ 'Please Mr Postman'/'It Won't Be Long'/'Roll Over Beethoven'/'All My Loving'—plus Lennon composing 'I'm In Love'.

In an era when many artists regard writing a song and making a video as a hard year's work, it is difficult to comprehend the sheer physical and mental strain imposed on The Beatles in 1963 and 1964. They toured constantly throughout that period—mostly in Britain at first, and then in 1964 all over the world. They performed almost weekly on British radio; made a full-length feature film; recorded four albums and twice as many singles; appeared regularly on TV; wrote songs for their friends and business colleagues; and dealt endlessly with the pleasures and perils of being the four most desirable young men on the planet, and the most recognisable.

Small wonder, then, that for their second album the band decided to maintain the format of their first, mixing eight of their own compositions with six cover versions. First, though, there was the small matter of their fourth single. Those present at the session confirm that 'She Loves You' sounded most unpromising as an acoustic guitar duet between Lennon and McCartney; and the blatant attempt to widen the scope of their me-mine-you-us lyrics with the introduction of a third character was scarcely a masterstroke either. But ask anyone who lived through Beatlemania: 'She Loves You', another back-seat-of-my-coach collaboration between Lennon and McCartney, is still the song which evokes those hurricane days of 1963. Lennon's flipside, 'I'll Get You', had a rather coy 'Oh yeah' introduction behind the harmonica work which was in danger of becoming a Beatles cliché; but it was a surprisingly flowing melody from a man who a few months earlier was still finding it hard to move from one section of a song to another. Here, the sheer liberation of the middle eight was a stunning contrast to the stumblings of 'Ask Me Why' and 'Hello Little Girl'.

Back at the album, Lennon ran up another near-single in the shape of 'It Won't Be Long'—again built around a simple repetitive chorus, though not quite as simple or repetitive as 'She Loves You'. Otherwise—not forgetting some remarkable rhythm guitar on McCartney's 'All My Loving'—Lennon concentrated on his covers during these sessions.

'Please Mr Postman' and 'You Really Got A Hold On Me' were both borrowed from the Motown stable in Detroit—from The Marvelettes and The Miracles, respectively. Just as with 'Soldier Of Love', The Beatles added pace and precision to the naïvety and charm of the originals, and non-purists would probably rather play their versions than the Americans'. 'Money' came from the same source, but after two years of regular practice The Beatles had transformed the rather lame rendition on the Decca audition tape into a tour de force. The track was now built around pianos, not guitars, and the band added a series of stop-start breaks which revved up the excitement.

Lennon's most incisive moment on the track came on the final chorus, however. His vocal was already raw and insistent, but then that was already expected. In what was probably a spur-of-the-moment vocal throwaway, though, he interrupted the repeated call 'Money, that's what I want', with the desperate plea 'I wanna be free'. You have to hear it to feel the impact; for a second, Lennon lays himself bare, before covering up again with the request for something which he already knew couldn't buy him love, let alone freedom.

No such drama infected another Lennon composition dating from this time. In a final act of generosity, Lennon manufactured another potential hit single for The Fourmost, looking for a follow-up to the début (Lennon-composed) hit, 'Hello Little Girl'. And so emerged 'I'm In Love', a chirpy, entirely uncomplicated tale of teenage romance gone right. Questioned about the song shortly before his death, Lennon remembered nothing; and it's hard to blame him for the lapse.

· **SEPTEMBER/OCTOBER 1963: *THE BEATLES*** recording '*I Wanna Be Your Man*'/'*Little Child*'/'*All I've Gotta Do*'/'*Not A Second Time*'/'*Don't Bother Me*'/'*Hold Me Tight*'/'*The Beatles' Christmas Record*'/'*I Want To Hold Your Hand*'/'*This Boy*.'

Three EMI recording sessions in the autumn of 1963 completed their second album, prepared the single with which they would conquer America, and produced a unique Christmas gift for all the members of their official fan club.

Of the songs awarded the 'Lennon/McCartney' credit, John wrote all or most of every one—with the exception of 'Hold Me Tight', the sole leftover from their February 1963 session for the 'Please Please Me' album. 'Little Child' and 'I Wanna Be Your Man' were true collaborations; the latter had been offered to The Rolling Stones in an unfinished state, and the couple wrote the chorus in half an hour while The Stones waited in the next room. 'Little Child' bore signs of similar haste; both of them said absolutely nothing, but won through on sheer enthusiasm. Lennon's rasping harmonica on 'Little Child' didn't harm matters, either.

'Not A Second Time' was an altogether more unusual piece of work. It was the first Lennon song which showed signs of having been written on piano, rather than guitar; Lennon was not as fluent on the keyboard as McCartney, but like Bob Dylan he evolved a style that fulfilled his own needs, rather than any technical criteria. From the start, the song had a slightly unsettling rhythm; and the lyrics matched it, with a hidden message that seemed to say: 'You made me suffer, and I'm going to let you do it again.'

'All I've Gotta Do' and 'This Boy' added more confirmation of Lennon's infatuation with American soul music. 'This Boy' was styled like a fifties doo-wop ballad—or at least like Smokey Robinson And The Miracles' adaptation of the same form. On record it sounded like a throwaway, but on stage Lennon turned its middle section into a catharsis, screaming out the elongated syllables of the word 'my' with anguished fervour. Ironically, in the original plan the middle section was meant to be filled by a guitar solo; Lennon's lyrics were only written during the recording session itself.

'All I've Gotta Do' was never performed in concert, but it was raised in the same school as 'This Boy,' though Arthur Alexander, and songs like 'You Better Move On', were the direct inspiration. Like a soul singer, Lennon stretched out the opening 'I' of the lyric over eight notes, and then repeated the trick with frills in the next line. His shift into a higher octave in the final chorus was a real trademark of confidence—and also an outcry of passion in a song which ended with the hatches battened back down, and order restored. More than his colleagues, Lennon was learning that singing could convey emotion, often at odds with the spirit of the words.

Such subtleties were soon proved irrelevant, of course, when 'I Want To Hold Your Hand' became The Beatles' biggest UK hit to date, and also their breakthrough record in the USA. In a way, it marked a shift between one era and the next; it was the last Beatles A-side for two years that was an obvious Lennon/McCartney collaboration, at the same time as it transformed the role of The Beatles—and indeed Britain—in the world arena.

Finally, 'The Beatles Christmas Record' inaugurated an annual tradition. The Beatles gathered around the Abbey Road microphones with a suitably effusive script prepared by their press agent, Tony Barrow. The band delivered it with the spice of sarcasm and expletives, before George Martin edited it down into something more tasteful. In itself, it's as irrelevant to the story of Lennon's career as the version of 'Tie Your Kangaroo Down, Sport' which The Beatles recorded with Rolf Harris at the BBC a couple of months later. But his adulteration of the Christmas carol 'Good King Wenceslas' towards the end of the disc, gave Lennon's fans advance warning of what they could expect from his literary efforts in the New Year.

• **JANUARY/MARCH 1964: *THE BEATLES* recording *'Komm Gib Mir Deine Hand'/'Sie Liebt Dich'/'Can't Buy Me Love'/'You Can't Do That'/'And I Love Her'/'I Should Have Known Better'/'Tell Me Why'/'If I Fell'/'I'm Happy Just To Dance With You'/'Long Tall Sally'/'I Call Your Name.'***

1964 was the most prolific year of John Lennon's songwriting career. McCartney had been consistently ahead in terms of quantity from the beginning, though by the second half of 1963 Lennon had begun to rival his output. The Beatles' third album, however, was dominated by Lennon, who also contributed the majority of the new songs for the fourth, also cut before the end of 1964.

What makes this outburst of creativity all the more remarkable is that it was shoehorned into two frantic songwriting binges—one at the start of the year, when The Beatles were on tour in France and then the United States, the other at the end of their world tour that summer. With the prospect of their first motion picture looming, The Beatles—and that meant Lennon and McCartney—were requested to come up with seven new songs. In fact, they wrote 13, which meant that the original idea for the *A Hard Day's Night'* album—that it should include not only the new material but also the older songs featured in the movie—had to be abandoned.

Of the songs on the eventual album, Lennon had the upper hand in the writing of 10. But none of them were ready when The Beatles entered the Odeon Studios in Paris at the end of January, to record German-language versions of 'I Want. To Hold Your Hand' and 'She Loves You.' Cut during the same session was 'Can't Buy Me Love', a McCartney solo effort.

By comparison, the band's February sessions showed a shift in emphasis. They produced Lennon's bluesy 'You Can't Do That'—an unashamedly raw piece of mock-R&B, with John himself playing the fiery bunches of notes which passed for a guitar solo, and suggesting the four-to-the-bar cowbell accompaniment that, as he later acknowledged, came straight off a Wilson Pickett record.

'I Should Have Known Better' was an exercise in craftsmanship, not inspiration—fashioned round a simple two-chord sequence on John's acoustic guitar. 'Tell Me Why' is aptly described by Lennon's 1980 account of its genesis: "They needed another upbeat song and I just knocked it off. It was like a black-New-York-girl-group song."

So that left 'If I Fell' as the session's real keeper. If McCartney had sung it, then no one would have doubted that he had written it—though if he had, he would no doubt have allowed himself a slightly less painful harmony part in the middle section. On the stereo mix, his voice cracks up completely as the tune reaches its height. Lyrically, the song was every bit as ambiguous as later Lennon non-romances like 'Norwegian Wood'. It seems straightforward enough at the start: Lennon's been hurt before, and wants reassurance. But as the song progresses, you gradually realise that this tender song—for all the world a ballad of weakness and need—is actually a quest for revenge. McCartney wouldn't have been so unromantic.

The remaining Lennon compositions from this batch of sessions were less weighty. Lennon himself dismissed 'I'm Happy Just To Dance With You' as a throwaway—"I couldn't have sung it," he announced later, in a sly dig at George Harrison, who could. And 'I Call Your Name' was The Quarry Men song updated—and with Lennon forcing the band into an approximation of a Jamaican ska rhythm for the guitar solo, something noticeably missing from Billy J. Kramer's version cut the previous year.

FEBRUARY 27, 1964: *MERSEY BEAT* publishes 'The Tales Of Hermit Fred' and 'The Land Of Lunapots'.

Barely three weeks before the publication of Lennon's first book, his old friend Bill Harry unearthed a couple of vintage Lennon poems from almost a decade earlier. The source? Apparently one of Lennon's schoolteachers, who had kept them ever since confiscating them when Lennon was in his mid-teens. Perhaps he always realised that John was a genius...

Despite Harry's announcement that Lennon had given him permission to print other writings from the same source, this was his last appearance in the pages of *Mersey Beat*. Neither piece cropped up in *In His Own Write*, though Paul McCartney's introduction to that book did allude—inaccurately—to the final line of *Hermit Fred*: 'As breathing is my very life to stop I do not dare.' The literary origins of this piece of parody range from Gilbert and Sullivan's 'A Wandering Minstrel I' from *The Mikado* to Wordsworth's 'The Leech Gatherer,' though quite likely Lennon had neither in mind. But phrases like 'I nit spaghetti apple pie' display the same manic wordplay as the 'semolina pilchard' of 'I Am The Walrus'.

'The Land of Lunapots' was pure nonsense from start to finish—Lear, Carroll and Swift crossed with the native surrealism of Liverpool. But with one of those flights of the imagination that brook no barriers, the teenage Lennon had concluded with a line that had a Yeatsian ring: 'I who sail the earth in paper yachts'.

MARCH 23, 1964: *IN HIS OWN WRITE* published in the UK.

The first book by John Lennon—'the writing Beatle' as he was helpfully credited on the American edition—was a publishing sensation. It topped the best-sellers' lists on both sides of the Atlantic; the first editions of

50,000 copies in Britain and 90,000 in the United States were soon exhausted.

The reviewers were equally enthusiastic–almost to a man. Although questions were asked in the Houses Of Parliament about the scandalous educational system in this country that could have produced such scant regard for standard English usage, most critics took the traditional Johnsonian line and were amazed to find a pop singer who could write. They were quick to place Lennon in a literary line that ran, eternally, from Lear and Carroll through James Joyce to James Thurber. The fact that Lennon pronounced that he had never read Joyce in his life did little to damage their confidence.

In retrospect, *In His Own Write* is scarcely a major work of literature. It is almost impossible to read at a sitting; hard enough, indeed, to take in more than a couple of its short pieces at a time. But it does sparkle with unrestricted imagination–a little short on form and discipline, maybe, but bursting with the enthusiasm of the recently liberated. Lennon himself was uncharacteristically modest about his brainchild; he figured that it might get reviewed alongside the week's new single releases, and can scarcely have imagined that he would turn up in the *Times Literary Supplement*. But he didn't allow his new-found critical credibility to go to his head.

On the evening of publication, Lennon appeared on BBC TV's *Tonight*, where he was interviewed by the critic and commentator Kenneth Allsop. During the course of a conversation in which Lennon mumbled some extracts from the book, Allsop wondered why none of John's fantasy and word-play had figured in his songs. Lennon had never considered the possibility; and though he shrugged off the query with his usual sarcasm, Allsop's remark bit deep.

It had not even been Lennon's idea to publish a book in the first place. He had shown his random scribblings to a friend–possibly Derek Taylor, then The Beatles' press officer, and later to host the expansive Press division of the Apple empire–who in turn had passed them on to the publishers, Jonathan Cape. In the context of the times, Cape would probably have published Lennon spelling out the alphabet; the fact that the book had some literary standing was an unexpected bonus.

With a contract signed, Lennon set about compiling this first anthology. He asked Bill Harry for copies of the issues of *Mersey Beat* which had contained his early work; while the rest of the text appears to have been written much more recently, most of it backstage during The Beatles' frantic criss-cross British tours in 1963. Little of that mix of elation and claustrophobia surfaces in the book; but there are enough personal clues to allow even the most amateur psychologist an insight into the man at work.

Divided roughly a third apiece between prose, poetry and drawings, *In His Own Write* revealed an obsession with violent death–fuelled by the tragic loss of his mother, no doubt, plus the natural ghoulishness of the adolescent male. Family disharmony–another obvious reference to his own life–was another theme of the stories; husbands murder wives, or simply disintegrate under their smothering embrace, as in the tale 'Nicely Nicely Clive', which not only tells us a lot about a man himself just beginning a shotgun marriage, but also ends with a husband coming home from sea—just as his own father, 'the ignoble Alf,' had done 20 years earlier.

Skipping the many rather negative references to 'jews' in the book's stories, we can find another general theme which had already been noted in Lennon's college days—his fascination with, and hatred of, cripples and spastics. Linked to the callous cruelty of 'Good Dog Nigel' and 'Randolf's Party'—in which a lonely soul is murdered by his friends on Christmas Day—this presents a picture of the author as sicko, the kind of man who collects pictures of corpses and is likely to pass his time pulling the legs off stray animals. Emotionally, however, Lennon was still a teenager; and teenage boys (girls too, for all I know) are apt to be cruel and—in their fantasies at least—violent with it. What's mildly charming about this aspect of the book is that Lennon seems to have been quite unaware how revealing it was.

Stylistically, it varied little from the work he had already published—the same frantic word-play or invention of a new language, the same twisting of sense and sentiment. There were jokes that simply ended before the punch line ('The Wrestling Dog' and 'The Famous Five Through Woenow Abbey'); mild social and political satire ('You Might Well Arsk' and 'All Abord Speeching'); even, ironically enough, an outsider's view of a wild party where the participants are under the influence of such obscene narcotics as 'hernia', 'odeon' and 'hump' ('Neville Club').

A word of warning, though, to me as much as you. When attempting to analyse Lennon's prose, beware the example of Dr James Sauceda—an American professor whose book, *The Literary Lennon*, is the only comprehensive study of Lennon's prose work. In it he devotes a section to the *In His Own Write* tale, 'The Famous Five Through Woenow Abbey'— convinced that the Famous Five in question are, of course, The Beatles and Brian Epstein. As every British reader of a certain age could have told him, the Famous Five were a bunch of teenagers whose adventures were told in a series of books by Enid Blyton—'Enig Blyter,' in Lennon's account, whom the innocent Sauceda assumes must be a travel agent.

These poems and stories should be taken in the spirit in which they were written—as the off-duty scribblings of an over-active brain. They are all restrictively short; Lennon obviously got bored very easily, and killed off his characters as soon as that happened. And the book's artwork is in the same vein—influenced by the shapeless figures found in James Thurber's work, but with the extra twist of Lennon applied, so that human faces are attached to unwieldy, joke-animal bodies, or else are distorted almost beyond humanity. The same hypnotic interest in cripples is repeated in Lennon's drawings—though there is more humour in the pictures, as in the illustration which accompanies 'Randolf's Party.' It shows Neanderthal men, some of them merely balloon heads attached to pieces of string, others boasting cubist profiles with one eye hovering just outside their faces.

Two illustrations stand out, however: the one which accompanies 'The Famous Five' for its humour—it has the Five (who are actually eight) standing 'by the light of their faithful dog Cragesmure', who is brightly luminous; the other, the uncredited sketch of a Lennon-like figure flying through the air, for its evocation of one of its artist's wish-fulfilment dreams. Dreams and nightmares make up most of *In His Own Write*; gradually they would be transferred from Lennon's scribblings into his songs.

Chapter 4

A P R I L   1 9 6 4   T O
S E P T E M B E R   1 9 6 5

· · · · · · · · · · · · · · · · · · ·

MARCH/APRIL 1964: *THE BEATLES filming A Hard Day's Night.*

Beatlemania was the working title of this project, in preparation since the autumn of 1963. United Artists signed The Beatles to a one-movie contract, and allowed the smallest possible budget for what they saw as one in a long series of pop exploitation vehicles. There was no point in wasting expensive colour stock on a bunch of here-today, gone-tomorrow pop singers, especially as the original deal was signed before The Beatles' remarkable success in America. And so it was that the most phenomenal pop group of the century were launched on the big screen with a black-and-white movie filmed just as cheaply as any quick-buck Elvis Presley multi-reel.

Lennon and The Beatles were aware of the pitfalls of the genre: they had watched Presley's decline from *Love Me Tender* to *Fun In Acapulco*, and the generally lamentable series of British pop movies starring the likes of Cliff Richard, Billy Fury and Adam Faith stood as a grim warning of what to avoid. So as Lennon told *Rolling Stone*'s Jann Wenner in December 1970, "We insisted on having a real writer to write it...we didn't want to make a fuckin' shitty pop movie."

After a brief meeting, Alun Owen—creator of the TV drama *No Trams To Lime Street*, which had been among the first British television plays to deal with life outside London in a realistic manner—was chosen, primarily because Beatles Lennon and McCartney, and no doubt the culture-conscious Brian Epstein, had seen his work. Lennon later described Owen as "a bit phoney...a professional Liverpudlian," and slated his script as a caricature of The Beatles' public images. He lamented "the glibness of it, and the shittyness of the dialogue."

And caricature Owen undoubtedly did—with Lennon portrayed as the unflappable, ever-dominant witty Beatle, always ready with a smart line in put-down or sarcastic humour. Tight-lipped (though certainly not ashen-faced), the screen Lennon exuded menace, sexuality and power—against the cuddliness or sheer naïveté of his Beatle colleagues. It wasn't that Lennon was a great actor; merely that his public image was a classic creation, and one which the movie script did little to subvert.

Lennon added a few ad-libs to scenes like the opening reel in the railway carriage, but was mostly content to play to a script that rammed home the message the world had already heard—this was a Beatle with a savage bite.

Beatlemania had been Owen's brief, of course, and despite Lennon's later criticisms, *A Hard Day's Night* proved to be the first pop movie (well, maybe excepting *Expresso Bongo* and *The Girl Can't Help It*) to take pop itself as its theme. Owen's Beatles were simultaneously trapped by and revelling in their stardom, chased by hordes of desirable teenage girls whenever they ventured a nose outside their dressing rooms, yet never losing their good humour or matiness. And by combining documentary-style footage with a series of clever set-pieces, director Dick Lester was able to make you believe that what you were seeing was real life—the Beatles off-guard, the four mythical moptops at work and at play.

Reality, of course, would have been a little harsher; instead of Lester, The Beatles might have needed Kenneth Anger as their interpreter. *A Hard Day's Night* hinted at sexual temptation, without raising the issue of groupies; but refreshments came no heavier than coffee, and sin no greater than failing to answer their fan mail.

Years later, Lennon remembered the filming rather differently: "I was on pills. That's drugs, bigger drugs than pot." Looking back at the movie, it's tempting to say you can see the signs in Lennon's unblinking stare, the speed of his vocal delivery; but then you could say the same for every early press conference or concert. After five years or more of pills on the road, speed had become normality, and an undrugged Lennon might have been rather less attractive to the eye.

In the end, *A Hard Day's Night* worked as entertainment, as the first step towards 'serious' rock films, and as the record of a social phenomenon. Lennon admitted: "It was a good projection of one facade of us, which was on tour. It was of us in that situation together, in a hotel, having to perform before people. We were like that."

As I've already mentioned, the filming of *A Hard Day's Night* not only slotted in neatly between tours, cutting down on their potential relaxation time; it also necessitated Lennon and McCartney coming up with seven new songs to fill the holes in the script. With McCartney only producing ballads fit for giving away to their friends, the onus fell upon Lennon; not for the last time, he took The Beatles' weight on his own shoulders, and didn't falter.

· · · **APRIL 16, 1964:** *THE BEATLES* recording 'A Hard Day's Night.'

If the movie had been called *Beatlemania*, there would probably have been no title song. As it was, Ringo let slip the 'hard day's night' malapropism during a sleepy interview after a hard day's filming, and Lennon it was who emerged with a song of the same title the next day. At this stage, the competition for such honours was still friendly; McCartney not only didn't mind (he was getting half the writing royalties, after all), but took over the lead vocal for the middle eight when Lennon found his own melody line too tough to sing.

The song opened with a clanging 12-string guitar chord of George Harrison's invention; then in came Lennon's masterful lead vocal, forcing out lyrics which shifted suddenly from exhaustion to relief. The exhaustion was probably real; the relief supplied to satisfy Lennon's own inner longing as much as the expectations of his audience. For the rest of 1964, Lennon's songwriting gradually began to rival the weary satiation of the 'Beatles For Sale' album cover.

· · · **JUNE 1/2, 1964:** *THE BEATLES* recording 'Matchbox'/'Slow Down'/'I'll Cry Instead'/'I'll Be Back'/'Any Time At All'/'Things We Said Today'/'When I Get Home.'

Two marathon sessions just before The Beatles set out on a world tour saw them complete the new recordings for the 'A Hard Day's Night' album; finish their one-and-only original EP, 'Long Tall Sally;' and send their drummer to hospital with tonsilitis.

There was no margin for error in these sessions, which makes it all the more remarkable that they produced some of The Beatles' most professional recordings of 1964. But the haste at which proceedings were conducted probably explains why Lennon's 'I'll Cry Instead', for example, was cut in two separate sections and then edited together afterwards by George Martin while the band were in sunnier climes.

'I'll Cry Instead' deserves attention for more reasons than that, however. It was the first of a string of 1964/65 Beatles songs that were obviously influenced by country music—or, to be more accurate, by rockabilly. Neither 'I'll Cry Instead' nor the later 'I Don't Want To Spoil The Party' had the pace or bite of Carl Perkins or Elvis Presley at their peak; the similarity was in Harrison's lead guitar playing, and in the rhythm work and chord changes evolved by Lennon.

'I'll Cry Instead', unlikely as it may seem, was also an unheralded slice of Lennon autobiography. The sheer admission of weakness was news in itself, but Lennon later saw the middle eight of the song—with its terror of being seen as weak, and desire to hide from the public gaze—as an honest personal statement. It's the corollary of Lennon's screen image, once again: Beatles couldn't be miserable, as that wasn't their role in life; least of all could the macho Lennon be seen to be lonely or misunderstood. The dawn of the self-pitying singer-songwriter was still some way hence; so Lennon could rest assured that his listeners would interpret his cry of emptiness as a metaphor for another teenage romance gone wrong.

Lennon's other three original songs were more interesting for their inspiration than their message. 'I'll Be Back' was his reworking of an unidentified Del Shannon song; 'When I Get Home' was R&B-based, like 'You Can't Do That;' and 'Anytime At All' shared a similar influence, with, in Lennon's memorable description, the chords shifting from "C to A minor, C to A minor, with me shouting." All three were supreme hackwork, exhibiting enough Beatles trademarks to pass muster without ever threatening to be memorable. If they still were, after all that, it was down to Lennon's ever more confident vocal work.

Since late 1963, when The Beatles discovered the art of double-tracking, Lennon had insisted on recording two parallel vocal lines for almost every song. He had begun to hate the sound of his own voice, so echo was also a necessity—a trait which assumed cavernous proportions in later years. From then on, it was a rarity to hear Lennon single-track his lead vocal, until he felt sufficiently sure of the truthfulness of his writing in the late sixties to be heard naked. Double-tracking became a standard part of the mid-sixties Beatles sound, giving them that air of class and ease which most of their beat group contemporaries lacked. But unconsciously or not, it was also—like the blunt wit and harsh demeanour—part of Lennon's defences against the outside world.

- **AUGUST 11/14, 1964:** *THE BEATLES recording 'Baby's In Black'/'I'm A Loser'/'Mr Moonlight'/'Leave My Kitten Alone.'*

The most hectic year of John Lennon's life had already seen him record an album, two singles and an EP; make a full-length movie; tour France, America, Europe, Britain, and Australia; and publish a book. Now, in the brief gap between the end of one tour and the beginning of a full-scale assault on the USA, The Beatles were asked to slot in another two days' of recording sessions.

Somewhere between Surrey and Sydney, Lennon and McCartney had found time to begin work on their next album. Two of the songs recorded this month were covers, both starring Lennon; the others were originals. 'Baby's In Black' was one of the last of the true Lennon/McCartney collaborations; as if to highlight the point, the pair shared a microphone on stage whenever they performed this rather old-fashioned and over-written melodrama, which could easily have been a leftover from The Quarry Men days exhumed to fill a gap in their schedule.

'I'm A Loser' was something else again. It still had its elements of exaggeration, but they were mingled with psychodrama as Lennon used the acoustic guitar/harmonica sound of Bob Dylan to soften the harder edges of his songwriting. Looking back in 1980, Lennon made light of the lyrics: "Part of me suspects I'm a loser, and part of me thinks I'm God almighty." But beneath the cynicism was a grain of truth. Once again, the super-confident Beatle was admitting defeat. The words sounded a little false—'What have I done to deserve such a fate/I realise I have left it too late' indeed—but the sentiments were real enough. Lennon couldn't leave

33

the message that bare, however: as on 'Misery' the previous year, the flow of the music, the exhilaration of the chorus, and the sheer enthusiasm of Harrison's Carl Perkins guitar fills, told against the sincerity of the song.

Lennon himself was the first to credit Dylan's influence on this song, and several more to come; but the inspiration is less obvious than you might think. By 1964 Dylan was moving away from political protest towards oblique comments on romance, and analysis of his own role as a singer and songwriter. Nothing Dylan wrote that year—well, perhaps 'Ballad In Plain D'—was as self-pitying as 'I'm A Loser.' For the moment, the Dylan influence went little further than a guitar, a harmonica and an attitude.

Beside the originals, Lennon used these sessions to record the Dr Feelgood R&B tune, 'Mr Moonlight'—with its throat-searing Lennon vocal undercut by some uncharacteristically leaden playing by his bandmates—and Little Willie John's 'Leave My Kitten Alone', most familiar to The Beatles through Johnny Preston's poppier cover version. 'Kitten' has become a legend among Beatles fans; it isn't perfect, as the rhythm section teetered on the edge of chaos, but Lennon's vocal was peerless, as powerful a piece of white R&B/rock 'n' roll as Britain produced in the sixties. Somehow, 'Mr Moonlight' made the finished album, and 'Kitten' was consigned to the vaults—where it remains at time of writing, despite valiant attempts to issue it in the eighties by EMI. Ironically, plans for it to appear as a Beatles single early in 1981 were stymied by Lennon's death.

• • • **SEPTEMBER 19, 1964:** *OXFAM print Lennon Christmas card.*

In the wake of the success of *In His Own Write*, Lennon received several requests for illustrations, both from charities and commercial organisations. Oxfam was the only recipient of Lennon's generosity, and a typically spherical robin adorned no less than half a million Christmas cards printed that autumn. Like most of Lennon's drawings, the Oxfam design must have taken all of five minutes to create.

• • • **SEPTEMBER/OCTOBER 1964:** *THE BEATLES recording 'Every Little Thing'/'I Don't Want To Spoil The Party'/'What You're Doing'/'No Reply'/ 'Eight Days A Week'/'She's A Woman'/'Kansas City; Hey Hey Hey Hey'/'I Feel Fine'/'Mr Moonlight'/'I'll Follow The Sun'/'Everybody's Trying To Be My Baby'/'Rock And Roll Music'/'Words Of Love'.*

The 'Beatles For Sale' album marks the pinnacle of British beat—and the exhaustion of a formula. The cover artwork told its own story: the smiles were gone, replaced by deadpan glares at the camera. In format, the album followed 'Please Please Me' and 'With The Beatles', just outnumbering the cover versions with originals. The Beatles brought a new polish to these recordings; but when the polish thinned, as on 'Mr Moonlight' and 'Everybody's Trying To Be My Baby,' the cracks were all too easy to see.

Five days of recording over three weeks saw the album completed, plus the taping of the band's eighth British single. McCartney took the B-side, with the playful and amateurish R&B romp, 'She's A Woman;' but it was Lennon's assured 'I Feel Fine' which stole the honours. The song was enough in itself, fashioned round a twisting, intricate and almost unplayable guitar riff inspired by Bobby Parker's R&B classic 'Watch Your Step.' (The same source fired the riffs at the heart of songs like 'Day Tripper' and 'Ticket To Ride.') But it was the opening whine of feedback which made Lennon proud. He claimed it as rock's first venture into deliberate distortion, and he was probably right. The session tapes prove that far from being an accident, as EMI announced at the time, the feedback was always meant as the introduction to the song; and that it was Lennon who not only dragged the sound out of his protesting amplifier but also insisted on re-takes until the howl had matched the noise in his head.

That same session saw Lennon and McCartney indulge their Buddy Holly fixation on a faithful, note-perfect recreation of 'Words Of Love.' Minutes earlier, Lennon had transformed Chuck Berry's 'Rock And Roll Music' from a rather lightweight R&B tune into a savage rocker that lived up to the promise of its title. Like two of the other classic Beatles rockers, 'Twist And Shout' and 'Long Tall Sally,' this was a first take; perfection was still coming easily to Lennon and his companions in 1964.

Earlier in the sessions, Lennon had shown off the fruits of another hurried writing binge. 'Every Little Thing' was a clear collaboration, though Lennon later denied any such thing—but the verse, a simple tale of romance, bears his melodic hallmarks, just as the more orthodox chorus carries McCartney's. Likewise 'Eight Days A Week,' which Lennon variously described as "lousy," "Paul's effort at getting a single," and "his initial effort, though I think we both worked on it." Internal evidence suggests they did: it is Lennon, after all, who sings the lead vocal throughout, which almost without exception is a clear sign of ownership. And though the song didn't mean much apart from the cute word-play of the title, it said nothing with considerable charm.

Lennon's authorship of 'No Reply' and 'I Don't Want To Spoil The Party' is in less doubt. I've already fingered 'Party' as a piece of slowed-down rockabilly in the 'I'll Cry Instead' mould; Lennon apparently associated country music with sadness, which was no doubt the inspiration for the rather tired lyric. Lennon's equally drained lead vocal deserved better. 'No Reply' was an altogether more convincing piece of songwriting, despite being one of Lennon's rare excursions into fake story-telling. The American song 'Silhouettes' provided the inspiration, as Lennon recalled: "I had that image of walking down the street and seeing her silhouetted in the window and not answering the phone, although I never called a girl on the phone in my life. Phones weren't part of the English child's life." But the subject was almost incidental alongside the power of the melody, and the effortless confidence of Lennon's vocals—and, to be fair, McCartney's harmony as well. The same confidence warmed the whole album.

· · · **FEBRUARY 15 TO 20, 1965:** *THE BEATLES* recording 'Ticket To Ride'/
'Another Girl'/'I Need You'/'Yes It Is'/'The Night Before'/'You Like Me Too
Much'/'You've Got To Hide Your Love Away'/'If You've Got Trouble'/'Tell
Me What You See'/'You're Gonna Lose That Girl'/'That Means A Lot.'

It's impossible to over-emphasize the pace at which The Beatles were
forced to work between 1963 and 1965; and small wonder that they cut
back their schedule as soon as they had the power to do so. Less than four
months after finishing 'Beatles For Sale', and having in the meantime
notched up a lengthy British tour and a three-week stint in The Beatles'
Christmas Show at the Hammersmith Odeon, they were required back in
the studio with another set of original songs, ready for their second
motion picture soundtrack.

At this point, no decision had been made about the title of the movie—
though producer Walter Shenson used this week to leak details of the
film's plot to the US press, and also to put forward his suggestion that it
should be called *Eight Arms To Hold You* (a weak word-play, presumably,
on the international hit 'I Want To Hold Your Hand').

So there was no immediate need for Lennon or McCartney to compete
for the honour of writing the movie's title song. What was taped during
these sessions was no doubt written with the movie in mind, but without
advance knowledge of the plot. It was hackwork, in other words, but it
had the potential to be much more than that.

In retrospect, The Beatles' 'Help!' album stands as their least
inspired—more tired, even, than the bleary-eyed cover of 'Beatles For Sale'
suggested that album might be. As events later that year revealed,
Lennon, McCartney and Harrison were on the verge of an artistic
breakthrough; but there was little sign of it here.

Of these 11 songs, no less than two—'I Need You' and 'You Like Me Too
Much'—were Harrison compositions, his greatest contribution to a Beatles
album to date. McCartney accounted for 'Another Girl', 'The Night Before',
'That Means A Lot', 'Tell Me What You See' and the original inspiration
(such as there was) for 'If You've Got Trouble', a Ringo Starr showcase
which has never been released.

That left Lennon with four new compositions on offer: 'Ticket To Ride',
'Yes It Is', 'You're Gonna Lose That Girl' and 'You've Got To Hide Your Love
Away.' 'You're Gonna Lose That Girl' was another in Lennon's homages to
New York girl-group pop—the answering vocals sounded as if they were
taken straight off one of John's favourite Shirelles' singles—and it was
only The Beatles' new-found production sheen, as on 'No Reply,' that
concealed the influence. Anyway, Lennon's adaptation of black pop styles
was now regarded across the world as Beatlesque; seen as trend-setters,
the group were now treated as if they were the inventors of all they
conveyed.

Even so, it wasn't hard to trace the links between 'Yes It Is' and 'This
Boy,' and from there back to American vocal group harmony records by
the likes of The Miracles or The Impressions. 'Yes It Is' was, at best,
unpolished: even after multiple attempts in the studio, the band's vocal

counterpoints were painfully off-key, and George Harrison's early use of a wah-wah pedal was more of a novelty than an innovation in this context.

'Ticket To Ride' needs no such apology, however. Lennon later saw it as a prototype for heavy metal, and certainly its mesh of rhythm guitars was as solid as anything recorded in England up to that point. He wrote in one of those R&B-styled riffs he borrowed from Ray Charles or Bobby Parker, and which were a hallmark of the band's singles between 1964 and 1966. McCartney added some stinging lead guitar, and a sterling harmony vocal; Ringo began each verse with an expert drum roll; and Lennon himself obliged with another perfectly assured lead vocal, with the dry, laconic, faintly weary air of control that had become his trademark. The result was as weighty as anything The Beatles had recorded to that date, and though 'The Night Before' might have been a more popular choice for radio play, the selection of 'Ticket To Ride' as a stop-gap single was an inspired move.

Finally, there was 'You've Got To Hide Your Love Away'—more acoustic guitar, more self-pity, but this time a recorder where Lennon's harmonica might once have been. The air of despondency was no doubt real enough, but Lennon translated it into a mythical lost romance, and so the lyrics have an air of fantasy which makes them, frankly, ludicrous when separated from the music, and the voice. The initial influence was Dylan, once again; but Lennon had yet to realise that sound and self-pity were not enough in themselves.

- **FEBRUARY TO MAY 1965: *THE BEATLES filming* Help!**

A Hard Day's Night having shattered box office records around the world, The Beatles were permitted the bonus of colour film for their second motion picture. And they were also sent on location, to the Bahamas (where with the logic known only to the film industry they made the final sequences of the film first, and therefore had to avoid a suntan that would look unrealistic in the early reels), and then to Austria—with a little filming at British studios tucked in along the way.

Director Dick Lester made the most of the increased budget; as Lennon noted in 1970, some of his comic-book parody sequences were a year or so ahead of the field. But although The Beatles were still nominally playing themselves, the caricatures of the first movie had become little more than cartoons in the second. Ringo Starr had stolen the critical plaudits in *A Hard Day's Night*, for the sequence in which he walked along a river bank kicking a stone. Ringo remembered little about it, as he was nursing a hangover the day that clip was filmed; but the belief that he was the actor of the four not only saw him launched on a solo movie career in the late sixties, but also made him the plot focus of *Help!*. Loosely, Ringo had a ring (surprisingly enough) which was sacred to the followers of the dreaded god Kaili, and...well, you can imagine the rest.

As a 1965 comedy, *Help!* stands up well enough. But as a vehicle for The Beatles' meagre acting talents, or a documentary of their progress so far, it was laughable in quite another sense. Lennon described the film in retrospect as "bullshit," and rated The Beatles' roles as being "bit players in our own movie." It's hard to disagree: Ringo's position as sacrificial victim aside, The Beatles had nothing more to do in *Help!* than sound witty and look like Beatles, which wasn't stretching their talents to excess.

So the same good humour which pervaded the first movie also hung over the second, though all but staunch Beatles fans were quick to note the drop in quality. Dick Lester made some attempt to place The Beatles' music in context, placing a couple of scenes at far-fetched Beatles' recording sessions (the group always made records on Salisbury Plain, of course). But generally the music was as arbitrary and meaningless as in any British pop film of the past. Ironically, when The Beatles met Elvis Presley a couple of months later, they berated him for the saccharine nature of his recent films. They were lucky that Elvis and the Colonel hadn't seen *Help!* first.

Backstage, Lennon found co-star Eleanor Bron to be a woman quite capable of matching his own wit and intelligence, and then some; he may well have noted the feelings of inferiority and curiosity which this novel experience aroused. More importantly, The Beatles spent time smoking pot. "*Help!* was made on pot," Lennon explained later. "We turned on to pot and dropped drink, simple as that." And back in London, Lennon, Harrison and respective wives were given their first taste of acid, unawares. For the moment, the experiences made them think. But *Help!*–the movie, not the song–was the last piece of work by the unselfconscious John Lennon. Pot, and then acid, unlatched a key into a room that he hadn't visited since his childhood. And everything he produced for the next few years stemmed from that trip, and what he saw there.

APRIL 13, 1965: *THE BEATLES* recording 'Help!'

Aside from an abortive second attempt to cut Paul's still unissued 'That Means A Lot' on March 30, this session was The Beatles' first since they had begun filming. The movie had been retitled *Help!*, and Lennon and McCartney went away–separately, of course–to write a theme song. As he had done the previous year, Lennon won the race, and so 'Help' was hurriedly put on tape so that Dick Lester could assemble the film's opening credits. The track was also saved for the band's next single, to be issued (like the soundtrack album) simultaneously with the worldwide release of the film.

'Help!' was commissioned to order then, which makes it ironic that it was Lennon's most personal song to date. It was also his most naked statement of his lack of direction, his nagging feeling that life as a superstar Beatle might be fun but didn't have a future. On the surface, Lennon was as apt to enjoy the pleasures of the road as freely as the rest: there are no tales of John demurely turning down a teenage groupie in favour of a book of verse or a jug of wine. But Lennon the artist–his imagination slowly being unlocked by his use of drugs, and the increasing time which he spent locked away in his music room at home,

3 8

just thinking or toying with his tape recorder—realised that this wasn't the whole deal. He wasn't going to turn it down, but he had more creative targets in mind.

It would be wrong to suggest that Lennon was alone in his voyage. Harrison was just as enthusiastic in his pursuit of the unknown through drugs, hallucinogenic or otherwise; his mental adventures led him to mysticism, to the spiritual texts of the East. McCartney was far more careful with drugs, though eventually he was the Beatle who went public about their LSD use; but he had cultural ideals of his own. He was beginning to investigate the avant-garde theatre, to build up contacts with gallery owners and writers, actors and classical musicians. Marooned in the Surrey stockbroker belt with a wife and child to keep amused, Lennon was cut off from Harrison's spiritual quest and the bachelor McCartney's delvings into the British underground. So he turned inwards—both in a literal sense, away from his family, and artistically in search of an inner truth.

And in the *Help!* movie theme, of all the unlikely places, he found it. In what Lennon came to recognise as his most honest style, the words of 'Help!' were quite straightforward: they said 'Help!' without any dressing. Behind the song was the realisation that what once had been natural had become a pose, that behind the superficial glamour of success lay emptiness and confusion, that the older Lennon became, the less he understood. (Or, as Harrison put it in an adaptation of a spiritual text on The Inner Light in 1968, "The farther one travels, the less one knows.")

"Instead of projecting myself into a situation, I would try to express what I felt about myself, as I'd done in my books," Lennon explained a few years later about the birth of his personal songwriting. "I think it was Dylan that helped me realise that: I had a professional songwriter's attitude towards songwriting. To express myself, I would write *Spaniard In The Works* or *In His Own Write*, the personal stories which were expressive of my personal emotions. I'd have a separate songwriting John Lennon who wrote songs for the meat market, and I didn't consider them to have any depth at all. Then I started not writing them objectively, but subjectively."

A decade later, Lennon described the song more succinctly: "I was fat and depressed, and I was crying out for help." But being a commercial songwriter with a hit record to make, Lennon allowed 'Help!' to become arranged like a rock 'n' roll song. It's one of the fastest records that The Beatles cut in the mid-sixties, and the beat effectively obscured the message. Anyway, no one was yet listening to Beatles singles for their autobiographical content, any more than they thought that Mick Jagger's contemporaneous cry of 'I Can't Get No Satisfaction' had any basis in fact. Songwriters wrote about love, in a way with which others could identify. Don't blame the critics, though: not even Lennon himself had caught on that 'I'm A Loser,' 'You've Got To Hide Your Love Away' and 'Help!' constituted anything more than three more steps towards another wall of gold discs.

• • • **MAY 10, 1965:** *THE BEATLES* recording *'Dizzy Miss Lizzy'/'Bad Boy.'*

In a rare piece of complete self-indulgence, The Beatles allowed themselves to record two of their final cover versions to fill up a forthcoming American LP. Used to seeing their work butchered by their US label, Capitol, they thought nothing of knocking off a couple of exuberant rockers for Stateside release. The outcry from British fans when it was announced that the tracks wouldn't be issued in the UK forced Parlophone to include 'Dizzy Miss Lizzy' on the 'Help!' LP and 'Bad Boy' as the sole titbit for long-term fans on the 'A Collection Of Beatles Oldies' album.

The purpose may have been cynical, but Lennon no doubt relished two cracks at the work of one of his favourite fifties rockers, Larry Williams. On 'Dizzy Miss Lizzy,' they accentuated the rhythm of the original, and made up for some rather hollow instrumental work with a rasping lead vocal. The transformation of 'Bad Boy' was much more dramatic, however, with Lennon relishing both the personal reference in the title, and the blatant Americanisms in the lyric. The track remains one of the classic Beatles rockers, with a refreshing lack of side that none of their own attempts at the same formula could match.

• • • **JUNE 1965:** *THE BEATLES* recording *'I've Just Seen A Face'/'I'm Down'/ 'Yesterday'/'It's Only Love'/'Act Naturally.'*

In three more days of sessions, after the end of filming and just before a European tour, The Beatles completed the 'Help!' album. With both 'That Means A Lot' and 'If You've Got Trouble' having been rejected, the projected album was light on McCartney songs; but he filled the gap with ease, recording 'I've Just Seen A Face', 'I'm Down' and 'Yesterday' in the same remarkable session. Lennon chose not to compete, offering 'It's Only Love' as his sole contribution to these recording dates. Judging by the way in which he talked about the song thereafter, dismissing it as "a lousy song...the lyrics were abysmal," this was hardly a labour of love, merely another day in the life of the trained songsmith.

• • • **JUNE 24, 1965:** *JONATHAN CAPE publish* A Spaniard In The Works.

Lennon book number one was written for fun; number two to fulfil a contract. The publishers obviously had no qualms about over-stretching their author: his original deadline for the book was Christmas 1964, which he missed handsomely. The early months of 1965 saw him briefly considering a spoken-word album of readings from this book-in-progress, and from *In His Own Write*; plus, more humorously, a proposed book of erotica composed with Gerry Marsden of The Pacemakers. Brian Epstein would no doubt have turned in his bed if that one had been published.

Instead, Lennon set himself to work to write *A Spaniard In The Works*, published to rather less critical applause than his first book, and proportionally fewer sales as well. "I wrote it with a bottle of Johnnie

Walker," Lennon recalled in 1980. "Once it became, 'We want another book from you, Mr Lennon,' I could only loosen up to it with a bottle of Johnnie Walker, and I thought, if it takes a bottle every night to get me to write...that's why I didn't write any more." Well, more or less, as we'll see later.

I'd love to know how many people actually read Lennon's books, rather than dipping into the stories, admiring the word-play, and moving on to less taxing fare. Parts of Spaniard are literally unreadable without a large bottle of Johnnie Walker, which probably figures. The mixed metaphors, shifts of (non)sense and provocative wit of the first book comes close to gobbledegook in Spaniard, while the increased length of the prose offerings—which seem to each represent an evening's writing, flat-out, ending only in medias res when the author loses interest—is not exactly conducive to reader participation.

But the book has its moments—with the wry satire of 'Cassandle,' a sarcastic parody of a popular British newspaper columnist; or the blatant cynicism of 'The General Erection' (obviously written in October 1964), with the country's leading politicians lampooned as 'Sir Alice Doubtless-Whom,' 'Harassed Wilsod' and 'Joke Grimmace,' and the whole pack aptly dismissed as 'the mentals of parliament.' The visuals which accompany this piece show, respectively, two blind men putting crosses on voting papers they can't see; two identical men (the bastions of left and right) in a pointless argument; and what is presumably Mrs Mary Wilson, naked and casting her vote down the lavatory.

In a similar vein, Lennon attacked the fake respectability of the church in 'I Believe, Boot...'—where the reference to 'St. Alf' must have hit at Lennon's wandering father—and threw in a cartoon in which a vicar can't help looking admiringly at the bare bodies of Adam and Eve. They are delightful visual puns to accompany the silly poem, 'The National Health Cow,' and in the 'I am blind/I can see quite clearly' cartoon spread. Elsewhere, you can read what you like into the fact that the character known as 'Snore-Wife' looks a little like John's wife Cynthia; that 'Araminta Ditch' in the story of the same name is drawn as if she was an untamed, hirsute maneater; and that one of the 'dwarves' in the 'Snore-Wife' story has three pairs of spectacles, just like John on the cover of 'Walls And Bridges' in 1974!

But the rest doesn't really bear too much attention. Poems like 'The Faulty Bagnose' and 'Bernice's Sheep' can have meant little to anyone apart from their author; while the lengthy title story and the Sherlock Holmes parody might have been funnier as straight parodies, without the interruption of endless word-play. The fact that the Holmes piece ends with an anti-climax is either a cunning piece of narrative subversion, or else sheer exhaustion on the part of its author.

A Spaniard In The Works also has far fewer personal references than Lennon's first volume. Perhaps he realised how much he had given away in In His Own Write. Second time around, nothing seems to have much relevance to anything, and Lennon was getting better at hiding his feelings, except when he wanted to show them off. Despite what he has said in interviews, there is far more of the real John Lennon in the mock-confessional songs of late 1964 and early 1965 than the written-to-contract verbal slapstick of *Spaniard*. With the manuscript delivered, however, Lennon duly signed a contract for a third book—to be completed by February 1966.

· · · SEPTEMBER 9, 1965: *PRODUCING* The Silkie.

In March 1965, Beatles manager Brian Epstein signed a group of university students from Yorkshire to his stable. The quartet were folksingers with a penchant for the work of Bob Dylan, an album of whose work they promptly issued at the end of the year. Initially Epstein approached Lennon and McCartney in the hope that they might donate a song for his new protégés, but when it wasn't forthcoming, he did inveigle them into spending an afternoon in the recording studio producing The Silkie's version of John's Dylanesque ballad, 'You've Got To Hide Your Love Away.'

In fact, it appears that John was nominally the producer of the session, with Paul (and George Harrison) actually down in the studio with the group, sharpening their arrangement and trying to dispel their nerves. The result was a slightly rough, atonal essay at the song, which lacked not only the blatant self-pity of Lennon's original version, but also its emotion. The novelty of the Beatle connection was enough to ensure it became a minor hit in Britain, and a more substantial success in the States, where it also served as the title cut of the group's album.

Chapter 5

OCTOBER 1965 TO
AUGUST 1966

. . . .

OCTOBER 12 TO NOVEMBER 11, 1965: *THE BEATLES* recording 'Run
For Your Life'/'Norwegian Wood (This Bird Has Flown)'/'Drive My Car'/'Day
Tripper'/'If I Needed Someone'/'In My Life'/'We Can Work It Out'/'Nowhere
Man'/'I'm Looking Through You'/'Michelle'/'What Goes On'/'12-Bar
Original'/'Think For Yourself'/'The Word'/'You Won't See Me'/'Girl'/'Wait.'

Few months in recording history have been as productive. Once again,
however, creativity was being squeezed out of The Beatles, not coaxed.
Their timetable since the end of filming in June had seen them finish
work on the 'Help!' soundtrack, undertake a European tour, and then set
out on a rather more extensive jaunt across the United States. A British
tour was booked for December; there was the prospect of the third Beatles
film, based on Richard Condon's western novel, *A Talent For Loving*,
which was slated for early shooting in November, and all the while John
had a February 1966 deadline for his next book to consider in the small
hours.

The Beatles' own aims had altered, meanwhile. No longer were they
content to record an album at speed, cranking out one near-perfect take
after another. They had not yet discovered all the potential of the studio,
and the majority of these recordings featured the standard Beatles' line-
up of guitars, bass, drums and an occasional keyboard. But in keeping
with the songs they were writing, the band were intent upon perfection.
February 1963 had seen them attempt 11 songs in a single day; now one or
at most two was considered ample.

This more relaxed schedule—in theory, at least—allowed the band time to think about what they were doing. And conscious thought was the ingredient these songs possessed which had not always been apparent in their predecessors. On occasion, the whirrings of The Beatles' minds was all too apparent on 'Rubber Soul': for the first time, they once or twice erred on the side of pretension rather than simplicity. But most of the album has the stunning clarity of a group of performers who have chanced upon a higher level of achievement, and have not had time enough to worry about its foundations.

'Rubber Soul' was certainly the first Beatles album—as against a mere collection of songs or, as on 'Please Please Me' and 'With The Beatles', a rough representation of their stage shows. In 1965, only one other recording artist—the ubiquitous Bob Dylan—was using a long-playing record as anything more than an extended single. His first all-electric album, 'Highway 61 Revisited', had shattered the boundaries of what was considered feasible inside the popular song. 'Desolation Row' extended the linear possibilities; 'Just Like Tom Thumb's Blues', or 'Tombstone Blues', or 'Ballad Of A Thin Man', had demonstrated what could be done with the poetic vision of Allen Ginsberg, a dose of amphetamines and a willingness to speak (however obliquely) from the heart.

By comparison, 'Rubber Soul' was a comparatively modest effort, though none the less impressive for that. Lennon, McCartney and the blossoming Harrison did manage, for the moment, to resist the temptation to echo Dylan's word-play and high-speed imagery: the combination of Lennon's acid wit and the scatter-shot verbiage of *A Spaniard In The Works* would have to wait for 'I Am The Walrus'.

But The Beatles' sixth album did shine with personal statements. Where even on the previous album, Lennon and McCartney had been content to compose imaginary tales of romance about imaginary people called 'you' and 'me', they were now laying themselves bare for the world to see. McCartney had a fight with Jane Asher: you could find out how he felt by listening to 'I'm Looking Through You'. Harrison was discovering that his closest companions were not always equipped for the spiritual journeys he was making: he used 'Think For Yourself' to force the point home.

As ever, Lennon was at once the most honest, and the most evasive. The emotional force of his writing was unmistakable, however, and that's what has helped 'In My Life', 'Norwegian Wood' and 'Girl' to their status as three of his most popular songs.

The 'Rubber Soul' sessions began, however, with a much less weighty Lennon tune. Its author always dismissed 'Run For Your Life' as a petty trifle—"a throwaway song that I never thought much of." And as Lennon was the first to admit, it was enough of a throwaway to 'borrow' a line from 'Baby Let's Play House', the A-side of Elvis Presley's fourth single for Sun Records in 1955. That performance marked Presley's realisation of his own sexual potency as a rock 'n' roll singer; when Elvis played house, he wasn't talking about spring cleaning.

The line that Lennon borrowed—'I'd rather see you dead, little girl, than to be with another man'—became less a threat than a petulant sneer in an overt attempt to cut short 'his' woman's independence. As some of the more basic sections of *In His Own Write* had already revealed, Lennon gave most away when he wasn't concentrating. The lyrics to 'Run For Your Life' show every sign of having been knocked off in five minutes—the verse that begins 'Let this be a sermon' is as weak and anti-climactic as anything he ever wrote—but these hurried lines are the clearest indication we have in song of what the pre-feminist (or perhaps that should be pre-Yoko) Lennon was like. Though he felt self-pity because no one understood him, it was clear that no woman would be offered the chance. As Lennon proudly announced in several Beatles interviews, "Women should be obscene and not heard." The target for groupies the world over, Lennon had his prejudices regularly confirmed. His come-uppance at the hands of A Strong Woman was still several months away.

Or then perhaps not. Recorded on the same day as 'Run For Your Life' was an early version of 'This Bird Has Flown', which was retitled 'Norwegian Wood' on the finished album. Begun while The Beatles were on a skiing holiday with George Martin earlier in the year, the song alluded to one of Lennon's more lasting extra-marital affairs. "I was very careful and paranoid because I didn't want my wife, Cynthia, to know that there really was something going on outside of the household," Lennon explained in 1980, "so I was trying to be sophisticated in writing about an affair." What makes the song unusual is that Lennon isn't in control of the affair; he ends up in the bath, fucked and forgotten just as crudely as any of the teenagers The Beatles enticed into their beds on tour. For once, Lennon is aware of the irony: 'I once had a girl/Or should I say/She once had me.'

On autobiographical terms, then, 'Norwegian Wood' is a fascinating song. What makes it a work of art, and Lennon's most satisfying composition to date, is the combination of words and music. Partly it's the way that John tells the story by omitting the action; we can see the bath, the bed, the Norwegian wood, and those details help us to imagine the rest. And for the first time, Lennon was able to use the folk guitar style of Bob Dylan to evoke something more than self-pity. Hinting at the strangeness of the experience, he allowed George Harrison to play a simple sitar line alongside his own acoustic guitar riff—one of the first occasions that the instrument had appeared on a rock record, and certainly the most influential.

The Beatles had two separate attempts at recording the song; it's the second which is on the record. The first shares a similar arrangement, though Harrison's sitar is double-tracked throughout, and also echoes Lennon's vocal melody at the end of each line far more clearly than on the more familiar arrangement. The difference, though, is in the atmosphere. Version One has a slightly more ethereal feel—finger-cymbals and bells giving it more of the authentic flavour of the Orient. But Lennon's vocal is (emotionally, not technically) flat—'dead' might be a more precise term. Version Two, the one that appeared on 'Rubber Soul', at least suggests that he has survived to learn from his experience; the original sounds like a slow moan of despair.

No such dramas surrounded the next song on the schedule, 'Drive My Car.' The impetus here was McCartney's, but it was Lennon who supplied the crucial metaphor, offering the blatantly sexual title line in place of Paul's much more juvenile 'wear my ring.' He also supplied some fine vocal harmonies–The Beatles' impeccable abilities as harmony singers are all too rarely mentioned–and helped to strip down the arrangement to rock and roll basics.

Bobby Parker's 'Watch Your Step' guitar riff–which had already fuelled 'I Feel Fine' and 'Ticket To Ride'–re-emerged in another revamped form on 'Day Tripper,' already selected as one half of the double A-sided single that was issued simultaneously with the LP. As on 'A Hard Day's Night,' McCartney took much of the lead vocal spotlight, hitting notes that were beyond Lennon's more limited range. But as John made clear in his 1980 interview with David Sheff, the song was his–"including the lick, the guitar break and the whole bit. It's just a rock 'n' roll song." The concept of the day tripper was all too familiar to British holiday-makers, but needed some explanation for American listeners, who in later years were quick to equate the trip with drug experimentation. More to the point, however, did John really write 'She's a prick teaser' in his original lyric, as legend suggests? McCartney does his best with the line to make it seem he did. The finished record was raucous and yet not out of control–just like the best American R&B records that inspired it. Otis Redding made the song's origins perfectly clear with his later cover version, while Lennon even incorporated a mock 'Twist And Shout' build-up into the guitar break as a nod to his black mentors.

Two days later, after prolonged work on the three-part harmonies of Harrison's 'If I Needed Someone,' The Beatles arrived at what proved to be the most durable song from these sessions–Lennon's 'In My Life.' In the wake of his murder in 1980, the song took on an almost unbearable poignancy, with Lennon's own admission of loss suddenly assuming a much wider significance.

In its original form, however, 'In My Life' was far less universal in its appeal. Back in mid-1964, you'll remember, interviewer Kenneth Allsop had suggested to Lennon that he should combine his literary imagination with his musical skill. A year later, under the influence of Bob Dylan and soft drugs, Lennon was ready to take the suggestion to heart. When it came to writing this song, as he recalled in 1980, "I had a complete set of lyrics after struggling with a journalistic version of a trip from home to downtown on a bus naming every sight."

Lennon's original manuscript for the song reveals, in fact, that the eventual first verse–a simple elegy to the past–was intact from the start. What followed was not quite as precise: 'Penny Lane is one I'm missing/ Up Church Road to the Clock Tower/In the circle of the Abbey/I have seen some happy hours/Past the Tramsheds with no trams/On the five bus into town/Past the Dutch and St. Columbus/To the Dockers Umbrella that they pulled down.' Brian Wilson of The Beach Boys might have been able to pull off the 'this-is-how-you-get-to-my-house' trick on 'Busy Doin' Nothing,' but Lennon's day tripper's guide to suburban Liverpool could scarcely have been turned into a public song, even if he could have made the verses scan. This early draft is really only valuable for the hint that it was Lennon, not McCartney, who first thought of making Penny Lane into a song.

John knew from the start that this approach was a road to nowhere: "But then I laid back and these lyrics started coming to me about the places I remember." McCartney helped structure the middle eight, preventing the song from turning into an endless succession of identical verses; and one of Lennon's all-time classics was eventually delivered.

In its final state, what had been a dewy-eyed remembrance of the past became a tribute to the healing powers of romantic love. The mixed emotions of the past survive, but are soothed by the presence of a lover. The key line, it seems to me, was 'These memories lose their meaning/ When I think of love as something new.' For the moment, something new was still a fantasy. When it became a reality, Lennon's break from the past was inevitable.

With one essay in understanding under their belts, The Beatles began work on another—'We Can Work It Out.' The basic song here was McCartney's, a plea for tolerance and common sense, as long as the girl involved agreed with him: 'try to see it my way...' It was Lennon who emerged as the more conciliatory: 'Life is very short, and there's no time for fussing and fighting.'

The same combination of McCartney melody and Lennon lyricism helped complete another memorable Beatles recording, 'Michelle.' The concept was McCartney's from the start: another love song to a non-existent woman. It was Lennon who brought things back to basics, with a middle section that cut through the French lyrics and simply says 'I love you.'

Further collaborations resulted in the updating of 'What Goes On', a Lennon country rocker originally composed in the late fifties, toyed with in 1963 as a possible contender for a single, and now revamped to give Ringo Starr his token vocal showcase on the album. The additional verses composed for this session include the memorable, meaningless couplet: 'I met you in the morning/Waiting for the tides of time.' Maybe that was what qualified Ringo for his composing credit on the song, alongside Lennon and McCartney.

On the same day that they recorded 'What Goes On', The Beatles also attempted their first serious instrumental since 'Cry For A Shadow' in 1961. '12-Bar Original' was a four-man composition, firmly in the style of the British blues boom; it is obviously the source of the long-held rumour that there was meant to be a 'Rubber Soul' title track. The music on the acetate which has survived lives up to that brand of inauthenticity: though George Harrison's experimental lead guitar work is fiery enough, it's the rhythm section, plodding along behind, which sabotages any ideas that The Beatles might have had of rivalling John Mayall's band in the blues-wailing stakes. Lennon's contribution to the piece was a Ray Charles-style rhythm guitar riff, which towards the end started to sound more like Carl Perkins. Now Country Soul—that might have been more like it...

Elsewhere on 'Rubber Soul', The Beatles showed clear signs of reflecting other recent developments in rock music. George Harrison's 'If I Needed Someone' was a clear nod to the folk-rock of The Byrds, and their intricate 12-string guitar patterns also seem to have inspired the instrumental work on Lennon's 'Nowhere Man', with some more traditional Beatles rockabilly thrown in during the guitar solo.

The song itself is powered by some gorgeous three-part harmonies; it flows as smoothly as anything Lennon had written to date. On first hearing, though, its blend of social comment and finger-pointing sounds cynical, even callous—as if we are being invited to mock some outcast from the norms of hip society, without any of the affection that, say, Ray Davies brought to a similar subject in 'Mr Pleasant'. Read the lyrics again, however, and it becomes obvious that Lennon had one specific target in mind as the 'Nowhere Man'–himself. In this context, the song looks ahead to 'I'm Only Sleeping' the following year, or even 15 years ahead to 'Watching The Wheels', in its portrayal of the author as a feckless dreamer, content to live in a fantasy world rather than worrying about the trials of everyday life. It was an indulgence that Lennon, in his Surrey mansion, found easier to make than most.

As October became November, and The Beatles demanded time for remakes of songs cut earlier in the 'Rubber Soul' sessions, the pressures on them intensified. To their credit, they didn't fall back on their past remedy, by delving into their bag of R&B singles for some suitable American songs to cover; they simply went away and wrote some more. The final days of the session saw Paul emerge with 'You Won't See Me', George Martin dust down the 'Help!' era tape box for McCartney's 'Wait', which was overdubbed to bring it up to date, and Lennon bring in two new songs for consideration, 'The Word' and 'Girl'.

Though it is Harrison who is usually pegged as The Beatles' resident mystic, it was Lennon who first put their spiritual discoveries into song; and being Lennon, he kept the ideas simple so that no one could miss the point. McCartney helped him finish the piece in the studio, but the framework was already intact, and 'The Word' was Love. The words, meanwhile, displayed a little breathlessness–'Everywhere I go I hear it said/In the good and the bad books I have read' mightn't have survived a lyrical revision–and the musical setting for Lennon's lesson was simple three-chord R&B. But the message was this time more important than the medium, and 'The Word' reflected The Beatles' discovery that smoking enough pot made everything much simpler. Lennon was always apt to reduce complicated issues into a slogan: here, for the first time, was the public announcement that all you needed was love.

What makes 'Girl' so staggering a piece of work is the speed with which it was written–and the fact that none of that haste is betrayed in the song. 'Girl' had the lazy tempo and feel of a narcotic haze, but the woman in question was unsettling enough to shock Lennon out of his reverie. Looking back from another country, Lennon decided that the song showed him "writing about this dream girl again–the one that hadn't come yet. It was Yoko." That implies that the song was a simple statement of longing–or else that his relationship with Yoko was as difficult as the one in the song. This is no fairy-tale romance behind his wife's back; like 'Norwegian Wood' 'Girl' is a song of incomprehension, of bafflement that a woman could be stronger than himself. Only by idealising her as The Girl could Lennon relate to her, and try to ignore the stigma of her blatant superiority.

The final verse of the song, though, moved matters into a different dimension. 'Was she told when she was young that pain would lead to pleasure?' Lennon asked in an apparent sideswipe at Catholic teaching, 'Will she still believe it when he's dead?' And all the while Lennon undercut the seriousness of the song with his heavy breathing during the chorus, and the 'tit tit tit' backing chorale in the middle eight.

Both 'Norwegian Wood' and 'Girl' showed that Lennon was becoming aware–at last–of the complexity of human relationships. He was still seeing love as a powerplay: either the woman would run for her life, or leave him in the bath to contemplate his nature. But while McCartney continued to idealise love, even when it was going wrong, Lennon's increasingly realistic attitude–and the insight that gave him into the state of his own marriage–meant that for the next two years, he scarcely wrote about romantic relationships at all.

And if the standard refuge of marriage or sex wasn't working, then Lennon would have to look elsewhere for his salvation, or his key to the mystery. Here began a search that dominated Lennon's work for the rest of the decade: the quest for a system that would validate or excuse his feelings of confusion and longing, for a panacea that would take away the pain, for a relationship that could take this complexity on board and channel it into creativity. The adventure was to lead him through drugs, primal therapy, meditation and religion, with each step of the way a response to the surprising changes that the next few years would bring to his private life. And in searching for a personal way out, Lennon–a born advertiser–couldn't help but push the world in his own direction.

• **DECEMBER 1965: *McCALL'S* publishes 'The Toy Boy.'**

In the rush to complete 'Rubber Soul', and then begin a British tour, Lennon had scant opportunity to work on the third book of poems and prose which he had been contracted to produce for Jonathan Cape by February 1966. That deadline came and went with Lennon admitting that he had composed only one piece; and by the summer of that year, plans to complete the book were dropped.

The poem which Lennon did complete wasn't wasted, however: it was sold to the American magazine *McCall's* in the autumn of 1965, and duly appeared in their December 1965 issue, tucked midway through the magazine without any cover-line to attract potential readers. What marks this piece out from the verse in *In His Own Write* and *A Spaniard In The Works* is both its length, and its lack of the extremely dense word-play which had become a Lennon trademark. The poem tells the story of a boy

49

and his toys, each of whom doubt the other's existence. The toys debate the question at night; the boy in the daytime, which is enough to have him certified insane by a psychiatrist.

On the surface, it's a typical piece of Lennon whimsy, with a cruel twist in the tale. But you don't have to be more than an amateur psychologist to draw the links between the boy who sees visions and is thought to be mad, and the Beatle who admitted in later years that he had been blessed with surrealistic visions from an early age. Just as Lennon would lash out at his Auntie Mimi in his 1970 *Rolling Stone* interview, for destroying his poetry and drawings when he was a child, so he uses the boy in this poem as a symbol of his own alienation. And he adds a tongue-in-cheek poke at the pretensions of artists, himself included: 'He was an artiste, so you see—He didn't like to chime for free!'

Why didn't Lennon finish his third book? There are several likely reasons—lack of time; boredom with channelling his thoughts into humorous stories for a public who didn't seem to be reading them, merely buying them; and, most probable of all, the simple fact that whereas Lennon's prose and verse writing had once been a form of exorcism, an outlet for feelings that he couldn't display in his public life, the shifting boundaries of rock songwriting now permitted him to write more or less honestly about his feelings in his lyrics. Not only had Dylan introduced the dubious concept of 'poetry' into rock; Lennon had also found out how to connect himself overtly to his songwriting, without use of the subterfuge, mixed metaphors and Freudian imagery of his prose work.

At the same time, Lennon was experimenting more seriously with hallucinogenic drugs, which affected almost everything he wrote for the next 12 months. The unreal worlds he had conjured in his prose were now assuming everyday reality: what mattered was not to relive them on the page, but to make sense of what he had seen on his trips, to relate it back to the self he had left behind. And Lennon chose to use the stripped down form of songwriting to express these vague, shifting feelings, rather than the more fixed medium of prose. Coupled with The Beatles' musical adventures, his songwriting became a three-dimensional foray into the unknown, where the LSD visions of his private life could be recaptured in words and—more importantly—in sound.

• • • **MARCH 1966: *RECORDING* 'He Said He Said.'**

International fame did have its advantages, and one of them was that The Beatles could buy whatever they wanted. Ringo Starr graduated towards film, and photography; during 1964 there was serious talk of a book of his portraits and tour snaps being published in the States, as a rival to *In His Own Write*. Lennon, McCartney and Harrison all bought cameras, too, but their major indulgence when it came to artistic home improvements was in the field of home recording.

By late 1965, all three Beatles had established well-equipped music rooms in their houses, where they regularly taped home demos of their latest compositions as a basis for the rest of the band to work from.

Lennon's studio in his Weybridge home was equipped with a bank of five tape recorders, allowing him as much freedom to multi-dub as most professional studios in Britain. Besides the expected guitars and keyboards, John had also bought violins, saxophones, and a variety of percussive instruments.

Both he and McCartney were beginning to experiment with sound itself, discovering the potential of tape loops as a source of pure noise, recording a piece of music and then running it backwards through one recorder and taping it on a second–anything in search of novelty, and to catch on tape the noises they heard in their heads during their ever more frequent drug experiments.

For the moment, Lennon kept his experiments to himself. Only close friends and Beatles ever got to hear most of what he taped at home from the mid-sixties onwards, until the advent of 'Johnandyoko' saw these ventures into the avant-garde being given a commercial release through the ever-benevolent Apple organisation.

More conventionally, Lennon began to use his tape recorders as a songwriting tool–something he continued to do right up until his death in 1980. He never learnt to notate music, and so rather than risk forgetting a tune or lyric in progress, he would tape entire songwriting sessions, recording over previous attempts with a wholesale disregard for posterity. Some of his earliest home recordings have survived, however, chief among them a batch of tapes which document the writing of one of his major contributions to the 'Revolver' album.

'He Said He Said,' as it was originally called, originated from an incident in August 1965, when The Beatles had taken advantage of a brief pause in their American tour to drop acid with some close friends at their house in the Hollywood hills. Alongside Byrds David Crosby and Jim McGuinn, the guests at that select party included jobbing film actor Peter Fonda, son of Henry and brother of Jane, but not yet himself a counter-culture superstar, as he became with *Easy Rider* in 1969. Stumbling around the room in a hallucinogenic haze, Fonda kept accosting the literary Beatle and mumbling the disturbing words, "I know what it's like to be dead," into his ear. At the time, Lennon must have been less than gratified: a successful acid trip was a delicate highwire act between paradise and panic, and Fonda's stoned remarks could have tipped Lennon over the precipice. Maybe for that reason, the phrase stuck, and by the early months of 1966, Lennon was using it as the basis of a new song.

As the composing tapes reveal, the original version of the song involved Lennon repeating the same phrase over and over again, to acoustic guitar accompaniment: 'He said, I know what it's like to be dead, he said.' At this stage, the line was taken at a fast blues tempo, with Lennon picking Dylanesquely in the background.

A couple of weeks later, Lennon had developed the song a little further. He'd slowed the tempo down, substituted a chopping rhythm guitar for the finger-picked original, and added some more lyrics–ad-libbing as he went along, so that gems like 'Who put all that crap in your hair' and 'It's

51

making me feel that my trousers are torn' were thankfully taken no further. Then Lennon put the song aside for further consideration, and went back to his sound-tapes.

APRIL 6 TO 22, 1966: *THE BEATLES* recording *'Tomorrow Never Knows'/ 'Got To Get You Into My Life'/'Love You To'/'Paperback Writer'/'Rain'/ 'Doctor Robert'/'And Your Bird Can Sing'/'Taxman.'*

In rock circles, it's become something of a critical commonplace to date the fragmentation of a shared popular culture from the release of The Beatles' 'Sgt. Pepper' album in June 1967. The artistry and imagination of that album, so the argument runs, divided musicians into those who wanted to take their experimentation a stage further, and delve ever-deeper into self-expression; and those who were content to bask in the cosier surroundings of pre-acid commercial music. There were those who straddled both camps, The Beatles among them, but the rock/pop divide gradually affected both the music and the way in which it was received, by public and media alike.

Given that 'Strawberry Fields Forever' was begun during the 'Pepper' sessions, and represents as well as anything on that album the gulf between traditional pop values and the new élite, that may be a more accurate benchmark of the Great Pop Divide. So 'Revolver' must represent the pinnacle of the old pop–four musicians and their studio aides thinking on their feet to create sounds as wild as the imaginations that had created the songs. 'Revolver' had its feet in The Beatles' past, but its head in the clouds of the future; and today it has a freshness, clarity and enthusiasm that little of The Beatles' other work can match.

Ironically, much of the songwriting on 'Rubber Soul' was more 'mature', or whatever adjective you prefer, than its 'Revolver' counterparts. Elements of the later album stood up more on attitude than on content. But there was an electric thrill to 'Revolver,' a richness of sound and production, that is still the peak against which all subsequent pop music has to be judged. In the end, it's the work of a band of equals, each contributing their own individual talents, and sacrificing themselves for the sake of the whole. As such, it could only have been made while The Beatles were still a unit–while they were a touring band in other words, a situation which came to an end (much to their collective relief) in August 1966. Thereafter, there were still Beatles records, but they were the work of four artists constantly aware that they had a life outside of the monolith. 'Revolver' was the last gasp of unity, and the finest testament to the strength of that brief collaboration.

Of the eight songs The Beatles cut during this fortnight, four were solo Lennon compositions, and another was written by Harrison with substantial assistance from Lennon. The latter was 'Taxman', essentially Harrison's song in concept and execution, but a number for which Lennon contributed the final verse ('Now my advice for those who die/Declare the pennies on your eyes'–proof of a decent classical education!), the 'Mister Wilson/Mister Heath' backing vocals, and also sharpened up Harrison's rhyming schemes in the middle section. Lennon later used Harrison's lack of acknowledgement of his help as a stick to beat his ex-colleague with in the 1980 *Playboy* interview.

It was the initial Lennon composition, however, which kicked off the sessions on April 6 and 7; and from the start it was obvious to all concerned that this was a different group, with a different purpose, to the one which had cut 'Rubber Soul' and the 'Day Tripper'/'We Can Work It Out' double A-side.

'Tomorrow Never Knows' (listed on the day's session sheet as 'Mark 1' and also known to Beatles insiders at the time as 'The Void') was so far removed from what had gone before, so obvious a step into new territory, that it is staggering to discover that it was the first 'Revolver' song to be recorded, before the far more basic 'Here, There And Everywhere' and 'Good Day Sunshine'. Lennon had doubtless prepared the song at home, though sadly the tapes don't seem to have survived; it would be fascinating to know how much of the concept of the recording was present on his original demo.

Even without the music, it's a remarkable song—proof of Lennon's venturing into the recesses of his own mind during one of the thousand acid trips that came close to fragmenting his personality; proof also that he was delving into the spiritual literature of the East, with its non-Christian concept of one eternal soul which survived all earthly life and death, and into the druggy ramblings of Timothy Leary, acid guru and apologist *par excellence*, and an occasional Lennon cohort until his imprisonment in 1969.

The first line sums up the ideal preparation for a trip: 'Turn off your mind, relax, and float downstream;' and the rest of the lyric describes the need to surrender to the unconscious so that you can grasp the oneness of being. 'The game existence' has to be played 'to the end of the beginning', and so we turn again on the great wheel of karma, amen. The central message was the same as on 'The Word', however: 'Love is all and love is everyone'. Turn on, tune in, and watch the problems of the world drift away.

As Mark Lewisohn's research for *The Complete Beatles Recording Sessions* revealed, the making of 'Tomorrow Never Knows' involved two off-the-cuff inventions of the EMI studio staff, ADT (automatic double-tracking, which saved the singer from having to overdub a second identical vocal if he wanted to thicken up the sound of his voice—as Lennon always did) and the use of the Leslie speaker (the part of a Hammond organ which gave it that distinctive swirly sound, and which when applied to a vocal brought a thin, distant, disembodied feel which was perfectly suited to a song about the insubstantiality of the physical being).

McCartney and Lennon also produced a whole series of tape loops from their home studios, which were mixed into the track on the second day of proceedings. The overall effect was—and still is—breathtaking. Heralded by a sitar-like drone, the track burst into life with the corporeal presence of white noise, which only repeated listenings separated into Ringo's unsettling drum pattern (with its hints of Indian ragas), and the squeals of over-amped guitars. But it was the tape loops which gave the track its nightmarish quality—shut your eyes and you could hear flights of prehistoric birds swooping across the speakers, or ghostly string sections echoing in the sky. The sound screeched and wailed, suggesting a desperate battle for the soul—while over the top, serene and surreal, lay Lennon's deadpan vocal, intoning the message of the collective subconscious.

It was a stunning performance, which could only be placed at the end of the 'Revolver' album; anywhere else, and it would have killed whatever followed. During the sessions, however, The Beatles moved straight on to record McCartney's soul number, 'Got To Get You Into My Life', and then Harrison's mock-raga, another essay in spirituality for the masses, 'Love You To'.

McCartney's 'Paperback Writer,' already picked out as the next single, returned the band to the here-and-now—with another skin-tight set of harmonies from Lennon, McCartney and Harrison to guide it home. The flipside of the single, though, harked back to the strange journey of 'Tomorrow Never Knows', in another acid-drenched attempt to remake the world in Lennon's own consciousness.

'Rain' remains a recording landmark for its use of backwards tapes over the final chords—an accidental discovery during a drug-induced haze at home, according to Lennon; George Martin's suggestion, in his account. But the record was so much more than that. Once again, it attempted to evoke the other-worldliness of the LSD trip—the feeling that the physical world was insubstantial compared to the world of the mind. The lyrics said it straight—come rain or come shine, Lennon didn't care, as 'it's just a state of mind'. The music matched it, with droning guitars, Lennon's voice stretched wearily out over six or seven bars intoning the same syllable—an effect which was achieved by recording the song at nearly 50 per cent faster than the finished record, and then slowing the tape down. And Ringo Starr's drumming, gradually assuming a life of its own on these revolutionary recordings—punctuated the dream with shotgun intensity.

'Doctor Robert' and 'And Your Bird Can Sing' were Lennon's other contributions to the first group of 'Revolver' sessions—neither of them matching the artistic depth of 'Rain' or 'Tomorrow Never Knows', but both evidence of the fabulous lustre of the finished album. 'Doctor Robert' was a blatant drug song—it didn't matter whether there was a real 'Dr Robert', or whether Lennon was simply referring to himself as The Beatles' in-house drug courier. The message was simple: take these strange pills, and you'll feel a new man. Only the dry cynicism of Lennon's vocal suggested that the prescription might have any side effects.

'And Your Bird Can Sing' was a throwaway—John's lyrics couldn't decide whether he was being indifferent and superior (the verse) or warmly sympathetic (the middle eight). But the imagery was a definite step beyond the moon/June rhymes of his early work, sounding portentous without suggesting any too restrictive meaning.

What linked 'Doctor Robert' and 'And Your Bird Can Sing', though, was the sheer aggression of the playing. Both were powered by searing guitar-work—'Doctor Robert' with its simple twist-and-turn R&B riff, 'And Your Bird Can Sing' with a more eclectic Harrison lead line. And the use of fuzz, echo and distortion gave the guitars a cutting edge that was a Harrison trademark from this record on. Equally incisive were Lennon's vocals: he had by now mastered the art of sounding devastatingly indifferent, overwhelmingly powerful, and slightly vulnerable, all at the same time, and seldom was his voice as gripping as it was throughout this album. Both songs buzzed with electricity, a quality they shared with the last of these April recordings, 'Taxman'.

As it turned out, this powerful version of 'And Your Bird Can Sing' was never released; after a few days' break, it was one of the songs which The Beatles completed during their second batch of 'Revolver' sessions.

APRIL 26 TO MAY 19, 1966: *THE BEATLES recording 'And Your Bird Can Sing'/'I'm Only Sleeping'/'Eleanor Rigby'/'For No One'/'Taxman'/'Got To Get You Into My Life'.*

From 'Revolver' onwards, The Beatles effectively abandoned the concept of cutting a single song in a single session. It was no longer enough to produce a recording in which the instruments and vocals were in tune and tempo; while there were fresh sounds to be added, or remixing to be done, no track was ever quite finished. They were attempting to pin down on tape a fleeting mental image of a sound, or an atmosphere; and increasingly they began to try every conceivable instrument and studio gimmick in the hope of shifting ever closer to the unattainable fantasy.

That's why recordings like 'Taxman' and 'Got To Get You Into My Life' reappear in this second batch of sessions, having been all but perfected earlier in the month. Likewise 'And Your Bird Can Sing', now converted to a smoother rhythm, with only the savage tone of George Harrison's lead guitar remaining from the original version. Gone, too, were the layers of harmonies which had adorned the first rendition of the track, to be replaced by a sparser vocal arrangement dominated by Lennon's laconic lead.

Lennon had already dominated the early 'Revolver' sessions; now he was content to lay back and let McCartney and Harrison bear the strain—after recording the masterful 'I'm Only Sleeping', that is. Lennon wrote the song on his acoustic guitar, which was also the basis of the first pass at the song. In this unfinished state, 'I'm Only Sleeping' stood as a sly, stoned dream vision, a confession of laziness that was more autobiographical than most Beatles watchers realised. Partly the song was a simple plea to be left alone, to be allowed to dip out of the rat race and dream; the same basic need which inspired 'Watching The Wheels' in 1980 to which lines like 'Everybody seems to think I'm lazy/I don't mind, I think they're crazy' clearly look ahead.

The not-so-hidden layer of the song, however, was drugs-based—pot, this time, rather than the more volcanic acid visions unveiled on 'Tomorrow Never Knows' and 'She Said She Said' (as it had now been retitled). On the first of those songs, Lennon had commanded his listeners to 'float downstream;' here the movement was in the other direction, though the self-fulfilling nature of the journey was the same.

So the sleep, and the dream, and what Lennon saw along the way, were a little removed from the usual shifting senses you'd experience as you went to bed. The challenge was to convey that in sound, to create that shifting perception which was at the heart of the dream and the trip. The Beatles had discovered on 'Rain' the unsettling effects of speeding or slowing voices and instruments: to heighten the gap between Lennon and reality, his vocal was speeded-up, while the backing track was slowed down, so that they seem to be swimming in different dimensions.

Stage two of the exercise in submerging the listener into the dream came via George Harrison's backwards guitar—pieced together painstakingly over a six-hour session, and actually ending up in the mix in three different places, depending on whether you heard the final track in Britain, America or France. The effect is identical, however—placing the listener on that sliding path into sleep where you are not sure what is and what merely seems to be.

While Lennon was using the increased range of the studio to delve into his mind, McCartney's approach was far more technical, though no less inventive. 'For No One' was his song entirely, on which he used classical brass player Alan Civil to transform a delicate love song into a piece of baroque. 'Eleanor Rigby' is another track for which he is generally given credit, though Lennon later claimed to have written the second verse. The story element of the song was certainly McCartney's conception; Lennon's contribution was to edit the plot, to help McCartney decide where the story was headed, and to turn the events in the song into characterisation as much as action.

• • • • **MAY 26 TO JUNE 8, 1966: *THE BEATLES* recording *'Yellow Submarine'*/'I Want To Tell You'/'Good Day Sunshine.'**

'Yellow Submarine', custom-made as Ringo Starr's solitary lead vocal for the album, was that rarity of the period, a true Lennon/McCartney collaboration. The actual taping of the track brought out the spirit of play which had united The Beatles in the beginning, and saw Lennon controlling the sound effects which were ultimately half of the record—the megaphone interjections, the blowing of bubbles, the sea noises, the general air of mayhem which eventually became an expected part of a Beatles studio outing.

It was McCartney who had concocted the childishly simple melody line; Lennon who helped knock it into shape, and who together with folk-rocker Donovan was there to polish off the lyrics. Charming though it was, however, it was too frivolous a piece of work for Lennon ever to take any great pride in it.

The other two songs taped in this fortnight, Harrison's 'I Want To Tell

You' and McCartney's 'Good Day Sunshine', pushed Lennon into the role of high-class sideman–adding superb high harmonies to both songs, and not even playing an instrument on McCartney's joyous love song.

• **JUNE 14 TO 21, 1966: *THE BEATLES* recording *'Here, There And Everywhere'/'She Said She Said.'***

With the sessions moving to an enforced close, as The Beatles had to play the first night of another world tour on June 24, Lennon and McCartney came up with one last composition apiece to complete 'Revolver.' Unlike 'Yellow Submarine', these were entirely solo efforts; Lennon loved McCartney's song, and would surely have claimed a piece of it as his if he could; but he didn't. Likewise, there was no question that 'She Said She Said'–now hurriedly finished off after Lennon had consulted his earlier demo–was a product of John's mind only.

Peter Fonda's paranoid rambling was still at the centre of the song, but by shifting the speaker from male to female Lennon placed this track into the same category of disturbing love song as 'Girl' or 'Norwegian Wood.' And in the final lines, Lennon shifted the paranoia from her to himself, as he repeats 'I know what it is to be sad/I know what it's like to be dead' over and over again.

Before then, he made an attempt to distance himself from the fear by evoking the past–not as on the 'Plastic Ono Band' album to come, by registering his credentials as an orphan, abandoned twice over by his parents; but by the simple statement that 'When I was a boy/Everything was right.' The song shifts tempo in a liberating burst of optimism as Lennon sings these lines, only to be sucked back into the fog as the verse takes control. It's a brilliant piece of arranging, no doubt done instinctively, but none the less revealing for that. And The Beatles' musical setting for this tale of reality cutting through fantasy was equally well chosen, with Harrison's lead guitar, distorted through a Leslie speaker, leading the band through a twisting spiral arrangement.

• **LATE 1966 ONWARDS: *MAKING* home movies and recordings.**

The Beatles bought a second set of executive toys in 1966–movie cameras and home editing equipment. John was already using his tape decks to demo his new compositions, and to create frightening collages of sound, as a dry run for the bizarre tape loops of 'Tomorrow Never Knows.' Now, with his 8mm Canon equipment, he could make pictures to match. What's surprising, though, is that Lennon chose not to indulge in the high-speed imagery of his songs–the lightning cuts and juxtapositions that attract most novices to film-making. Bruce Conner's *Cosmic Ray* and *Vivian* were two of the experimental films in vogue: they raced a succession of dazzling images across the eye, leaving no single shot on the mind, just the visual sensation of assault.

Lennon saw the Conner films, and wasn't impressed. They were too slight, too fast to have any meaning. He set out to create the opposite effect—lingering images from which there would be no escape. He worked with films which would last 10 minutes at normal speed, then projected them in slow motion. And his subjects—which could be anything from one of his family to an object in the room—were captured in lengthy, unbroken shots that showed little movement or pace. Editing on the camera, he was able to superimpose other images, using the same technique of multi-dubbing that he had perfected on his tape recorders. Then, when these languorous but unsettling combinations of pictures were ready, Lennon would put music to them—Stravinsky's 'Rites Of Spring', the musique concrete of Stockhausen or his acolytes, and eventually, when he had grasped the finer points of the process, his own dramatic soundscapes, culled from the darker reaches of his narcotic imagination.

Lennon didn't know it, but in New York a school of film-makers and artists were working on very similar principles. The Fluxus group shared his preoccupation with the single, held shot—and his use of noise as a substitute for music. One of the most enthusiastic Fluxus film-makers was a naturalised Japanese-American—Yoko Ono.

Chapter 6

SEPTEMBER 1966
TO AUGUST 1967

. . . .

- **SEPTEMBER 5 TO NOVEMBER 7, 1966:** *FILMING How I Won The War.*

"That's it: I'm not a Beatle any more," announced George Harrison on August 30, 1966, the day after The Beatles' final live concert at Candlestick Park, San Francisco. He was speaking with relief, not sadness; and though his was the most extreme reaction, the speed-crazed treadmill of touring had long lost its appeal for all four Beatles.

Back in Britain, Harrison made plans to travel to India to learn the sitar with maestro Ravi Shankar; Paul McCartney began composing the film score to the movie *The Family Way*. And Lennon? His was the most obvious move away from The Beatles, taking on a solo acting role in a movie by Dick 'Beatles Films' Lester, shot almost entirely on location in Celle, West Germany in September, and then Carboneras in Spain for the rest of the autumn.

How I Won The War was scripted by Charles Wood—shortly to become famous as the author of *The Graduate*—from a novel by Patrick Ryan. What attracted Lester, and Lennon, was its strong anti-war message: the plot concerns a beleaguered and forgotten bunch of British squaddies who are on a mission to build that most British of defences, a cricket pitch, behind German lines in the Second World War. It belongs to that same anarchic, *non sequitur* brand of British comedy as Spike Milligan (compare the film *The Bed-Sitting Room*, for instance), and as the Goons—also Milligan's invention—were one of Lennon's loves as a teenager, the script must have shone alongside the four-lads-together synopses which were continually being submitted as a possible third Beatles film.

Making the film entailed not only a break away from The Beatles—enough in itself to win headlines about a possible fissure in the group—but also a change of image. The WW2 soldier required shorter hair than a Beatle, so Lennon submitted to the film crew's barber in front of a phalanx of photographers, and emerged with his most closely-cropped haircut since the late fifties. He also used the opportunity to adopt the National Health 'granny specs' which later became a trademark; previously, only a handful of Beatles photos had caught Lennon wearing (horn-rimmed) spectacles, as he preferred to squint or wear contact lenses in public.

Being removed from the centre of The Beatles hurricane, and physically transformed for his role, must have sent Lennon deep inside his own mind, searching for a key to the madness he had endured, and his own complicity in it; and wondering all the time whether he had a future outside of the performing flea circus. That doubt and introspection surfaced in a song which Lennon began at this time, 'Strawberry Fields Forever.'

Between the interminable delays while shots were set up and the sun arrived at the right place in the sky, Lennon did a little filming—not as much as his later star billing in the movie might have suggested, but enough to make sure he was noticed. Charles Wood had made a few unfortunate concessions to Lennon's fame; references to his past as a musician made uneasy listening amidst the social comedy and stark satire of the wartime theme. And he was not required to develop a character, or act outside his own experience: most of his speech was chopped into neat one-liners, delivered in the same sarcastic tone as his interjections in *Help!* or *A Hard Day's Night*. Other actors—notably Michael Crawford and Roy Kinnear—carried the weight of the plot, and furthered their growing reputations as comic performers. It was difficult to escape the feeling that Lennon was there for his name—and perhaps because director Dick Lester simply enjoyed his company off-set. The suspicion that Lennon was being exploited must have been confirmed in his own mind when the film company, United Artists, issued a soundtrack-single from this non-musical film, credited to Musketeer Gripweed (Lennon's film role) and the Third Troop, and containing just one second of Lennon's on-screen dialogue during its two-minute duration.

How I Won The War eventually capsized beneath the weight of its own heavy-handed satire—but not before Lennon had, unwittingly, provided the film's most dramatic moment. As the troops are gradually wiped out trying to carry out their pointless mission, the wisecracks of Musketeer Gripweed serve as an ironic comment that life continues while there's humour. When he is suddenly killed by a stray bullet, the anti-war message of the film is thrown back into perspective. Seeing Lennon dead now has different connotations to those it had in 1967; then he was a symbol of youth, life and hope, and his fictional demise was as shocking an epitaph on the futility of war as any of Charles Wood's more obvious attempts at political commentary.

The film eventually opened to lukewarm reviews, and has only rarely been seen on television since. It did little to further Lennon's acting career; henceforward he only appeared in films alongside the other Beatles, or under his own direction. But by helping him to realise that he had an independent life away from the Beatle-faced hydra, *How I Won The War* was a pivotal event in Lennon's career. It confirmed the conclusion which George Harrison had already suggested: the tight-knit Beatles were no more. In their place were four individuals, whose efforts to make space for their own activities slowly pulled the group apart.

• **OCTOBER 27, 1966: *PENGUIN publish* The Penguin John Lennon.**

As an admission that his literary career was at an end, Lennon consented to the issue of his two books as a single paperback, complete with all the original drawings–though their proportions in relation to the text were in many cases altered for this edition. At least three different cover designs were used for this book over the next four years: one showing Lennon dressed as Superman, another with his face covered in pairs of spectacles (compare, once again, the illustration for 'Snore Wife' and 'Several Dwarfs' in *A Spaniard In The Works*, and the cover of 'Walls And Bridges'); and the last, introduced in 1969, a distorted, pinched facial photograph of Lennon the stern guru, hidden behind waves of hair and a flowing beard.

• **EARLY NOVEMBER 1966: *RECORDING* home demos of 'You Know My Name' and 'Strawberry Fields Forever.'**

Lennon arrived back in London on November 7; the next Beatles recording session was already scheduled for a fortnight hence. While Lennon had been away, McCartney had been writing; the pattern for the next couple of years was set, as Lennon later explained: "Paul had a tendency to come along and say he'd written his 10 songs, let's record now. And I'd say, well, give us a few days and I'll knock a few off."

According to Lennon, this happened with 'Sgt. Pepper' and 'Magical Mystery Tour.' For the latter, he scarcely made the effort: for what eventually became 'Pepper,' he set to work to finish the song which had been nagging him in Spain.

Begun at the same time, however, was a simple set of chord changes which evolved into one of The Beatles' most bizarre recordings. For the moment, 'You Know My Name (Look Up The Number)' was merely a few stabbing chords on the piano, with (on the surviving composing tape) Lennon feeling desperately for the changes and more often than not missing them, while he repeated the title again and again.

Putting this aside, he spent some time translating the bare beginnings of 'Strawberry Fields Forever' into a song. Setting up the Studer recorders in his music room, he rolled the tape while he worked through the basic structure of the song with his acoustic guitar. The first few takes all came to a halt a few bars into the first verse, as Lennon searched for the rhythm which would help the words flow. Hitting a feel that he liked, he dived straight from one verse into another and then on into the chorus without a pause, before repeating the entire structure again.

Switching to electric guitar, he established a chopping, insistent rhythm rather than the gentler picking of his early attempts, at the same time adding a little speed and urgency to his rendition. This time he repeated both verses twice—presumably allowing himself room to add more later on—before one run-through of the chorus and another repeat of the first verse.

That was the tape, stark and unassuming, which Lennon played to the other Beatles in the studio in late November, and which became the blueprint for one of the band's most complex and rewarding recordings. The simplicity of these demos belied the depth of the song.

As Lennon recalled in 1980, 'Strawberry Fields Forever' was a conscious attempt to put one of his persistent childhood suspicions into words: "The second line goes, 'No one I think is in my tree'. Well, what I was trying to say in that line is, 'Nobody seems to be as hip as me, therefore I must be crazy or a genius'. It's that same problem I had when I was five: 'There is something wrong with me because I seem to see things other people don't see'." And Lennon went on to repeat the assertion he had made many times before, that he had seen surreal visions as a child, that he had been aware of a different way of seeing the world to those around him, and that this realisation that he didn't conform was at first frustrating, and then terrifying.

LSD had merely repeated the process, with greater intensity than before. Once again, Lennon was seeing things that he couldn't place in words, and which no one else could see. 'Strawberry Fields Forever' was his attempt to bridge the gap between reality and acid dream, between what he saw under the influence of LSD and the concrete world. Lennon had already written several songs that expressed one point of view in the verse or chorus, another in the bridge. Now he changed his mind in every line—'It's getting hard to be someone but it all works out/It doesn't matter much to me' and 'I think I know I mean a "Yes" but it's all wrong/That is I think I disagree'. With the way he thinks and feels constantly shifting, what there is to hold onto is the past—for which Strawberry Fields, a landmark site in his area of Liverpool, is a potent symbol, though no more than that.

So the chorus relates back to Lennon's childhood, and invites us all to go along—though nothing there is real, and there's nothing to get hung about. It's the way in which Lennon constantly pierces his own bubble, flounders in his misunderstanding, that makes the lyric so disturbing, and so emotional. In this early form, with the eventual first verse still to be written, 'Strawberry Fields Forever' was part nightmare, wholly a dream, and as stunning a link between reality and fantasy as anything written by Shelley or Coleridge. But this was merely the skeleton: in the studio, The Beatles added the flesh, and gave it life.

• • • **NOVEMBER 24 TO DECEMBER 22, 1966: *THE BEATLES* recording**

'Strawberry Fields Forever'/'When I'm 64'/'Everywhere It's Christmas'.

Once The Beatles had recorded 11 songs in a day; now it took 11 sessions in the month up to Christmas 1966 to record two songs for their next project, plus one improvised mock-carol for their annual Christmas flexi-disc for Fan Club members.

Studio time was no problem; EMI had already learned from 'Rubber Soul' and 'Revolver' that The Beatles should be given a free hand to create whatever they wanted, at whatever speed felt most comfortable. From here onwards, there is no suggestion that the record company made any attempt to intrude upon the band's artistic decisions. (The same did not always apply to Lennon's later solo recordings.)

The Beatles were in such a heightened state of consciousness, through fair means or foul, however, that they found adding to an existing track easier than finishing one. The next experiment might always be the one which transformed an interesting recording into a perfect one; and the long, difficult process of taping 'Strawberry Fields Forever' was proof that this rather haphazard procedure was something more than self-indulgence.

When The Beatles regrouped for the first of their late 1966 sessions, they had no direct blueprint for what they were doing. The assumption was that they would record an album, and that along the way a single would materialise in a puff of smoke, like a Pope from a Vatican conclave. But with no timetable to respect, and no initial concept for their album, the band were at liberty to take the sessions at their own speed.

So it was, then, that on November 24, 1966, The Beatles finished a six-hour session with less than three minutes of tape—the first take of 'Strawberry Fields'. Lennon had extended and rearranged the song he had played on his home demo; there were now three verses, the first of which was more didactic and definite than the other two, spelling out a message to himself and anyone else who cared to listen: 'Living is easy with eyes closed/Misunderstanding all you see'. This rebuttal of the dream world of 'I'm Only Sleeping' set up the later verses, with their self-probing analysis of Lennon's reaction to his uncertain future, and their honest account of his mixed emotions.

At home, Lennon had become one of the first people in Britain to install a mellotron—an instrument which acted as a rather cumbersome precursor to the synthesiser and sampler we know today. "It's all done by tapes," he explained at the time. "There are dozens of reels of tapes inside, and when you pull these knobs and press the keys they start playing."

Lennon probably got no closer to understanding the process than that, but he soon began to use the mellotron for his home recordings. He also brought it into the studio for this first pass at 'Strawberry Fields', and it's the faintly unearthly sound of this instrument, like a dying concertina, which began the take, and underpinned the first verse. For the second, Lennon substituted a gentle electric guitar, combining both instruments for the chorus. His vocal was left high in the mix, an island of calm in an ocean of shifting currents and sounds; but for the third verse he was

6 3

joined by a bank of luscious vocal harmonies, wavering under the melody line like a dissolve into a dream sequence. Back through the chorus again, and it was already time to fade on a meandering series of mellotron wheezes, heading slowly in no particular direction.

Lennon could have issued this recording as it stood, and 'Strawberry Fields Forever' would still have been one of The Beatles' most remarkable recordings. Instead, he thought about it over the weekend, and when The Beatles resumed recording four days later he was ready with a new arrangement.

Take one had been little more than a solo rendition; thereafter, Lennon designed the song round the band. The initial musical setting was still simple enough, however, with the pulsing mellotron that opens the finished record in place as early as take two, backed by exuberant drum fills from Ringo Starr, while George Harrison played a Byrdsian guitar jangle behind Lennon's deadpan, deadbeat vocal. Take one had a sense of wonder; this second arrangement was an emotional wasteland, with Lennon reciting the lyrics as if they were simply too tough to register.

Equally stunning in its way as the original version, the second 'Strawberry Fields' still didn't match Lennon's vision of the song. So after an interlude of just over a week, he and The Beatles prepared a third arrangement. The major difference was the tempo: this version was decidedly faster than its predecessors, requiring Ringo to dig deep into his resources for the drum fills that augmented the simple guitar and mellotron backing. Ringo came into his own on the fade-out, with a series of pulsating rolls around the kit that acted as an urgent call to arms—answered by the stabbing brass and flowing cellos that were overdubbed across the whole track a week later.

At the end of that latter session, Lennon overdubbed a suitably manic vocal—with an intensity quite missing from the previous rendition. Supported by the rushing brass and drums, it turned an elegiac piece of reflection into a crazed amphetamine rush of neurosis; the invitation to go to 'Strawberry Fields' suddenly felt more like a threat than a promise.

Lennon still wasn't satisfied, however; he liked both the claustrophobic atmosphere of the final take, and the spacy, melancholy tone of version number two. The solution, as all Beatles historians will know, was for producer George Martin to marry the first half of the slow version and the second half of the fast—speeding up the former and reducing the tempo of the latter to discover, quite by chance, that whereas they had been recorded a semitone apart, they were now in the same key. And so was born one of Lennon's—and The Beatles'—most compelling recordings: one which so astounded their fans when it was issued as a single that the record became their first since the start of 1963 not to top the British charts. Not for the last time, Lennon was moving too fast for his public.

No such worries attended the recording of 'When I'm 64'—a McCartney song begun in the late fifties, for which he had more recently written a new set of verses. Just as McCartney had supported Lennon on his song, so Lennon did likewise—without adding any notable creative input.

• **DECEMBER 29, 1966 TO JANUARY 20, 1967:** *THE BEATLES recording
'Penny Lane'/'Carnival Of Light'/'A Day In The Life.'*

'Penny Lane' was McCartney's answer song to 'Strawberry Fields'–
though in its lyrics it actually came closer to the original draft of 'In My
Life', the version which attempted to give a guided tour of Lennon's
Liverpool. McCartney's song achieved that object far more successfully;
but by comparison with Lennon's ambiguous relation to the past, 'Penny
Lane' was unashamedly nostalgic.

'Carnival of Light' was the name of a psychedelic event at the
Roundhouse in London for which McCartney had promised a special
Beatles contribution. Under his direction, the band spent one session
assembling a barrage of noises, tape loops, screams and assorted
madness, which Paul then mixed and gave to the event's organisers–since
when it has never been aired in public again. Lennon went along with the
idea whole-heartedly; his home tapes no doubt contained many similar
ventures into noise as an art-form. But it's worth noting that it was
McCartney who not only conceived of the project and directed its
completion, but who also had the avant-garde art world connections in the
first place. By all accounts, Lennon–based in the plush stockbroker belt
of Surrey–was jealous. The event no doubt fuelled his suspicions that
there must be more to life after marriage than bringing up baby and
hiding in his music room; and a certain Japanese artist was ready to take
up the slack.

On the day that The Beatles finished recording 'Penny Lane', January
17, 1967, Lennon read in the *Daily Mail* a report about the discovery of
several thousand holes in the streets of Blackburn, Lancashire. This
minor scandal–food for a lively borough council meeting, no doubt–was
one of the prime sources of inspiration for a song which The Beatles
began recording two days later. 'A Day In The Life'–originally called 'In
The Life Of'–was a wry piece of autobiography, which reflected Lennon's
recent film role in Spain, the death in a bizarre traffic accident of a friend,
and then the news report from the *Daily Mail*. Placed together in
apparently random succession, they provided a frightening vision of a
world in which one sensory perception was just like another, and where
strange happenings lurked around every corner. Emotionally, Lennon
chose not to get involved: 'And though the news was rather sad', he wrote,
'well I just had to laugh.' And the final surreal comment about the holes in
the Albert Hall made a chilling link into that dubious invitation, 'I'd love
to turn you on'–a line actually provided by McCartney, who'd been
searching for a song to put it in.

Thus arranged, 'A Day In The Life' was taped by Lennon on acoustic
guitar, in another laconic, matter-of-fact vocal that expressed no sense of
involvement in the bizarre workings of the world. McCartney's simple
piano supported the guitar, while Ringo turned in another epic display of
drumming, using his fills as a comment on the proceedings. After the
second verse, The Beatles left 24 bars spare, with aide Mal Evans
counting them off in an increasingly echoed voice, while an alarm clock

marked the end of the gap left for something to happen. For the moment, the middle section was left bare, filled by piano and drums, before Lennon resumed with the third verse, and another 24 bars ensued to bring the recording to a close. Satisfied with work so far, The Beatles took the best part of two weeks off, before regrouping at the beginning of February.

LATE JANUARY 1967: *RECORDING* home demo of 'Good Morning, Good Morning.'

The Beatles' most complex album to date, 'Revolver,' had been recorded over a period of two-and-a-half months, with occasional breaks included. Two months into the sessions for their next album, they had succeeded in taping just three complete songs, plus the skeleton of another. Already, in response to the need for a new Beatles single, the group had given EMI finished mixes of 'Penny Lane' and 'Strawberry Fields Forever'—which were then removed from consideration for the album.

That was ironic, as they were probably the two finest tracks to come out of these sessions—and also two of the only songs which had been written before The Beatles began recording in late November 1966. The search was now on for new material, and while McCartney hit upon the tune which would become the eventual theme of the album, Lennon was ensconced at home in front of the TV. There he heard a banal commercial for Kelloggs' cornflakes, which used the phrase 'Good morning, good morning' as its tag. Later that night, Lennon began writing a song—a piece which sounds at first like a trip into the mind of a bored businessman, before you realise that Lennon was once again singing about someone closer to home.

'Nothing to do to save his life, call his wife in', Lennon's lyric began; clearly marriage and romance were not regular bed-partners in his scheme of things. The rest of the lyric reflects a search for meaning, for anything which will break him out of the rut; in the end, only 'watching the skirts' brings him 'in gear' and Lennon openly admits his interest in a-woman-not-his-wife.

Lennon cut his basic demo on keyboards, combining a staccato piano part with the hazy tones of his mellotron, which came into its own in the middle section, giving the song a lazy, stoned feel perfectly complemented by his laid back, amused vocal. Though The Beatles' recording added decoration to the song, the essential ingredients were already intact.

FEBRUARY 1 TO APRIL 1, 1967: *RECORDING* home demos of 'Being For The Benefit Of Mr Kite'/'Lucy In The Sky With Diamonds;' *THE BEATLES* recording 'Sgt. Pepper's Lonely Hearts Club Band' (and 'Reprise')/'A Day In The Life'/'Good Morning, Good Morning'/'Fixing A Hole'/'It's Only A Northern Song'/'Being For The Benefit Of Mr Kite'/'Anything'/'Lovely Rita'/'Lucy In The Sky With Diamonds'/'Getting Better'/'Within You, Without You'/'She's Leaving Home'/'With A Little Help From My Friends.'

Once established back in the studio on February 1, The Beatles continued recording solidly for two months, working almost every day, with only three separate gaps of four days apiece as longer breaks. In the process, they completed one of the most celebrated albums in music history—a record which has consistently been voted as the best album of all time, in both public and critics' polls, and which is often used as a touchstone for subsequent developments in rock music.

Lennon, it has to be said, was never convinced by the 'Pepper' myth. "It was a peak," he said in 1970, "but I don't care about the whole concept of 'Pepper.' It might be better, but the music was better for me on the double album, because I'm being myself on it." Ten years later, he was more precise: "'Sgt. Pepper' is called the first concept album, but it doesn't go anywhere. All my contributions to the album have absolutely nothing to do with the idea of 'Sgt. Pepper' and his band." The concept was McCartney's, at any rate, and Lennon never disputed it; and it was the idea of the concept, if that's not too vague, which got people excited, rather than the actual links between the songs.

And Lennon is accurate to say that, 'A Day In The Life' aside, this wasn't his finest hour with The Beatles. His work on 'Revolver' and 'Rubber Soul', then again on 'The Beatles', has much more of him and less of the professional songwriter; and during his solo career it was self-expression which became Lennon's constant judgement tool for his own work.

What 'Pepper' does have is imagination—a rich, playful experimentation with sound and lyric that opened the eyes of the audience and fellow musicians alike. 'Pepper' was merely a reflection of the colour and excitement of the new psychedelic culture; but as the first record to catch that spirit of optimism—what would later be termed the Summer Of Love—on vinyl, it came to look as if it had invented the era rather than documenting it. Suffice to say, though, that the story of 'Pepper' the icon belongs in a book on McCartney; by the start of February 1967, Lennon was all too consciously creating new material out of desperation, and any raw materials he had at hand.

While in Kent to film the promotional clip for 'Strawberry Fields Forever' on January 31—which together with the film for 'Penny Lane' accounted for the break in the 'Pepper' sessions—Lennon had wandered into an antique shop and been taken by a poster for a 19th century circus. Intrigued by the names and skills of the acts on offer, he translated the circus bill into song, adding a few linking lines like the one which received separate billing on the 'Pepper' back cover—'A splendid time is guaranteed for all'.

The new song was titled 'Being For The Benefit Of Mr Kite', and Lennon wanted, as George Martin remembered, "to smell the sawdust on the floor." To achieve this object, Lennon, McCartney and Martin prepared a series of tape loops from the workings of an old musical steam organ, threw them into the air, and stuck them back together, to produce the puffing, ungainly waddle of sound which supports Lennon's song.

Similar ingenuity went into the recording of 'Good Morning, Good Morning'—based, as I've already said, on Lennon's home demo (as 'Mr

Kite' had also been), but with the Sounds Incorporated brass section and a tearing George Harrison lead guitar solo added in. Then for the fade, Lennon requested a panoply of animal noises—heard in succession so that each animal should be capable of eating its predecessor.

Meanwhile, The Beatles had also concocted a way to fill the Blackburn-style holes in 'A Day In The Life.' Paul McCartney played Lennon his own day-in-the-life-of-a-doper middle section, which Lennon agreed was a perfect foil for his own lyric; and after a couple of passes, the first of which McCartney ended with an unscripted "Oh shit," the section was recorded. A week later came one of the most famous recording sessions of all time—the orchestral overdubs for 'A Day In The Life,' which saw the musicians performing in fancy dress garb and being encouraged to fill the song's two 24-bar holes with a sliding romp from the lowest note in each instrument's range to the highest. Dismissing the original idea of a massed hum to end the song, The Beatles eventually hit upon a four-part piano chord, overdubbed several times, and allowed to fade naturally away to bring the musical element of the album to a close.

Other songs were McCartney's brainchildren—'Fixing A Hole,' for instance, which proved him to be Lennon's equal when it came to meaningful vagueness, the two versions of the 'Sgt. Pepper' theme, 'Lovely Rita,' a mischievous ode to a traffic warden, 'She's Leaving Home' and 'Getting Better.' Both the last two songs were collaborations, however, at least up to a point. Lennon wrote and then sang the ironic counterpoints to the tale of an errant teenage girl in 'She's Leaving Home;' taking the part of the parents rather than the child, they gave a rather one-dimensional song an unexpected depth. Likewise 'Getting Better,' with Lennon self-consciously contributing the lines about 'beating his woman' in the second verse, and answering McCartney's optimistic chorus with a grudging 'can't get no worse.'

George Harrison presented the 'Pepper' sessions with 'Within You, Without You,' on which he was the only Beatle to appear; and then 'Only A Northern Song,' which was left unfinished for the time being. Ringo's major role at this time was recording a 22-minute drum track, named 'Anything,' for no apparent purpose whatsoever in the session after The Beatles had recorded the 'Day In The Life' piano chord.

Under pressure from McCartney's sudden burst of songwriting, Lennon did come up with one more new tune during these sessions. As he told the story, his young son Julian had come home from nursery school with a drawing. When asked what it was, he announced it was a class-mate, Lucy, in the sky with diamonds. Like composers in all the best Hollywood musicals, Lennon felt a song coming on; and by the end of February he had taped a home demo of a slightly contrived exercise in psychedelia, named after his son's picture.

'Lucy In The Sky With Diamonds' is difficult to separate from the era which produced it. Lennon later expressed dissatisfaction with the way it was recorded, but that was somehow secondary to the message of the song. Except that the more you examined the words, the more you realised that there was no message merely a string of unconnected fantasy images, a kind of adult fairy-tale filled with 'marmalade skies', 'newspaper taxis' and 'tangerine trees'. The words are there for their sound, and for the acid glow they suggest, rather than to be taken as literal images—which is probably why 'Lucy' seems to have dated less well than Lennon's other contributions to the album.

As every casual fan of The Beatles knows, the initials of 'Lucy In The Sky With Diamonds' were taken to mean that Lennon was eulogising the use of hallucinogenic drugs; in the same way, 'A Day In The Life' received little airplay because of McCartney's tag line, 'I'd love to turn you on'. To the end of his days, Lennon continued to deny the allegation: as with his vehement rebuttal of the rumours that he had a homosexual affair with Brian Epstein, it's difficult to see why Lennon kept the story up for so long when he had confessed to so much else. Denial in 1967 was one thing; this was still prior to The Beatles' admission that they had taken LSD. Thirteen years later, the story of Julian's painting would have been more newsworthy if he had denied it.

It took just two days to record 'Lucy In The Sky With Diamonds', lightning work in comparison with other 'Pepper' cuts. Listening to the tune again in 1980, Lennon winced at the amateurishness of the recording; and one of the reasons he agreed to help Elton John record the song in 1974 was that it was a chance to do the song justice after seven years. But from the opening notes on McCartney's Hammond organ through to the synthesised whistle that closes the song, 'Lucy' is as redolent of 1967 as anything The Beatles taped that year.

That left 'With A Little Help From My Friends'—a McCartney conception, finished in the studio with suggestions from anyone who was around. Lennon came up with the only lines in the song that suggested more than they said—'What do you see when you turn out the light/I can't tell you but I know it's mine'—and also chipped in some of the questions put forward by his and Paul's backing vocals. As the photographs from this session show, The Beatles were using any instrument they could find in the Abbey Road studios; having experimented with various harmonicas and keyboards, Lennon opted to play cowbell on this song.

On April 1, the band recorded the 'Sgt. Pepper' reprise, the last element in the jigsaw make-up of the album named after that song. After supervising the mono mixing, which was the version of the album which The Beatles considered to be the most important, they left the more gimmicky stereo mix to George Martin and his engineers.

• **APRIL 20/21, 1967: THE BEATLES** recording 'Only A Northern Song'/end piece for 'Sgt. Pepper.'

The album wasn't quite finished, however. After a further session of overdubs and re-recording on Harrison's 'Only A Northern Song'– presumably a last attempt to salvage it for 'Pepper'–the band regrouped to record a selection of random dialogue which could be inserted at the end of the album, and would play endlessly on manual gramophones until the needle was lifted bodily from the record. Lennon's final contribution to

'Pepper' was even more bizarre: it was he who suggested that the engineers add a high-frequency whistle to the end of the second side of the LP, too high for humans to hear, and therefore accessible only to passing dogs.

· · · **APRIL 25 TO MAY 3, 1967:** *THE BEATLES recording 'Magical Mystery Tour.'*

With 'Pepper' finally complete, and set for release on June 1, The Beatles were free to begin work on another project. By his own later account, Lennon would rather have rested, or taken time to digest the copy of Yoko Ono's book *Grapefruit* which lay by his bedside. McCartney was now the effective leader of the group: it was he who had supervised the making of the 'Pepper' cover, and he also who came up with the idea that instead of making another big-budget feature film, The Beatles should write and direct a more experimental movie of their own.

Magical Mystery Tour was adopted as the title from the start; and for a while all four Beatles were intrigued by the project, which they hoped would put paid to the constant media speculation about the nature of the film still owed to United Artists under the terms of their original 1964 contract. But it was only McCartney who kept his enthusiasm going, and so it was no surprise that he arrived at the studio in late April with a projected title song for the film.

Lennon's injection to the proceedings was small; he added some backing vocals and rhythm guitar, but otherwise McCartney directed the sessions.

· · · **MAY 9 TO JUNE 25, 1967:** *THE BEATLES recording untitled jams/'Baby You're A Rich Man'/'All Together Now'/'You Know My Name'/'It's All Too Much'/'All You Need Is Love.'*

A fortnight after deciding to make *Magical Mystery Tour*, The Beatles were obliged to sign another film contract: this time guaranteeing their participation in the making of a cartoon film based on their song, 'Yellow Submarine.' The deal meant that they had to provide at least four new songs for the film, plus unlimited use of their other recent recordings. The film company were no doubt hoping for four Beatles gems; in practice, every time The Beatles recorded something that was vaguely unsatisfactory, it was mentally filed away for the movie.

These sessions were also witness to The Beatles' only known attempts to record avant-garde instrumental material. Two full days were devoted to taping long, meandering and apparently aimless pieces of musical concrete, no doubt inspired by what Lennon had seen and heard of the performance by fellow EMI recording artists Pink Floyd at the 24-Hour 'Technicolour Dream' event at London's Alexandra Palace on April 29 (where one of the performers was Yoko Ono); and also by the copy of 'The Velvet Underground And Nico' album which manager Brian Epstein had been playing incessantly for weeks. (Epstein was negotiating to take over The Velvet Underground's management at the time of his death.) Those who have heard the jam sessions state, however, that The Beatles' journeys into the avant-garde lacked any rudimentary form, or even respect for the art of staying roughly in tune.

Luckily, several more illuminating recordings did emerge from these post-'Pepper' recording dates. They varied from the instantly catchy bubblegum of McCartney's 'All Together Now' to the full-blown acid rock of Harrison's 'It's All Too Much', which was enlivened by Lennon and McCartney's ridiculous backing vocals. Note also Lennon's opening shout of "To your mother" as the guitar feedback takes control.

Several days of recording were given over to perfecting the bizarre backing track of 'You Know My Name (Look Up The Number)', a Lennon 'composition' for which he had already taped a home demo the previous autumn. Having written no more words for the song, Lennon decided to make the instrumental track a work of art in itself; and from the heavy staccato piano and echoed drums of the opening section, the song moved in succession through a bossa nova rhythm, what sounded like an out-take from a bird warblers' convention, and then back into another Latin shuffle, before taking in a spirited saxophone solo by The Rolling Stones' Brian Jones. With the track complete, the song was placed to one side while Lennon came up with some more lyrical ideas.

His only other new song at this point was recorded in a single day on May 11, with Lennon leading the rather erratic accompaniment on piano and clavioline (another recent invention which gave a keyboard the sound of a Turkish street market). The song was bathed in a swirl of dense, faintly eerie sound, with the clavioline adding the feel of a demented soprano sax across the surface. Deep in the mix were some half-hearted handclaps, a stoned mickey-take of the rhythmic clapping which had been a feature of the early Beatles records.

What they were creating was 'Baby You're A Rich Man'—by legend a paean to the demoralised Brian Epstein, though there seems no truth to the cruel rumour that Lennon turned one of the song's final choruses into 'Baby you're a rich fag jew.' Despite the fact that on paper the lyrics read like a straightforward enquiry—'How does it feel to be one of the beautiful people?'—Lennon's icy vocals gave the song an ironic bite. Ultimately, though, 'Rich Man' works better as a record than as a song, which was probably why it was relegated to the flipside of their next single.

That record turned out to be another Lennon solo composition—written on guitar, round a chord sequence which he revisited for 'Instant Karma!' in 1970, but which he played in the studio on harpsichord. 'All You Need Is Love' was, like 'A Hard Day's Night' and 'Help!' before it, written to order. The Beatles had been chosen to represent Britain in the first global television link-up, a lengthy and rather tedious programme called *Our World* which was transmitted on June 25. Their brief was to write a suitably simple song, which could be understood by viewers who didn't speak English; and then to record the track live on the show.

What Lennon concocted at short notice was little short of an anthem for the optimistic summer of 1967. 'All You Need Is Love' was a rather naïve reaction to world affairs, as subsequent events demonstrated; but Lennon expanded the theme with a moralising lyric which preached that nothing was impossible if you would only try. The same spirit invested work as late as 'Double Fantasy' in 1980. The repetitive melody and gently punning lyrics interacted well enough, and over the fade Lennon left a gap for improvisation—filled on the night by an off-the-cuff rendition of 'She Loves You', written when the concept of love was a little narrower.

The broadcast duly went out on time, showing The Beatles and heavy friends apparently making the record. In fact, only the lead vocal and guitar were not already on tape, though McCartney and Starr also double-tracked their existing parts, and the orchestra brought in for the session also played over what they had already recorded. The arrangement actually owed more to George Martin than to The Beatles, as he added depth to one of The Beatles' simplest rhythm tracks of the period, and also thought up the idea of using a burst of the French National Anthem to open the track. One delicacy lost in the overdubbing was the rare sound of Lennon playing the banjo—the instrument on which his mother had taught him to play rock 'n' roll songs over a decade earlier.

After the live recording was completed, Lennon took the opportunity to patch up a few lines of his vocal, before the track was mixed for release.

• • • **MID-JULY 1967: *RECORDING* **'*We Love You*' *with The Rolling Stones.*

Mick Jagger and Keith Richard had been among the backing vocalists on the TV broadcast of 'All You Need Is Love', Lennon and McCartney returned the compliment when The Stones recorded their summer of love anthem, which served the dual purpose of thanking fans for their support during The Stones' recent conflicts with the law. John and Paul added their distinctive falsetto harmonies to 'We Love You;' three years later, John took the opportunity of telling Jann Wenner of *Rolling Stone* that the song was nothing more than an imitation of 'All You Need Is Love'.

• • • **AUGUST 22 TO NOVEMBER 2, 1967: *THE BEATLES*** *recording 'Your Mother Should Know'/'I Am The Walrus'/'The Fool On The Hill'/'Blue Jay Way'/'Flying'/'Hello Goodbye'; Lennon producing 'Shirley's Wild Accordion' by Shirley Evans; Lennon recording 'Jessie's Dream'.*

The sessions were long and disconnected, and The Beatles rarely worked for more than a day or two a week, but during the last few months of 1967 they did complete the musical half of the *Magical Mystery Tour* project. Along the way, outside events had intruded. At the end of August, their manager Brian Epstein was found dead at his London home. That same week, The Beatles had attended an introductory meeting about Transcendental Meditation, held by the Maharishi Mahesh Yogi; and while Epstein was dying in the capital, his boys were in Wales, at an intensive TM induction course also run by the Maharishi. From here until their rather unhappy stay at the Maharishi's camp in Rishikesh, India, the following spring, TM played an increasingly important part in

The Beatles' lives, supposedly encouraging them to abandon the use of narcotics and spend several hours each day concentrating on their own personalised mantras.

Little of that influence found its way into the band's music, any more than they ever referred to Epstein in song. But the dreamy mental state brought on by TM did invest George Harrison's 'Blue Jay Way' and the group's instrumental 'Flying', which was cut down from a strange nine-minute-plus jam into a tighter but still mostly ethereal mood piece for the *Magical Mystery Tour* film.

McCartney's contributions to the soundtrack were characteristically lightweight, at least in tone. 'The Fool On The Hill' was one of his most striking ballads, and John added some colourful harmonica playing to the instrumental track for the song. His mellotron was at the heart of 'Flying', suggesting that this may have been the initial inspiration for the song. More interestingly, he was credited on an EMI session sheet for the first time as producer, during a session in which accordion player Shirley Evans taped 'Shirley's Wild Accordion' for the *MMT* soundtrack. This track was copyrighted as a Lennon/McCartney composition, and involved Evans double-tracking her accordion parts while Ringo Starr played drums and Paul McCartney added maracas and vocal encouragement. The ensemble discussed what an accordion would sound like played backwards; John Lennon corrected Evans when she crept away from the arrangement that had been written out for her. But after a busy session comprising 15 takes of the instrumental, it seems not to have been used in the *Magical Mystery Tour* film.

There is also some doubt about the origin of another piece of *MMT* incidental music, 'Jessie's Dream'. Not recorded at EMI but concocted at one of the group's home studios, it was listed as a four-man Beatles composition. It accompanies the nightmare in which 'Jessie', a lady of rather weighty disposition, is overwhelmed by the swill-like food shovelled onto her restaurant table by the ever-smiling waiter, John Lennon. The image is sufficiently disgusting to make it easy to ignore the musical accompaniment, but isolate the sound and what you'll hear beneath the dialogue sounds like an early run at the avant-garde tape-play of the 'Two Virgins' album—full of discordant pianos and echoed guitars, chopped into a loping, unearthly rhythmic pattern. On aural evidence, 'Jessie's Dream' sounds like the world's first airing of one of Lennon's experimental home recordings—taped, it should be noted, several months before John first invited Yoko Ono to his home.

'Jessie's Dream' was taped in the middle of a batch of sessions for 'Hello Goodbye'—a McCartney song tailored as the group's next single, although its final section was also played over the credits of the film. It began a run of McCartney-composed Beatles singles that—with one major exception—ran unbroken until the group split two-and-a-half years later. Lennon had enjoyed a similar series of A-sides from 1963 through to late 1965; then, as now, the identity of the author of The Beatles' hits was also a clue to who was controlling the group's overall direction.

The flipside of the single, and also Lennon's only major contribution to the film soundtrack, was altogether more substantial: 'I Am The Walrus.' When Lennon had made the connection between writing for himself, as in his books, and writing for an imagined public, the results had reflected more the personal content of *In His Own Write* than the surrealistic word-play and nonsensical imagery. 'Walrus' represented a rare dip into that second stream, with its gushing flow of puns, innuendo and sheer invention—assembled, according to Lennon's long-time friend Pete Shotton, as a deliberate riposte to the more pretentious of The Beatles' critics, those who were already examining 'Sgt. Pepper' for insight into the universe.

The initial inspiration was more prosaic, however: the recurrent two-tone whine of a police siren, passing Lennon's Surrey home. That musical motif survived on the final recording, in the form of the riff that underpins the basic instrumental track, and the repetitive melody line to which Lennon recited his stream-of-nonsense lyrics. And the policeman who lines up his troops in the final verse was another obvious nod to the song's origins.

Like the pastiche artist he was, Lennon put together the rest from a variety of sources—the walrus from Lewis Carroll's 'The Walrus And The Carpenter' (though Lennon later acknowledged that he'd misunderstood the poem and chosen the villain of the piece as his 'hero'); the Hare Krishna from the religious leanings of Beatle Harrison; the 'I'm crying' chorus line, stretched out over several bars, from The Miracles' soul ballad, 'Ooh Baby Baby;' 'Lucy In The Sky' from his own son (and song); and the opening statement of common identity—'I am he as you are he...'—from the Buddhist and Taoist scriptures into which he'd dipped during his acid-led search for spiritual enlightenment. But the construction was the product of a mind tuned to the message of the unconscious: the sound of the words was as significant as their meaning, or lack of it.

Lennon later rated 'I Am The Walrus' as his favourite Beatles song. It wasn't the most meaningful, merely the one that gave him the greatest pleasure to record—just as McCartney looked back on the equally playful 'You Know My Name (Look Up The Number)' with particular relish. For a record that was awash with sound effects and bizarre asides, however, the backing track was remarkably simple—recorded with, for the time, a standard line-up of Beatles instruments, guitars, drums and keyboards. Only after the lead vocal was added did the music begin to rival the lyrics. George Martin arranged an orchestral score for the song that included long, atonal slides up the scale, and plenty of gloomy, diminished chords; then a choir added the 'oompah oompah' backing vocals and John's wry assertion that 'everybody's got one.'

Lennon's mind only resumed control of the piece in the final mixing, when he added in a broadcast of Shakespeare's *King Lear* being broadcast on the BBC Third Programme at the time. It might just as easily have been the cricket commentary, in which case Beatleologists would have had an entirely different set of theories to investigate.

In retrospect, 'Walrus' was a turning point in the Beatles' career—and Lennon's. Issued at the end of 1967, it was their last full-blown excursion into psychedelia; subsequent Beatles visions were always tinged with sentiment ('Rocky Raccoon') or cynicism ('Piggies'). In the new year, Lennon continued to experiment in sound; but increasingly he would indulge in the formless collages that he had already begun to assemble at home, rather than try to capture that hallucinogenic chaos in words. And early in 1968 he found a willing partner in Yoko Ono—someone who could not only enjoy his experimentation, but who could give it intellectual justification.

Chapter 7

SEPTEMBER 1967
TO MAY 1968

. . . .

SEPTEMBER 11 TO NOVEMBER 1967: *FILMING Magical Mystery Tour.*

Conceived during a transatlantic plane trip in April 1967, *Magical Mystery Tour* was a McCartney brainchild: he wrote the rough shooting script, or at least the bare bones of one; he evolved the idea of The Beatles and friends travelling through the West Country on a bus; and he composed most of the soundtrack music. All four Beatles supervised the shooting and then the editing, particularly Paul and Ringo; Lennon's main contribution was to go along with the idea, and to map out a couple of scenes in the film which McCartney offered him as a sop to his own domination of the project.

Lennon rarely discussed the film in later years; he talked more about the 'soundtrack' album concocted by Capitol Records in the States than he did about his own first experience of movie direction. But this 50-minute TV film seems to have been a project which he allowed to happen, rather than controlled. True, he did improvise his own scenes in the film, but then so did everyone else, within the basic framework dictated by McCartney. Only a couple of scenes betray more than casual interest on Lennon's part, though he still managed to capture more screen time than Harrison, for example, whose glazed eyes and stoned expression suggested that he had prepared for the filming a little too heavily.

The background to the project is well known. McCartney's initial enthusiasm, which had led The Beatles to begin recording the title song back in April 1967, had dimmed over the summer. Only when he felt the band drifting apart after the death of Brian Epstein did he resurrect the project, setting the unrealistic deadline of Christmas for a British TV première. A few days of filming in the West Country produced a batch of chaotic, disconnected vignettes, which had to be cobbled into some form of narrative logic in the editing studio. In the end, McCartney was forced to resume shooting to create visual settings for Harrison's 'Blue Jay Way' and his own 'The Fool On The Hill', which with their imagination and trickery far outshone the original location footage.

As we've seen, Lennon became sufficiently involved in the movie to donate 'I Am The Walrus' to its soundtrack; produce Shirley Evans' elusive 'Wild Accordion;' and dig into his archive of home recordings for 'Jessie's Dream.' He also narrated the early stages of the story, and showed his gift for character in a number of brief cameo roles—like the ticket seller, and the evil Italian waiter in the dream sequence. With its anarchic distortion of everyday convention, that dream/nightmare scene, with Lennon attempting to drown the unfortunate Jessie in food, has the feel of some of Lennon's early prose pieces; just as the film clip that accompanies 'I Am The Walrus', a vain but amusing attempt to match the surrealism of the song, was based on the wilder corners of Lennon's imagination.

Otherwise, it's difficult to see any guiding influence at work on some of the film's *longeurs*—the marathon race round a deserted airfield, Victor Spinetti's sergeant-major routine, the sing-song on the coach. What's also noticeable is the sheer amateurishness of the camera work and editing— the work of people who were totally unfamiliar with the medium they were using, but who were sufficiently in thrall to their own mystique not to worry. Though the best of the film's humour looks forward to *Monty Python's Flying Circus*, far too much was self-indulgent, aimed at an audience of four and their wives and close friends. Small wonder, then, that the movie attracted such a critical pasting; and that one of its four co-directors chose to pretend that it had never actually happened.

- **OCTOBER 11 TO NOVEMBER 14, 1967: *LENNON sponsors* Yoko Plus Me.**

On November 9, 1966, John Lennon attended the preview of an exhibition at the Indica Gallery in London, to which he'd been invited by his friend, gallery owner John Dunbar. The exhibition was the work of Yoko Ono—a Japanese performance artist who was now a leading member of the Fluxus group in New York. Equating performance art with the prospect of sex, Lennon was intrigued; then bewildered, as he found no hint of an orgy in progress, merely a set of minimalist sculptures— 'Hammer-A-Nail', a white board which invited the onlooker to do just that; an apple on a stand; most invitingly, a ladder which you climbed, to find a spyglass revealing the message: 'Yes'.

Lennon and Ono exchanged a few remarks, made mental notes of the other's existence, and then went on with their lives. Over the next few months, they met casually at other openings, while Yoko became a mini-celebrity as a result of the furore surrounding her *Film No.4*, or as it was better known, *Bottoms*. The film was simply a collection of behinds, shot one after another from an identical position, complete with the bemused comments of the participants on the soundtrack. Earlier Ono films had been even less dramatic, concentrating on a single event or observation in the accepted style of the Fluxus group.

Yoko had also published a book of her 'instructions', keys to her conceptual art, suggestions for happenings or events or films. The book was called *Grapefruit*: Yoko had a copy delivered to Lennon during the 'Sgt. Pepper' sessions. When the pair next met, Yoko happened to mention that she was looking for a sponsor for an exhibition at the Lisson Gallery. Lennon agreed to help out: and while the exhibition was being planned, found that he had been chosen to participate in Yoko's *13 Days Do-It-Yourself Dance Festival*, in which selected people received conceptual instructions through the post, and chose whether or not to follow them.

On, significantly enough, Lennon's 27th birthday, Yoko Ono opened the exhibition of her work at the Lisson Gallery. Her media profile in Britain had already been heightened by the publicity surrounding *Film No.4*; now her coy announcement in the event's programme that the exhibition had been financed by John Lennon guaranteed her of further column inches. Despite its title, Yoko's show—also known as *Half-A-Wind*—had no direct input from Lennon: eager to avoid being linked too closely with the artist, he had made his financial contribution of £5,000 anonymously, and was perturbed when his name was, after all, mentioned in connection with the event. In fact, it appears that he didn't even visit the exhibition once it had opened.

He missed the opportunity to view a retrospective of Yoko's work to date. One floor was devoted to her 'Stone Piece'—featuring the artist, or so one presumed, occupying a white bag in a stone-like posture. At this point, the concept of 'bagism' had yet to be invented, but the game was already in play. Another section of the exhibition featured a selection of equally familiar Ono pieces—including the 'Hammer-A-Nail' sculpture which had initially attracted Lennon's attention at the 1966 Indica Gallery show, and the apple on a stand.

The focus of the show was on the top floor of the gallery, however, where Yoko presented 'Half-A-Room'—items of household furniture neatly sawn down the middle, but otherwise arranged in conventional relation to each other.

These were the concepts, the conceits, which Yoko brought to her artwork with John. Their novelty intrigued him—and for a while he was content to treat her artistic world as an adventure playground. His sponsorship of this show meant that he had paid his entrance fee.

• • • **NOVEMBER 1967:** *LENNON/McCARTNEY produce 'Dear Delilah' by Grapefruit.*

As has become increasingly apparent in recent years, The Beatles' Apple company began life as a financial manoeuvre to lessen their tax obligations. The ideal of an artistic utopia came later. From the start, however, Lennon and McCartney wanted to play with their new toy. On

November 11, they signed the members of a new pop group, named Grapefruit, to their Apple Publishing division—the first bricks in their intended empire. Lennon himself had named the fledgling group, significantly drawing their title from Yoko's bedside book.

Taking their duties as publishers seriously, for the moment at least, The Beatles also agreed to help produce the band's first single, 'Dear Delilah'. Lennon and McCartney weren't credited; Terry Melcher's name was on the label. But observers agree that it was the two Beatles who controlled the session, McCartney assisting with the arrangement while Lennon made sure that some of the band's sparky energy made it onto tape. Surprisingly, perhaps, the resulting record has little overt evidence of Beatle involvement: there are no backwards tapes, or excerpts from BBC radio broadcasts. To show that they had forgotten none of their old tricks, John and Paul simply came up with a clear, punchy production, enough to win the group a minor hit single.

NOVEMBER 24/28, 1967: *RECORDING tapes for* Scene Three Act One; THE BEATLES *recording* 'Christmas Time Is Here Again'.

On October 3, 1967, the newly-opened National Theatre in London announced to a bemused theatrical press that they would shortly be staging a dramatic adaptation of John Lennon's two books, *In His Own Write* and *A Spaniard In The Works*. A few weeks later, serious work began, with the play's title already fixed as *Scene Three Act One* (from an amusing playlet in the first book), and Lennon co-opted as one of three writers on the project.

As it transpired, Lennon's involvement with the finished play was fairly slight. But as early as November 1967 he did begin to prepare sound tapes and spoken-word recordings for use in its production. One session was devoted to the actors from the cast reading extracts from the script while classical music was inserted as a backdrop. Another saw Lennon supervising The Beatles as they recorded Christmas party noises, which consisted of mock-chatter and much clinking of glasses, with the ensemble breaking into 'Knees Up Mother Brown' at the close. Another tape was filled with 'Working Noises'—miscellaneous knocking and scraping sounds, with added tape echo. 'Electronic Noises' mingled with the rubbing of wine glasses with high pitched whistles; while for 'Celeste (Children's Hour)' George Martin played short spurts of BBC-style incidental music. Lennon and McCartney directed proceedings throughout.

Lennon's second session for *Scene Three Act One* took place after The Beatles had recorded their 1967 Christmas Fan Club Record. Previous Christmas discs had either been spoken word messages or mock pantomimes: the 1967 effort followed the second course, but interrupted proceedings with an excerpt from a six-minute Beatles song, 'Christmas Time Is Here Again'. Credited to all four Beatles, the track had the air of a McCartney throwaway, with the same chorus repeated over and over again, like a rehearsal for 'Hey Jude' the following year. But Lennon and the others entered into the spirit of the occasion, chipping in weird sound effects and character voices as the performance gradually slid into mayhem.

FEBRUARY 3 TO 11, 1968: *THE BEATLES* recording 'Lady Madonna'/ 'Across The Universe'/'The Inner Light'/'Hey Bulldog.'

Ever since the previous September, The Beatles had been trying to schedule a trip to the Maharishi Mahesh Yogi's meditation centre in Rishikesh, India—only to be forced into postponement because of their commitments to the *Magical Mystery Tour* project. A new departure date was set for February 15: by then, The Beatles had to record a new single, to be issued in their absence, which they hoped would fulfil the expectations of their audience (and EMI) through to the end of the summer, when they might conceivably have had time to record a new album.

Just like the old days, Lennon and McCartney submitted rival songs for consideration. Paul's 'Lady Madonna' was started first, with Lennon supporting this pastiche of fifties rock 'n' roll on fuzz guitar and backing vocals. The following day, they began to record Lennon's 'Across The Universe'—stage one in a process which eventually became a saga.

Lennon regarded the song as one of the few where the lyrics stood up by themselves, as poetry; though he took little personal credit, claiming that the entire song had come to him one night as he lay in bed, seething over an argument with his wife, Cynthia. None of that conflict surfaces in the song: its subject, instead, is the process of writing. Like much of the best romantic poetry, 'Across The Universe' celebrates what critics are apt to name the Muse—the inspiration, in other words, of the writing, the creative process whereby the words form in the mind and are transferred on to the page.

What's striking is not the subject, but the power of the imagery, and the complete lack of the overblown lyricism that most writers would have brought to the subject. 'Across The Universe' is one song that can safely be given to those who doubt rock music's credentials as 'serious' art; yet because it came out of instinct, rather than conscious thought, it has none of the faults that attend most attempts to be 'serious' in the rock field. As Lennon recalled, "I didn't want to write it...it wrote itself. It drove me out of bed...It's like being possessed, like a psychic or a medium...Letting it go is what the whole game is. You put your finger on it, it slips away, right?"

Sadly, little of that ease, of that yielding to the power of the art, survived in the recording of the song. It's difficult to imagine how commercial 'Across The Universe' might have been as a single; it was a Beatles record, so it would have sold, but it lacks the common touch of 'All You Need Is Love' or 'Hello Goodbye.' As The Beatles were supposed to be recording a single, maybe some of that doubt crept into their performance in the studio. Either way, what began as one of Lennon's most cherished songs ended up, in his words, as "a lousy track...The Beatles didn't make a good record out of it. The guitars are out of tune and I'm singing out of tune because I'm psychologically destroyed and nobody's supporting me or helping me with it, and the song was never done properly." Lennon added that he felt McCartney was subconsciously trying to destroy his work at this period; though there's nothing to support that on the original session tapes.

The basic recording of 'Across The Universe' was done in a day, with George Harrison playing sitar to support the Eastern mysticism of the lyric, and two fans dragged in off the Abbey Road doorstep to sing high harmonies. In an inspired move, Harrison spent a couple of hours writing out and then performing little flurries of backwards guitar, which were inserted into the mix—transforming the song into a psychedelic haze—and then just as quickly removed. By the end of the session, and after some additional overdubs four days later, Lennon was unable to avoid the conclusion that 'Universe' could not be issued as a single.

So the song languished in the vaults for 18 months, until George Martin dug it out as The Beatles' contribution to a World Wildlife Fund charity album, and overdubbed some bird sounds over the opening seconds. The following year, when Phil Spector was called in to assemble the 'Let It Be' album, he also went back to the original 'Across The Universe', and produced an entirely different mix of the song. George Martin had speeded up the original Beatles' recording by about five per cent; Spector slowed it down by the same amount, and then added a heavenly choir and a full string orchestra to support the majesty of Lennon's lyrics. The author wasn't consulted, but voted his thanks by asking Spector to produce his next three albums.

We're getting ahead of ourselves, however. Back in February 1968, once The Beatles had decided to release 'Lady Madonna' and Harrison's 'The Inner Light' as their next single (their last 45 not to feature a Lennon song on either side had been 'Love Me Do!'), they made arrangements to film a special promotional clip, to be shown on TV while they were off in India. The original plan was to portray The Beatles at work on 'Lady Madonna', but rather than waste a day in the studio they chose instead to record a new song, Lennon's 'Hey Bulldog', written to order for the 'Yellow Submarine' soundtrack.

Watched by Yoko Ono, who complained that The Beatles always used such simple rhythms, the band built the song around a rewritten walking blues riff, that once again harked back to the R&B songs of Ray Charles. Lennon's lyrics trod a fine line between nonsense and inspired nonsense, and the gusto of the performance, and the sheer chaos of the fade-out, made this one of the warmest, most enjoyable Beatles recordings of the era. In a way, it's another landmark in their career, another milestone on the road to dissolution. Rarely in the future would they approach a session with such boyish enthusiasm. The disillusionment of the Rishikesh fiasco seemed to remove the last of the group's Four Musketeers spirit, that one-for-all camaraderie and mutual support which had seen them through every crisis from the sacking of Pete Best to the critical panning of *Magical Mystery Tour*.

FEBRUARY TO MAY 1968: WRITING 'I'm So Tired'/'Yer Blues'/'The Happy Rishikesh Song'/'Child Of Nature'/'Julia'/'Sexy Sadie'/'The Continuing Story Of Bungalow Bill'/'Dear Prudence'/'Revolution'/ 'Everybody's Got Something To Hide Except For Me And My Monkey'/ 'What's The New Mary Jane'/'Look At Me;' recording home demos of 'Julia'/'Sexy Sadie'/'Child Of Nature'/'The Happy Rishikesh Song'/ 'Everybody's Got Something To Hide Except For Me And My Monkey'/ 'Look At Me;' recording demos of new material with The Beatles.

John Lennon spent three days short of two months in India early in 1968, most of that time at the Maharishi Mahesh Yogi's retreat in Rishikesh. The four Beatles had made the often-postponed trip to seal their pact with Transcendental Meditation: in the land where the Maharishi had developed his theory, transcendence ought to have been easier to find than in London, where growing business commitments and personal anxieties were eating into their peace of mind.

John travelled to India with his wife, Cynthia; he admitted later that he had tried to find a way to take Yoko as well. As it turned out, two months' separation from Yoko seem to have kindled his interest, and within a month of his return they had begun an affair.

Meanwhile, Lennon and the other Beatles threw themselves into the Maharishi's regime, each spending hours alone in their rooms, contemplating the infinite and repeating their individual mantras. It was a rare respite from the frenetic pace of life in the fast lane; separated from the trappings of stardom, and from the hallucinogenic drugs which had become a regular method of escape over the last two years, Lennon was forced to look at himself, and his relationship with the rest of the world.

The Beatles had taken acoustic guitars to India, and they used their time of relaxation to write. By the time they had all returned in early April, McCartney announced that they had composed 30 songs in India, and that the best of these would shortly be recorded for an album called 'A Doll's House', set for release by the end of the year.

Harrison was already using his music as a vehicle for his spiritual beliefs; his experiences in India merely strengthened his commitments. McCartney seems to have remained untouched by the experience; or at least he wasn't able, or ready, to translate his thoughts into song. He approached the leisure time as a professional tunesmith, cranking out a series of well-crafted, rounded songs which revealed little of his inner self.

Lennon did not find subterfuge as easy, however, or as satisfying; and the songs he wrote in India were necessarily a reflection of his own life. Seeing himself and the world with heightened clarity—induced as much by the absence of chemicals as by the Maharishi's teaching—he took the process of self-discovery he had begun with his prose writings and his songs on 'Rubber Soul' a stage further.

What emerged were the same feelings of guilt about his marriage, loss over his shattered family life, confusion about his own direction, and hope for the future, which he had being trying to suppress—or twist into psychedelic visions—for the past three years. This time, however, the messages emerged without any metaphors. Lennon found himself, secure in a haven of inner peace, confronting his most virulent demons. Slowly these emerged in music and lyrics, in songs like 'Yer Blues' and 'I'm So Tired'—ironic offspring of a venture which was supposed to bring harmony and contentment.

At the same time, Lennon made a conscious attempt to persuade himself that the meditation process was working its magic. Two songs, both of them rejected for release when John realised that they were insincere, painted an entirely optimistic portrait of the meditation experience, untroubled by the nagging pain of Lennon's real feelings. He recorded both of them when he returned to Britain in April, but neither of them were attempted during The Beatles' recording sessions that stretched from June to October.

'The Happy Rishikesh Song' had the same mantra-like simplicity as The Beach Boys' meditation songs, themselves the product of time spent with the Maharishi. Lennon's demo has a lightness of touch missing from most of his work, as he works through the repetitive guitar chords and a set of lyrics which parrot the Maharishi's slogans without real understanding. Lennon's irony surfaces in the middle section, however, with its recognition that despite meditation, 'everybody needs a woman.' And the final lines of the song reveal his realisation that blind acceptance of TM was just another drug: 'swallow this, that's all you've got to do.' Significantly, John borrowed one of this song's lines for another blast at unthinking faith, 'Serve Yourself.'

The second meditation song, 'Child Of Nature', lacked the irony of 'The Happy Rishikesh Song'. Set to a melody which was later used for 'Jealous Guy,' it offered an embarrassingly fulsome tribute to the Maharishi's teachings, with a title that harked back to the 19th Century Romantics' view of the natural boy uncorrupted by society. Lennon's proclamation that TM has returned him to such a state, however, is firmly punctured by the other songs that emerged during his stay in India—while the pomposity of his home demo, with dramatic mandolins and an affected lead vocal, adds to the inauthentic air.

These songs were the work of a man writing what he felt he *should* be writing. The rest of his work from India is altogether more authentic, and more painful. 'I'm So Tired' is a blunt successor to the dreamy 'I'm Only Sleeping;' fashioned like an acoustic blues, with a self-pitying lyric to match, it bursts into violent, electric life during the chorus, with its blatant appeal: 'I'd give you everything I've got for a little peace of mind.' Second time through, Lennon's voice rises uncontrollably as he cries out, 'I'm going insane', nailing any idea that this was merely the suffering of the Romantic.

'Yer Blues' said it even straighter: 'Feel so suicidal, even hate my rock 'n' roll', which was about as desperate as a rock star could get in 1968. The grim imagery of the verses, with their 'black clouds' and 'blue mists', were only slightly redeemed by the mocking reference to 'Dylan's Mr Jones', the butt of Bob's 'Ballad Of A Thin Man'. Those were the most blatant of

Lennon's self-examinations, the darkest visions unleashed by his solitude and inner searching.

Also written in India were two of his most affecting ballads, 'Julia' and 'Look At Me' Lennon recorded a series of almost identical, double-tracked demos of 'Julia' when he returned to England; like 'Look At Me', they demonstrated his new-found skill as a guitar-picker. The same simple acoustic riffs, taught to Lennon by a fellow meditator, Donovan, could be heard behind several songs over the next couple of years, from 'Sun King' to Yoko's 'Remember Love:' the Indian spring obviously gave Lennon the chance to improve his musical skills as well as his songwriting.

'Julia' eventually emerged on the 'White Album' in the same form as it had been recorded at home, though it wasn't until he began his affair with Yoko that he followed the name of his mother, Julia, with a translation of Yoko's name, 'Ocean child' in the song's lyric. Without the knowledge of his mother's name, Julia sounded like a poetic ballad of love; but Lennon never invented characters for his love songs, unlike McCartney's 'Martha My Dear' or 'Michelle' What's surprising, in retrospect, is the idealisation of his mother, achieved without any of the pain which emerged on his 'Plastic Ono Band' album. It's a gap only partly bridged by our knowledge that John was also writing about his lover-to-be.

'Look At Me' was more straightforward in its message: 'Who am I supposed to be?' asked Lennon, in what was musically a continuation of 'Julia' The question was obviously still relevant when John finally recorded the song in 1970, but as early as 1968 he could see the hint of a solution in his new relationship: 'Nobody else can see/Just you and me'

Not all of Lennon's songs from India were quite as personal. Three, in particular, continued the tradition of semi-nonsense lyrics begun the previous year. 'Everybody's Got Something To Hide Except Me And My Monkey' was a sturdy rocker built around a set of contradictions: at its most basic level, it said that the new Lennon didn't need any disguises, something of a manifesto for the years to come.

'What's The News Mary Jane' is altogether more mysterious, and lightweight. It's a stream of unconsciousness series of riddles, which may or may not poke fun at one of Lennon's friends who was somewhat slow to catch on to psychedelic drugs. For once, the drug imagery–'Mary Jane' for marijuana–was probably deliberate; but the message didn't go any deeper than that.

Likewise 'The Continuing Story Of Bungalow Bill' Lennon explained in 1980: "That was written about a guy in Maharishi's meditation camp who took a short break to go shoot a few poor tigers, and then came back to commune with God. There was a character called Jungle Jim and I combined him with Buffalo Bill. It's a sort of teenage social-comment song and a bit of a joke." With its musical simplicity and singalong chorus, it also works well as a children's song–children being ideally placed to appreciate Lennon's cruel sense of humour.

Another, more pathetic fellow meditator inspired the beautiful 'Dear Prudence' The woman in question was Mia Farrow's sister, who had meditated herself into her room and wouldn't come out. Lennon was chosen as the man to persuade her back into the real life, and wrote the song as a simple message that the world outside was beautiful, and so was she, so why wouldn't she come out to play? Its initial impetus aside, 'Dear Prudence' is as clear and convincing an advertisement for TM as Lennon ever created, with its childlike appreciation of the natural world, clarity of thought and open generosity—only slightly undercut on John's home demo for the song by a spoken ending which turned poor Prudence into a candidate for the funny farm. Otherwise, once again, the way that Lennon taped his double-tracked acoustic demo was the way that the song was recorded in the studio.

'Sexy Sadie' is the song which remains Lennon's clearest and most memorable picture of the Maharishi episode, however. Beatles associate Magic Alex Mardas convinced the group that the Maharishi was showing far too carnal an interest in the women in their party; when Harrison, the band's biggest advocate of TM, started to believe the story, then Lennon was sure it must be true. As they made their plans to leave, teasing the baffled Maharishi with his lack of universal knowledge of their thoughts, Lennon composed a vicious song of hatred—the cry of the abandoned follower (or the deserted child). 'Maharishi', he wrote in the original draft, 'you little twat/Who the fuck do you think you are/Oh you cunt'.

Back in Britain, Lennon mellowed a little, changed the title of the song to the more obscure 'Sexy Sadie' to avoid legal complications, and turned a gut reaction into a song. The finished result mixed sarcasm ('She's the latest and the greatest of them all') with aggression ('You'll get yours yet'), but couldn't dispel the aggrieved tone of the disappointed disciple. Lennon later admitted that he had seen the Maharishi as a kind of father-figure, a substitute for the ignoble Alf; and it's the child's burning resentment at being betrayed by someone who was supposed to protect him that is the song's underlying theme.

Lennon spent much of April recording home demos of most of these songs—generally doubling up his vocal and acoustic guitar parts, concentrating more on feel than accuracy or timing. The demos have a clarity sometimes missing on the final record—and a slightly trippy feel that suggested that John had lost no time in returning to the comforting arms of Mary Jane. There are slight differences between these demos and the finished records, but they are usually a matter of decoration rather than conception: The Beatles may have embellished the songs, but they didn't change them, though the home recording of 'Dear Prudence' repeats the middle section, for example, while The Beatles' take does not.

In mid-May, The Beatles regrouped to prepare for their own proper recording sessions. Over two or three days, they cut more rough demos of their new songs, only slightly more complicated than Lennon's solo work, and again with a high, stoned atmosphere that suggests the band were taking things very comfortably indeed. If they had been a little more precise and together, then these demos might have made a better album than 'The Beatles' eventually turned out to be: they have a communal feel entirely missing from the proper recording sessions, where (as has been noted many times in the past) each of the group effectively used the others as sidemen on their own compositions. At these demo sessions at George Harrison's house, they gave even their darkest new compositions a frivolity that came from co-operation and mutual understanding.

One of the most impressive of The Beatles' demos from this week was another new Lennon song, written just days before it was recorded. 'Revolution' was an instant, slightly confused response to the student uprisings on the streets of Europe, and the battles in the USA over the American Army's naked involvement in the civil war in Vietnam.

'Revolution' saw Lennon as a gradualist, urging caution rather than full-blooded commitment to violent solutions. 'But when you talk about destruction/Don't you know that you can count me out', ran one of the key lines, which caught Lennon midway between the need for a radical change in society, and the hippie ideal that everything could be achieved through love. The song was understood by student radicals as a rather patronising piece of anti-realism: they felt that Lennon's repeated chorus line, 'Don't you know it's gonna be alright', could only have come from someone not personally affected by the problems which fuelled the student protests. In purely political terms, however, the lyrics made sense in quite another way: backing the line of the traditional Western Communist parties that revolution had to evolve rather than be imposed in a single direct action, as the ultra-left (the Trotskyists) were recommending. Whatever Lennon's true motives, The Beatles' first off-the-cuff recording of the song was wonderfully inappropriate, full of joyous harmonies that sounded like a celebration rather than a warning. Only later would Lennon find a more suitable setting for his lyrics, and question his own ambiguous feelings about political violence.

Chapter 8

MAY 1968 TO
DECEMBER 1968

. . . .

MAY 20, 1968: *RECORDING* 'Two Virgins.'

Conveniently, both sets of spouses and children were out of the country. That left Beatle John Lennon free to invite avant-garde artist Yoko Ono to his Surrey home, ostensibly to play her his home recordings. Lennon made sure that his boyhood friend, Pete Shotton, was also in the house to lessen his own nerves. But when Shotton left the shy couple alone, they retired to Lennon's home studio upstairs. Lennon ran his tapes, Yoko recognised a kindred spirit, and the couple spent the night recording what was later issued as 'Two Virgins', before making love at dawn. By the time that Cynthia Lennon returned from Greece, her place in her husband's life and home had been supplanted.

There's an Edenic, mythic quality to this episode that seems somehow typical of the John and Yoko story. But we have the recording as proof of their first night together, plus the fact that a couple of days later they made their first joint appearance in public, at the opening of the Apple-financed tailoring business in London's Kings Road. That same week, they attended Yoko's happening at the Arts Lab in Drury Lane, where she was exhibiting 'Objects To Be Taken Apart Or Added To.'

As we already know, Lennon had been creating his own tapes of noise and nonsense at home for some two years before Yoko entered his den. Her experiments with sound went back to the fifties. It took a while for the two visions to coincide, however, and 'Two Virgins' remains the least convincing of the partnership's forays into the avant-garde, more interesting as a personal document than in its own musical right.

87

Some copies of the finished 'Two Virgins' album attempted to break the 30 minutes of sound into separate tracks, numbered from 1 to 10 for convenience. In fact, though, 'Two Virgins' had no recognisable form at all. It merely extracted around 30 minutes from an audio vérité record of the night's work, a jumbled assemblage of voices, distorted musical instruments, sou... effects tapes and the hum of the home studio. It's difficult to know how much of the album was recorded 'live', that is without any overdubs or editing, and how many of the more bizarre sound effects—explosions, bird song, thirties' music hall ditties—were added afterwards. Comparing the instrumental sounds of the album to 'Jessie's Dream' in *Magical Mystery Tour*, though, you find many similarities—the same tone of treated, reverbed guitar, the same plinkety-plonk piano. It's likely, then, that Lennon merely set up several of his tapes and loops on various recorders, and then he and Yoko improvised over the top.

Those improvisations immediately distinguish the professional avant-gardist from the novice. Yoko soon chimes in with her unique style of vocalising, letting out a ghostly wail which John answers with feedback guitar, then bursting into a full-blooded scream, which Lennon vainly attempts to match. While her contributions are as whole-hearted as any of her later recorded work, Lennon sounds ill at ease, tantalised by what he is doing but unable to turn off his irony. So while Yoko wails, John plays nursery rhymes on the piano, or invents everyday conversations in an exaggerated Lancashire accent. 'It's just me, Hilda, I'm home for tea', he announces at one point—to be answered by Yoko drifting as ever into the mock-philosophical, calling out 'Tea's never ready.'

Other highlights include John unable to find a tin-opener; the sound of collapsing buildings; and some genuinely fascinating moments when Yoko echoes the shifting sands of Lennon's guitar pedal with some heady bursts of vocal noise. But such moments are interrupted by periods of tedium, with only the whistle of the tape and the clunking of microphones to disturb the silence. It's this air of chaos which makes 'Two Virgins' of minor artistic interest. But amidst the crashing barrage of noise and the half-hearted attempt at catharsis, you can hear two cultures, two views of the world in collision—the tight, ironic rock 'n' roller, and the sure-footed performance artist. It was the effect she had on him which gives these early ramblings their significance.

Whether the tape should ever have been released, however, is another matter. As Yoko said, "It was a bum album," though she was also referring to the cover photograph, showing John and Yoko stark naked, in full front and back views. EMI in the UK and Capitol in the States refused to distribute such a scurrilous album cover, even when wrapped in a brown paper bag with the description of Adam and Eve's nudity from Chapter II of *Genesis* printed on the back. As this was The Beatles' first album release on their Apple Records label, it did not exactly bode well for the new company's artistic independence, though eventually two small labels, Track and Tetragrammaton, did send the record to the shops. Even then, some 30,000 copies of the album were seized by police in New Jersey early in 1969, under local obscenity laws.

Lennon's closest colleague in The Beatles was also apparently unhappy by the couple's willingness to be pictured in the nude. Despite that, however, Paul McCartney was quoted on the album sleeve: 'When two great Saints meet it is a humbling experience. The battles to prove he was a saint' Whether this grammatically obscure tribute was directed at the Lennons, of course, was a moot point.

For John, sainthood didn't come into it. The album cover was a gesture of nakedness—"We felt like Adam and Eve," he commented later—and a way of showing the world that they had nothing to hide, that they were just like anyone else. Though the second half of this manifesto was soon forgotten, the attempt at complete openness sparked most of Lennon's public activities, and art, through to the end of 1970.

LATE MAY 1968: *RECORDING* 'The Maharishi Song.'

'Sexy Sadie' wasn't Lennon's sole response in song to the Maharishi. A few days after recording 'Two Virgins', he and Yoko taped this virulent little spoken blues over electric slide guitar backing. Yoko's role was to entice John through a searing attack on the supposed hypocrisy of the guru and his followers, fingering everyone from the Beatle wives and their infatuation for a leather-clad American actor to the Maharishi and the women who queued for a private consultation. 'I wrote 600 songs about how I feel', Lennon notes in an aside; 'I felt like dying, crying and committing suicide, but I felt creative.' Mostly, though, 'The Maharishi Song' is a vicious assault—another cry from the heart of a man betrayed. It was never taken any further, as the sheer act of committing it to tape proved cathartic enough. But 'The Maharishi Song' confirms that Lennon had expected spiritual transport from the Rishikesh experience, and felt he had been sold short.

MAY 30 TO JUNE 25, 1968: *THE BEATLES* recording 'Revolution 1'/'Don't Pass Me By'/'Revolution 9;' John recording sound effects and poetry.

Despite the unprecedented pre-production for the album, in the shape of the demo sessions at George Harrison's house in late May, 'The Beatles'—alias, 'The White Album'—took almost five months to complete, with the band working regular five-day weeks in several London studios.

Despite its commercial potential, Lennon had decided to abandon the light-headed arrangement of 'Revolution' recorded a week or so earlier, in favour of a slower, lazier version which accentuated the message of the song. In its original form, however, as Mark Lewisohn's researches in the EMI vaults revealed, 'Revolution 1' was some 10 minutes long. The first four minutes of that version, complete with rowdy electric rhythm guitar and some sleepy 'shoo-be-doo-wah' backing vocals from Harrison and McCartney, were issued on the 'White Album.' Lennon overdubbed his lead vocal lying on the floor of the Abbey Road studios, and altering the lyrics slightly from one take to the next—first you could count John 'out' when it came to violence, then it was 'in'. On the finished recording, he hedged his bets, slurring 'out, in' as his comment on the necessity for violence in the overthrow of the state.

Not satisfied with the song itself, Lennon then took the final six minutes of the original take, and used it as the bedrock for a remarkable sound collage, also titled 'Revolution'–though this time it was 'No. 9'. Just two weeks after the amateurish efforts of 'Two Virgins', Lennon and Ono were assembling an altogether more convincing portrait of chaos, the sound of society in tumult, of political demonstrations, explosions, gunfire, disintegration. Rambling in and out of the noise were the voices of John, Yoko and George Harrison, throwing in *non sequiturs* and ironic asides. To begin the tape, Lennon dug out an EMI test tape, with an engineer reciting 'Number nine' in a lugubrious voice. Then on June 20 and 21, the trio knitted the pieces together, using all three studios at Abbey Road to play the tape loops which were at the heart of the recording, and then taking another day's session to mix the results. Significantly, the piece was completed while one of its main critics, Paul McCartney, was on holiday in the United States.

'Revolution 9' remains the least popular of all The Beatles recordings, and the most accessible of John's sound collages. By comparison, 'Two Virgins' was indulgent and directed inwards, aimed at those who had made it rather than the rest of the world. 'Revolution 9' may have been a waste of valuable Beatles vinyl, or not; but at least it achieved its stated purpose, painting a violent revolution in sound. As such, it's a much more truthful record of the summer of 1968 than, say, The Rolling Stones' much-fêted show of sympathy with the radical left, 'Street Fighting Man'.

On the same day that he began 'Revolution 9', Lennon taped a second set of noises and effects for the theatrical adaptation of his two books, originally staged late in 1967 as *Scene Three Act One*, now ready for presentation at the Old Vic a fortnight hence under the more obvious title, *In His Own Write*. (Adrienne Kennedy and Victor Spinetti's script was subsequently published in its own right as *The Lennon Play*, though John seems to have had no hand in the adaptation.)

Lennon's work on the play's incidental music seems to have involved raiding the EMI library of sound effects for suitable pieces of orchestral and Hammond organ music to accompany Lennon vignettes like 'Last Will And Testicle' and 'The Neville Club;' and finding tapes of applause and party noises to be heard during other scenes in the play.

JUNE 26 TO OCTOBER 13, 1968: THE BEATLES recording *'Everybody's Got Something To Hide Except For Me And My Monkey'/'Goodnight'/'Ob-La-Di, Ob-La-Da'/'Revolution'/'Don't Pass Me By'/'Cry Baby Cry'/'Helter Skelter'/'Sexy Sadie'/'Hey Jude'/'Not Guilty'/'Yer Blues'/'Rocky Raccoon'/ 'While My Guitar Gently Weeps'/'Back In The USSR'/'Dear Prudence'/ 'Glass Onion'/'I Will'/'Birthday'/'Piggies'/'Happiness Is A Warm Gun'/ 'Honey Pie'/'The Continuing Story Of Bungalow Bill'/'I'm So Tired'/'Julia' (NB: Other songs were recorded by various members of the Beatles during this period, but without any contributions from Lennon.)*

The remaining four months of sessions for the 'White Album' also produced the epochal single, 'Hey Jude'/'Revolution'—the flipside being an entirely new, much raunchier version of the song the band had already recorded once. Dominated by distorted fuzz guitars, this 'Revolution' was a 'count me out' rendition, despite the aural evidence that Lennon was all for chaos and mayhem.

Like all The Beatles, John wasn't present at all the 'White Album' sessions; he missed the recording of several Harrison songs in early October, while Ringo Starr actually left the band for 10 days during the taping of 'Back In The USSR' and 'Dear Prudence'. For much of the time, Lennon was content to play sideman to McCartney—adding a nifty jazz guitar solo to 'Honey Pie', for example, bass to 'Rocky Raccoon', organ to Harrison's 'While My Guitar Gently Weeps' in its original incarnation, and then joint lead guitar with Eric Clapton on the remake, saxophone on the frenzied 'Helter Skelter,' and inventing tape loops of animal noises for Harrison's satirical 'Piggies', to which Lennon also added the lines about the pigs 'clutching forks and knives/to eat their bacon'.

'The Beatles' remains the band's richest treasury of songs, a potpourri of musical styles from country and western to music hall, rock 'n' roll to sentimental ballads, all of them performed with just a hint of satire. It lacks the formal unity of 'Sgt. Pepper' and 'Abbey Road', or the air of community which marked all The Beatles' albums up to 'Revolver.' But it declared to the world that the group were capable of anything, and the performances ranged from ultra-tight, carefully arranged productions, to off-the-cuff ditties on the verge of falling to pieces.

Though Lennon was always a champion of the spontaneous, recording 'I'm So Tired' and 'Bungalow Bill' in a single session, his work was as diverse as anyone else's in the band, and the new songs he contributed during the sessions varied between the lush children's song, 'Goodnight', and the self-mocking rocker, 'Glass Onion'. Even though Lennon had already worked out rough arrangements for his other songs during the demo sessions, that didn't mean he wasn't open to embellishments: so 'Dear Prudence' was soaked in three-part harmonies, some characteristically stabbing electric guitar (few albums in history have such a dirty guitar sound), and McCartney's finest drumming on record. 'Bungalow Bill' was given a flowing Spanish guitar introduction, while everyone in the studio—including Yoko—joined in on the chorus, and Yoko even had a whole line to herself.

From which you will also gather that Yoko was now a part of The Beatles' recording team, much to the disgust of the other band members. In the past, wives and girlfriends had known their place: now wherever John went, Yoko would follow. Leaving aside their feelings for John's wife, Cynthia, the other Beatles found Yoko's presence a distraction; they resented her suggestions that they might vary their tempos, or (as during 'Sexy Sadie') simply pull their socks up; and they found John more willing to listen to Yoko's comments than their own. For the first time, The Beatles began to feel uncomfortable about criticising each other's work: the outspokenness which had been their in-built defence mechanism against over-indulgence was put on hold.

On tape, Yoko's contribution was most obvious on 'Revolution 9', and on a song which was left off the final cut—'What's The New Mary Jane'. John, Yoko, George and Mal Evans taped this late one night at Abbey Road, adding bizarre percussion to the basic instrumental line-up of piano and guitar, while Lennon chanted the off-the-wall lyrics over the top (in more ways than one). A three-minute mix of the song was prepared, and John and Yoko took the acetate home; but Paul vetoed its inclusion when he and John stayed up 24 hours assembling the final running order of the album.

Yoko had a less direct influence on Lennon's most brilliant song from these sessions—'Happiness Is A Warm Gun'. The name came from an American gun magazine which George Martin showed to John; one of its features was headlined, 'Happiness is a warm gun in your hand' which duly became the song's working title. Lennon used the phrase, and its sexual symbolism, as the basis for a piece of mock doo-wop, a throwback to the vocal groups of the fifties, written around those familiar C-Am-F-G chord changes. He then tied it together with two other song fragments, the first another stream-of-nonsense lyric put together with Apple publicist Derek Taylor, the second—'Mother Superior jump the gun'—an early reference both to John's nickname for Yoko, and to Yoko's domination of their relationship.

Rather than being assembled in sections, however, the song was recorded whole—with the frequent changes of tempo requiring many re-takes. It began with Lennon reverting once again to his favourite piece of guitar-picking, this time on electric rather than acoustic, interrupted by Harrison's blasts of fuzz guitar. Then came a bluesy linking section, the lyrics of which broke several taboos simultaneously: 'I need a fix cause I'm going down/Down to the bits that I left uptown;' and finally the band fell playfully into the doo-wop segment, with John, Paul and George answering Lennon's raw vocal with a three-part harmony of 'bang bang shoot shoot'. The lasciviousness of Lennon's vocal left no doubt that the lyrics' guns and triggers were merely metaphors for an altogether more basic human occupation.

Like much of John's work from the late sixties, 'Happiness Is A Warm Gun' suggested much more than it stated. Likewise 'Glass Onion', Lennon's ironic tribute to the group he was slowly beginning to leave behind. Its lyrics referred to a sheaf of recent Beatles recordings, from 'Fixing A Hole' to 'The Fool On The Hill;' while the most quotable line revealed that 'The walrus was Paul'—a gesture of respect and sympathy to the man who had been his closest friend, and who he would never be as close to again. The rock beat of the song, the aggression of Lennon's vocal, and the sleepy string arrangement, all conspired to hide the fact that this was another of Lennon's production line jobs, spliced together like a dovetail joint.

'Cry Baby Cry' was constructed in the same manner—with a hook-line taken from a TV commercial (Lennon frequently watched TV while he was trying to write songs), and a story-line that reads like a missing chapter from 'Alice Through The Looking Glass'. Lennon thought so little of this acoustic folk song that, being reminded of the song in 1980, he commented: "Not me. A piece of rubbish." But his prints were clearly on the gun.

'Goodnight' was a precursor to 'Beautiful Boy' on 'Double Fantasy'—a lullaby for a five-year-old son. First time around, it was meant for Julian Lennon, not Sean, and John gave it to Ringo to sing, backed by a full concert orchestra. Like McCartney's 'Honey Pie', 'Goodnight' sounded like a standard the first time you heard it; Bing Crosby might have sung it back in the thirties.

The last song recorded for 'The Beatles' was 'Julia'—almost the first number Lennon had written for the project. Taped on October 13, it was an entirely solo performance—the only time John did this on a Beatles record. The arrangement was unaltered from the demos recorded back in April, so why did Lennon hold back the song for so long? Speculation is fruitless, but it's tempting to think that this might, after all, have been too personal a statement even for John Lennon. The publication of Hunter Davies' authorised Beatles biography during the recording sessions alerted the world to the fact that Julia was the name of Lennon's mother; maybe John felt he couldn't make his love song to her, and Yoko, public. And maybe the fact he was about to issue an album with his full-frontal naked picture changed his mind.

JUNE 15, 1968: *ACORN EVENT* at the National Sculpture Exhibition, Coventry.

In late May, John and Yoko requested that they be allowed to exhibit a work of art in the National Sculpture Exhibition, staged by Fabio Barraclough in the grounds of Coventry Cathedral. Rather than the tangled metal and plastic favoured by the leading artists of the day, the Lennons contributed a piece of 'living art'—two acorns, to be planted in the ground, one facing East, the other West, as symbols of the couple's union, and as a message of hope and spiritual growth for the future. The idea was Lennon's, though it was clearly influenced by Yoko: Lennon was catching on to the idea that a concept was as powerful as an object.

Barraclough was willing to indulge the pop star, but only so far; the Lennons could plant the acorns, but they wouldn't be mentioned in the catalogue. So John and Yoko prepared their own, fronted by a photograph of the couple apparently growing out of the acorn pots, and with a simple text by John: 'This is what happens when two clouds meet'. Once again, the inspiration of Yoko's book *Grapefruit* was unmistakable.

At the Cathedral, the couple's extra-marital relationship meant that they were not allowed to plant their acorns in the main exhibition, which was on consecrated ground; nor, in the event, did the Canon allow the Lennons' catalogue to be distributed. But the acorns were finally laid to rest, beneath a plaque that read: '*Yoko* by John Lennon/*John* by Yoko Ono/ Sometime in May 1968'. Photographers duly captured the event, winning it far more publicity than the rest of the Sculpture Exhibition.

The aftermath was a clear indication of the rocky path that lay ahead, however. After a few days, the acorns were removed by an intruder: when the Lennons sent a replacement set, 24-hour security was called in to prevent a repetition. Acorns? Two clouds meet? The papers hinted that Lennon had gone crazy. Two decades or more later, it is likely that John and Yoko's living sculpture has been more productive than any of the metaphorical constructions or abstracts submitted by the rest of the artists in the Exhibition.

· · · · **JUNE 18, 1968: *IN HIS OWN WRITE* play staged.**

Beyond writing the original books on which this adaptation was based, and recording some background noise for the production, Lennon had no real involvement in this one-act play, or in its predecessor *Scene Three Act One*, staged in November 1967. But while he was in New York in May 1968, announcing the foundation of the Apple Corps to the world's press, Lennon let slip that he was writing a film script based around the same material. When the play proved unpopular, the film was abandoned; and no vestige of Lennon's script has surfaced since.

· · · · **JULY 1, 1968: *YOU ARE HERE* exhibition opens.**

"John has these crazy ideas all the time," Yoko commented when this exhibition opened at the Robert Fraser Gallery in London's West End. "He just didn't use them. It was just a personal joke for himself. He has about 20 ideas in 20 minutes. So I say, 'Well, that idea is good, why don't you just do it?' and he had never thought of actually doing it, physically. The point is, when you do something, something happens, the concept is simple, but then you get all sorts of reactions and you've started something."

That's a very precise description of Yoko's influence on Lennon in 1968—translating fantasy into reality, and provoking a critical response. In the spirit of the Fluxus art movement she had joined a few years earlier, John's *You Are Here* exhibition was based around a single theme—expressed in a large white canvas hanging on a gallery wall, on which John had scrawled 'You are here.' As a diversion, Lennon had assembled an array of charity collection boxes—once a common sight in British stores and streets, usually soliciting money for the blind or the care of animals. They made a surreal complement to Lennon's own charity appeal, a hat placed on the ground with a handwritten sign, 'For the artist.'

Like most conceptual art, the *You Are Here* piece was probably better imagined than staged; certainly the critics felt so, suggesting that Lennon was completely in thrall to his oriental artist friend, to whom the show was dedicated: 'To Yoko from John, with love.' Outside the exhibition on opening day, Lennon let loose 365 helium-filled balloons, to each of which was attached a reply card, asking for comments. As the cards slowly returned from around the Home Counties, John and Yoko began to feel the force of the public's disapproval, both of his abandonment of his wife, and of his open dalliance with a Japanese woman.

The opening was filmed, at the Lennons' request—the first of their joint ventures into that medium. Snippets of the film have since been shown in various documentaries about the couple.

- **CIRCA AUGUST 1968:** *FILM NO. 5 (SMILE)* filmed.

Smile was the Lennons' first authentic collaboration on film, as the footage of the *You Are Here* opening was never edited into a distinct whole. The subject of the film was simple enough—it documented the birth and life of a John Lennon smile, filmed on a high-speed camera in a few seconds' real time, which played back through a normal projector increased the length of the movie to just over 50 minutes.

As usual, the concept had come first. In the manner of her film scripts in *Grapefruit*, Yoko had wanted to capture every person in the world smiling. Gradually, she lowered her horizons, settling on the nearest subject at hand—John Lennon. He saw himself as a representative of the human race, and the film as a statement of optimism for the future: "A symbol of today smiling—that's what I am, whatever that means. I don't mind if people go to the film just to see *me* smiling because it's not that harmful. The idea of the film won't really be dug for another 50 or 100 years."

With its single sustained shot of Lennon's head, backed by a soundtrack made up of the natural sound of his garden—tweeting birds occasionally disturbed by passing airliners—*Smile* made for gentle reflective viewing. Despite its title, in fact two smiles were observed—the only action of note being Lennon blinking three times half-an-hour into the film, and then letting slip a brief glimpse of his tongue. The fascination was in tracing the minutest flickers of expression across his face, and the eventual satisfaction of seeing Lennon smile.

Credited as an Apple film, *Smile* was premiered at the Chicago Film Festival in December 1968; it remains the simplest of the Lennon/Ono films, but that simplicity was a blueprint for what was to follow.

- **CIRCA AUGUST/SEPTEMBER 1968:** *TWO VIRGINS* filmed.

Like *Smile*, *Two Virgins* was filmed at Lennon's Kenwood home in the summer of 1968, and first shown in public four months later in Chicago. This was the couple's first official film together, and Lennon's initial experiment in working with 16mm film, not the 8mm he had used for his home movies in the past. As we've seen, those Lennon solo movies had been the pictorial equivalent of his musical collages, but Yoko persuaded John to strip his work bare, and leave the central statement of each artwork—its concept—clear. It took John some time to incorporate Yoko's suggestion into his music; there were too many layers of tradition and skill to cut through first. But in film, Lennon was happy to follow her lead, and retain the Fluxus characteristic that each piece of art should concentrate on one happening or observation.

Using sections of the as-yet-unreleased 'Two Virgins' tapes as its soundtrack, John and Yoko produced a film that accentuated their similarities, and their innocence. They hired a film crew to shoot them both in turn against an identical background, centring on head-and-shoulders shots that could be juxtaposed and merged. When the two sets of film were edited together, John and Yoko dissolved into two faces of the same being, superimposed on beautiful shots of clouds. The result was a stunning evocation of uncomplicated love, that gave the couple an ethereal distance from the real world. Towards the end of the 21-minute film, the faces separated for the final time, the camera moved back, and the couple were seen in a lengthy, slow-motion embrace. Clad in white, the Two Virgins smiled beneficently at the camera throughout, secure in their mutual love. And as in *Smile*, the simplicity of the action merely heightened its sincerity.

CIRCA OCTOBER 1968: *RECORDING* The Beatles' '1968 Christmas Record!'

As if to highlight the fragmented nature of the group, after four months of exhausting sessions recording 'The Beatles', the band recorded their contributions to their 1968 Fan Club record separately, for the first time. DJ Kenny Everett was given the task of collating the individual offerings into some kind of coherent whole.

The Lennons recorded two spoken pieces, 'Jock And Yono' and 'Once Upon A Pool Table'. The latter was a bizarre collection of puns, metaphors and nonsense word-play, like a translation of one of the pieces in *A Spaniard In The Works* into another language. Biographically, it's 'Jock And Yono' which is of most interest—as it is a thinly disguised fairy-tale nightmare about John, Yoko, and their supposed friends in The Beatles camp. As John recalled in 1970: "They all sat there with their wives, like a fucking jury, and judged us, and the only thing I did was write that piece about 'some of our beast friends' in my usual way, because I was never honest enough, I always had to write in that gobbledegook."

That line comes from 'Jock And Yono': 'They battled on against overwhelming oddities/Including some of their beast friends', and in retrospect it's remarkable that the first public criticism of the other Beatles' conduct towards Yoko should emerge on a Beatles record. Lennon could still end on an optimistic note, however: 'They lived hopefully ever after (and who could blame them)!'

NOVEMBER 7, 1968: *WRITING* A Short Essay On Macrobiotics.

The essay was actually a cartoon strip, written as a puff for a health food store in London, and originally published in the macrobiotic magazine *Harmony*, before being reprinted in an American magazine and then in the book *Lennon Remembers*. The strip caricatured John and Yoko's 'Two Virgins' cover, and amusingly portrayed the transformation in the Lennons' shape as they adopted macrobiotic food at Greg's, and read *Harmony*. The strip ends with John and Yoko high in the sky, just like those two clouds meeting in the Acorn Piece back in June.

From this point onwards, Lennon accompanied almost every autograph or drawing with a quick caricature of himself and Yoko, made up of eyes, smile and spectacles. After the birth of Sean Lennon in 1975, the caricature was widened to include the new member of the family.

• **MID-NOVEMBER 1968:** *RECORDING* 'No Bed For Beatle John'/'Baby's Heartbeat'/'Radio Play'/'Song For John.'

On October 18, 1968, the Lennons were busted in Ringo's West End flat for possession of cannabis resin. Though it fuelled the public's growing dislike of the couple, the case at first seemed to have few long-term ramifications; but it was eventually to become the excuse for the US government to carry out an apparent vendetta in the early-to-mid seventies, by refusing to grant Lennon permanent visa status. In the short term, the stress surrounding the case and the initial court hearing must have contributed to Yoko Ono's miscarriage on November 21, nearly three weeks after she had been admitted to Queen Charlotte's Hospital in London.

Even the loss of a six-month-old foetus, which was named John Ono Lennon II and buried secretly in a coffin, did not prevent the Lennons from continuing their artistic exploits. Lennon had remained by Yoko's bedside throughout her three-week stay in hospital, staying overnight in a sleeping bag by her bed when the ward ran out of spare beds. It was this event which, a week or so before the miscarriage, prompted the recording of 'No Bed For Beatle John.'

The track was in the style of a Gregorian chant, with Yoko and John reading stories from the British press about their activities, from the bed episode to the release, after long delays, of 'Two Virgins.' On the same day, Lennon used his portable recording equipment to tape a few seconds of the unborn baby's heartbeat in Yoko's womb, which he later extended in his home studio until it lasted for more than five minutes.

Finally, John devoted more than 12 minutes of tape to the sound of someone violently turning the switch of a transistor radio off and on, while he and Yoko made phone calls in the background. This was 'Radio Play,' not a play for radio, you understand; and no doubt of enormous artistic significance, though it escapes me for the moment. The Lennons were beginning to feel that, as artistic outcasts from society, their every movement and statement was worthy of documentation. The next three years saw them taking this manifesto to extremes: for the moment, this record of an unhappy period in the Lennons' lives was saved for release on the couple's second 'avant-garde' album, 'Life With The Lions'—its title an ironic hint at the antagonistic media circus in which John and Yoko were now being asked to perform.

Omitted from the album, but recorded on the same day as 'No Bed For Beatle John,' was Yoko's 'Song For John'—actually a medley of three of her compositions. She ad libbed her way in distinctive style through a minute or so of 'Let's Go On Flying', continued with a brief snatch of 'Snow Is Falling All The Time' (which would eventually be recorded by the Lennons under a different title), and concluded with two minutes of 'Don't Worry Kyoko', the first known rendering of a song which she performed several times the following year.

Together with 'No Bed For Beatle John' and 'Radio Play,' 'Song For John' was issued on a flexi-disc distributed with the Spring/Summer 1969 edition of *Aspen*, an American arts magazine. 'Baby's Heartbeat' was offered to a students' magazine in London run by young entrepreneur Richard Branson, but never appeared; instead, a court case ensued, and Apple and Lennon were forced to concede appropriate costs, having failed to provide the musical offering which they had originally promised.

EARLY DECEMBER 1968: *WRITING* and recording home demos of *'Everybody Had A Hard Year'/'A Case Of The Blues'/'Don't Let Me Down'/ 'Oh My Love'.*

No sooner had the Lennons lost a baby than they were dragged into court to plead guilty to a charge of drugs possession. With hostile media attention increasing all the time, Beatles fans apparently turning against him, and his efforts to have a child with his lover brought to a tragic conclusion, small wonder that the songs Lennon wrote during these weeks were a cry of pain, a last search for refuge against despair. A BBC film clip shot at the time shows Lennon in his garden performing 'Everybody Had A Hard Year' on acoustic guitar; the song has since erroneously been bootlegged as an extract from the soundtrack of the Lennons' film, *Rape*. There is also a home recording of the same song, which ended up as Lennon's contribution to The Beatles' 'I've Got A Feeling'. In this initial form, it consisted of a series of repeated verses written around John's acoustic guitar picking, a succession of universal statements sung in a dull, depressed voice that only goes to confirm the personal application of the song's title.

'A Case Of The Blues' was an attempt at channelling the same emotions into positive creativity—and one of Lennon's final ventures into psychedelic imagery, with slightly surreal lines like 'There'll be no coloured glasses wearing knock-kneed shoes' set to an insistent acoustic guitar rhythm that isn't so far removed from his early essays at 'Mean Mr Mustard'.

'Don't Let Me Down' probably wasn't known as such in December 1968, as Lennon had yet to hit upon the title line and chorus. On his two composing tapes for the song, he simply repeats the basic lines of the first verse over and over again, searching for the right chord changes. There are none of the rhythmic breaks of the final song, so—like 'Everyone Had A Hard Year'—it just flows through the verse and back to the beginning again. Stage two of the writing process sees Lennon introducing the middle section for the first time, with the lines 'I'm in love for the first time/Don't you know it drives me mad', before moving into another set of changes that were axed from the final version. The overall effect is more melodic than the record would be; perhaps Lennon felt that the melody was getting in the way of the message, which was a simple song of love for Yoko—as much wish-fulfilment as a statement of fact in the bleak final weeks of 1968.

But the most dramatic and direct expression of the Lennons' sadness came in the initial setting of a song which was completely rewritten two years later for the 'Imagine' album. It was Yoko who wrote the original lyrics for 'Oh My Love;' Lennon set them to music, and broke down the emotion into verse form. Such niceties were irrelevant, however, alongside the naked self-exposure of the words.

Though Lennon sang two of the three home demos recorded at this time, the song was written for Yoko's voice. 'You had a very strong heartbeat', the couple sang to their miscarried child, 'but that's gone now/ Probably we'll forget about you but whoever you were, you were an angel' The rest of the lyric described the mother's bonding with her child, and offered the wish that the experience of loss would make her a stronger woman; but the tone of Lennon's voice undermined the hope.

• **DECEMBER 1968: *FILMING* Film No. 6–Rape.**

Rape was the most professional, and successful, of all the Lennons' ventures into the milieu of film—perhaps because it was a movie to which their major contribution was the concept, not the technique or execution. Just as John's songs from the end of 1968 were cries of rage and pain, so *Rape* also conveyed some of the misery, the cocoon of madness that surrounded the Lennons at this time. Its subject was persecution by media—something of which they had recent experience. As a perverted mirror of their own tribulations, the couple sent cameraman Nick Knowland into the streets of London to locate an attractive young woman, who luckily for the film spoke no English. Knowland then pursued his prey across London, chasing her in a car as she tried to escape in a taxi, and eventually cornering her in a room from which she has no escape. That's the 'rape' of the title: not the sexual assault which it might suggest, but defilement by camera, the systematic breaking of a personality through constant invasion of privacy. The innocent subject's descent from amusement to suspicion, panic and then blind despair, mirrored the way in which the Lennons had seen their public personas change from clowns to buffoons to convenient targets.

There was a difference, of course; John and Yoko had chosen to play their games in public, and had invited media publicity by their choice of careers. Their complaint might have carried more weight had it come from people less willing to place themselves in the public eye. And the morality of the actual filming technique also left a little to be desired. But *Rape* attracted positive reviews when it was premièred on Austrian TV in March 1969, and again after a screening in London that autumn. It also spawned a sequel, *Rape Part 2*.

The second *Rape* was a short—unlike the 77-minute duration of the original film. Shot necessarily with a hand-held camera, the only dialogue in German, and with the last 45 minutes filmed in a darkened room, *Rape* was an endurance test for any audience. The relentless pursuit of the camera was broken only by the change of reels: the film forced the viewer into the role of voyeur. The audience was trapped inside the film—both metaphorically, as the 'rape' takes place, and literally, by the sheer grinding pressure of the movie's length and lack of accessibility.

Lennon was credited as one of the film's sound engineers, and also with music—which was simply a few seconds of 'Radio Play' which accompanied the closing credits.

· · · **DECEMBER 10/11, 1968:** *PERFORMING 'Yer Blues'/'Jam' at The Rolling Stones' Rock 'n' Roll Circus.*

As an illustration of The Beatles' increasing fragmentation, Lennon chose to make his début as a solo performer in the week when the group were supposed to begin rehearsals for their comeback live gigs at the Roundhouse in London—shows which were eventually cancelled as the 'Get Back' project was proposed in its stead.

The occasion was the filming of The Rolling Stones' TV film, which brought many of The Stones' favourite performers together in a circus tent. Lennon chose to perform with Yoko, of course, backed by Keith Richard on bass, Mitch Mitchell on drums, and Eric Clapton on guitar. (The impromptu group performed under the name of Winston Legthigh And The Dirty Macs, incidentally.) Tapes exist of their rehearsals on December 10; the following day, they performed a searing version of 'Yer Blues' in front of the cameras, with a passion that lived up to the anguished potential of the song's lyrics—helped, once again, by recent days in the life. The song segued into a blues jam, where Yoko's screams competed for space with a keening violin solo by a guest musician, before the band roared to a halt. Small wonder that The Stones themselves felt intimidated, and felt their performance paled by comparison: as a result, the movie was never completed, though The Stones are still threatening to do so one day.

· · · **DECEMBER 18, 1968:** *JOHN AND YOKO perform at the Alchemical Wedding.*

'Perform' as in 'performance art' was the order of this day, as the Lennons' solo contribution to what was billed as the Christmas party of the British underground—in the august surroundings of the Royal Albert Hall, no less—was to cavort on stage encased in a white bag. Yoko had already adopted the bag disguise as her own way of dealing with sticky situations: film exists of her walking through the streets of London in a bag, being greeted warily by passers-by. Indeed, *Bagwear: How And When To Wear It* was the title of one of the pamphlets on offer in the infamous *Yoko Ono Sales List*. From there, it was only a short step to Bagism, and then to naming John and Yoko's production company Bag Productions. Subsequent bag appearances will only be listed if they are accompanied by more notable artistic events, however.

Chapter 9

JANUARY 1969 TO
SEPTEMBER 1969

. . . .

. . . **JANUARY 2 TO 31, 1969:** *THE BEATLES* filming *Let It Be*; recording *'Going Up The Country'*/*'Dig A Pony'*/*'I've Got A Feeling'*/*'Don't Let Me Down'*/*'Rocker'*/*'Save The Last Dance For Me'*/*'She Came In Through The Bathroom Window'*/*'Get Back'*/*'Blues'*/*'Two Of Us'*/*'Teddy Boy'*/*'Maggie Mae'*/*'Dig It'*/*'Dig It 2'*/*'Bye Bye Love'*/*'Let It Be'*/*'For You Blue'*/*'Shake Rattle And Roll'*/*'Kansas City'*/*'Miss Ann'*/*'Lawdy Miss Clawdy'*/*'Blue Suede Shoes'*/*'You Really Got A Hold On Me'*/*'Tracks Of My Tears'*/*'The Long And Winding Road'*/*'Isn't It A Pity'*/*'Oh Darling'*/*'The Walk'*/Billy Preston demos/*'Love Me Do'*/*'The One After 909'*/*'I Want You'*/*'Not Fade Away'*/*'Mailman Bring Me No More Blues'*/*'Besame Mucho'*/*'God Save The Queen'*/*'Lady Madonna'*/**LENNON** writing and rehearsing (besides songs listed above) *'Suzie Parker'*/*'Shakin' In The Sixties'*/*'Mean Mr Mustard'*/*'Child Of Nature'*/*'Sun King'*/*'Gimme Some Truth'*/*'Polythene Pam'*/*'Madman'*/*'Watching Rainbows'.*

The 'Get Back'/'Let It Be' project could fill a book by itself—a boring book, but a book nonetheless. The full, tangled story of this Beatles project can be found in Mark Lewisohn's *The Complete Beatles Recording Sessions*: all that's relevant here is that, having abandoned the idea of performing live shows, The Beatles decided to play a concert for TV, and to film the rehearsals. Along the way, the project changed shape, and became a documentary of the band at work in the studio. After a month of painful and mostly fruitless work, The Beatles gave up, leaving assorted engineers and producers to pick up the pieces. Eventually, after 16 months of delays, Phil Spector assembled the 'Let It Be' album, Michael

Lindsay-Hogg the accompanying movie; and The Beatles called it quits.

The first fortnight of January 1969 was spent at Twickenham Film Studios, where The Beatles performed, bickered and chatted under the gaze of the harsh movie lights. No proper recordings were made during this period: all that exists (in profusion) are bootleg recordings made from off-cuts of the film found abandoned while the movie was being edited. On January 22, The Beatles relocated to Apple, where they set about making a studio album—also watched by the cameras. On January 30 they performed live on the Apple roof; a day later they repeated the exercise inside the studio.

The eventual 'Let It Be' album was not exactly their most creative. Contributions from Lennon included a remixed 'Across The Universe' from early 1968; two humorous jams, 'Maggie Mae' and 'Dig It;' 'I've Got A Feeling', which married Paul's unfinished song of that name with his own 'Everyone Had A Hard Year,' as taped at home the previous month; 'The One After 909', a late fifties Quarry Men song unearthed for the occasion; 'Two Of Us', a McCartney song to which Lennon added some of the lyrics in a last show of creative unity; and 'Dig A Pony.'

John later dismissed this last song as "another piece of garbage," but he took it seriously enough at the time, a blend of nonsensical imagery ('I do a road hog...I pick a moon dog') and encouraging philosophy, which repeated the underlying message of 'All You Need Is Love' (you can do whatever you want) with a dash of well-earned cynicism.

Given the harrowing events of recent weeks, Lennon's other new compositions aired this month were surprisingly lightweight. They were proof that for The Beatles, at least, he was still ready to act the part of hack tunesmith, churning out 'Mean Mr Mustard' (as yet unperfected) about a miser mentioned in a press story, and 'Polythene Pam' loosely about an attempt a year earlier to inveigle him into an orgy with a bondage queen. Two other songs later destined for 'Abbey Road' also surfaced in early form, but at this stage 'Sun King' was merely an instrumental based around his trademark guitar-picking, and 'I Want You' was little more than the title and a riff.

Thankfully, Lennon had thought to finish off 'Don't Let Me Down', and the song remains his most poignant work from this month of intensive sessions. The basic structure of the verses remained from his December 1968 demo, but Lennon had tightened up the middle eight with a touch of idealism ('It's a love that lasts forever/It's a love that has no past') and then inserted the chorus line both as a desperate plea for security, and an admission that dreams can easily be destroyed.

At the same time, Lennon began work on 'Gimme Some Truth'—the title of which rapidly became a manifesto for his work over the next two years or more. The words had yet to come, as had the middle section, but the core of anger was what sparked the song into life—the fact that Lennon was sick and tired of being pushed around and treated as an object of contempt, both by the public and (as 'Jock And Yono' had already shown) by his fellow Beatles as well. It took two years before Lennon had sharpened his vision sufficiently to finish the song, and make an incoherent rant into a searing attack on hypocrisy and double-dealing.

Two other songs premièred during the session showed promise, if no more than that. 'Madman' was essentially a one-verse idea–'There's a madman coming gonna do you no harm/wearing pink pajamas and he lives on a farm'–based around a catchy two-note riff that shared a rhythmic base with (once again) 'Mean Mr Mustard'. 'Watching Rainbows' was even more intriguing. It was powered by the same three-chord pattern that opened The Everly Brothers' 'Wake Up Little Susie', and which ended up underneath Yoko's 'Don't Worry Kyoko'. (One version of 'Madman' also ran accidentally into an identical riff.) What's more, there was a song attached–a rather draggy one, admittedly, that suggested an off-key version of 'The Mighty Quinn', but one which had a theme and a chorus line ('Instead of watching rainbows I'm gonna make me some'). And with an ironic twist of fate, it ended with Lennon calling out 'you've gotta shoot me', before The Beatles jammed off into the distance.

Most of the rest was chaos–half-finished ideas that were never knocked into shape, or off-the-cuff ramblings that were by chance captured on film, and hence assumed an importance out of keeping with their ephemeral nature. Examples in circulation include John's 50-second dig at music publisher Dick James in 'Shakin' In The Sixties;' the faintly obscene rock 'n' roll song 'Suzy Parker' preserved in the *Let It Be* film ('when you get to Suzy Parker, everybody gets well done'); two entirely different and equally pointless jams called 'Dig It', to which the phrase 'Can you dig it' is almost a complete lyric sheet; and endless variations on 'White Power' and 'Commonwealth', all of which were sparked by the initial set of lyrics for McCartney's 'Get Back', which were a parody of British racism long before they assumed their more familiar shape (which Lennon interpreted as a subliminal message to himself and Yoko).

Oh yes, Yoko. During pauses in the session, Yoko had her chance to jam with The Beatles, who did their best to look and sound enthusiastic about creating a barrage of feedback and assorted mayhem behind her piercing screams. Mostly, though, they ignored her, and she sat bored at Lennon's side or feet, reading, knitting or simply looking aloof.

Lennon, meanwhile, had his moments of communal feeling: these were, after all, the men with whom he had conquered the world. But for every 'Two Of Us' rehearsal in the *Let It Be* film, with Lennon and McCartney playfully egging each other into Elvis Presley impressions, there are countless moments like the agonisingly uninspired attempt to improve on 'Across The Universe', with Lennon ultimately giving up the ghost himself and leading the band into 'a fast one' as an escape route.

All The Beatles put more enthusiasm into their amateurish renditions of rock 'n' roll standards–and a few of their own. Lennon himself led the band into impromptu versions of 'She Said She Said', 'You're Gonna Lose That Girl', 'Help!' and 'Please Please Me', all unrecognisable as being the same musicians who had recorded the originals. He also pulled his colleagues into performing a remarkable array of cover versions–including 'Honey Hush', 'Hi-Heel Sneakers', 'C'mon Everybody,' 'Good Rockin' Tonight', 'Fools Like Me', 'You Win Again', 'Tennessee', 'What Do

You Wanna Make Those Eyes At Me For,' 'Bad Boy,' 'Sweet Little Sixteen',
'Around And Around', 'Almost Grown', 'School Day,' 'Johnny B. Goode',
'Milk Cow Blues Boogie', 'Little Queenie', 'Blue Suede Shoes', 'Soldier Of
Love', 'Rock And Roll Music', 'Sabre Dance', 'A Shot Of Rhythm And Blues',
'Devil In Her Heart', 'Don't Be Cruel', The Who's 'A Quick One', 'New
Orleans', 'Mailman Bring Me No More Blues', 'Move It' and 'Digging My
Potatoes'. And those were simply Lennon's offerings to the sessions...

Lennon later complained that the *Let It Be* film was "set up by Paul for
Paul...the people that cut it cut it as 'Paul is God', and we're just lying
there. I knew there were some shots of Yoko, and me, that had been just
chopped out of the film for no other reason than the people were oriented
towards Engelbert Humperdinck." That's an exaggeration, but it's
symptomatic of Lennon's attitude to McCartney, to The Beatles, to the
whole damned myth. In the event, his contribution to the project was
slight because that was all he was prepared to put in. He was saving his
energy for his work with Yoko: art-work, in other words, not what he
considered hack-work.

- **FEBRUARY 1969: *WRITING* '*Bag One*' poem.**

It was art critic (and future Lennon assistant) Anthony Fawcett who
introduced John to the joys of lithography, short-cutting the laborious
effort of drawing directly onto the plates and allowing him to create
images on paper that could then be transferred onto litho blocks. John
took away a supply of the requisite materials, and promised to return soon
with a set of drawings which could be issued as a collected edition of his
work. As a gesture of commitment to publisher Ed Newman of the
Curwen Press, he engraved a poem directly onto a plate this month, to be
used as a preface for the collection.

The result was an acrostic, of the kind used to teach small children
their alphabet—albeit a subversive one, where 'A is for Parrot which we
can plainly see' and 'K is for intestines which hurt when we dance'. It ends
like any nursery rhyme should: 'This is my story both humble and true/
take it to pieces and mend it with glue'.

- **FEBRUARY 22 AND APRIL 18, 1969: *THE BEATLES* recording 'I Want
You (She's So Heavy)'.**

Less than a month after the collapse of the 'Let It Be' sessions, The
Beatles regrouped to attempt another album. The first song to be
completed was one which they had rehearsed during their January
sessions—Lennon's uncluttered message of love for Yoko. Whereas his love
songs had once been as opaque as 'Girl' and 'Norwegian Wood', 'I Want
You' said it straight, with no metaphors or imagery to get in the way. The
Beatles' performance was equally direct, veering from a bluesy shuffle in
the verses to the multi-guitar powerhouse which closed the song,
repeating the central riff over and over like an inescapable warning of
doom. Just as the tension became unbearable, with synthesiser white

noise seeping out from under the guitar chords, Lennon cut the tape in mid-note: silence, as he was to discover on 'Life With The Lions', said as much as noise.

• • • **MARCH 2, 1969: *PERFORMING* 'Cambridge 1969.'**

The scene? Lady Mitchell Hall, Cambridge University. The occasion? A concert of experimental, left-field music. "This is a piece called 'Cambridge 1969'," announced Yoko Ono, before emitting an unearthly bellow that sounded like the rasp of twisted metal. Behind her, almost hidden in the darkness of the stage, John Lennon wrenched his electric guitar around his amplifier, producing howls of feedback that acted as dissonance to Yoko's lengthy cries of atonal sound. Gradually her long, single notes gave way to cackles, screams and groans, all matched by Lennon's guitar. As the couple built towards a climax—Yoko screaming at precise intervals, Lennon forcing a wall of white noise from the amps—they were joined on stage by a percussionist and sax-player, who squealed ineffectually in support, and were then left exposed as the Lennons packed their avant-garde credentials and went home.

Pure noise was nothing new for Yoko: at a concert at London's Royal Albert Hall a year earlier, she had performed with saxophonist Ornette Coleman—creating a mutated soundscape of passion which was sampled on 'Aos', included by John on Yoko's first LP. For Lennon, though, Cambridge was a revelation—his first experience as an avant-garde performer, not a Beatle, in contrast to the usual routine where Yoko was seen as the intruder on his territory. The Lennons were using noise as a statement of emotion—without sophistication, or direction, admittedly, though the gist was easy to follow. Yoko's screaming had liberated Lennon's guitar work; this was a far cry from the tentative feedback of 'I Feel Fine' (though much closer to McCartney's 'Helter Skelter'). Next would come the freeing of his voice—and then his writing.

'Cambridge 1969' formed one side of the 'Life With The Lions' album. The other was taken up by the recordings made at Queen Charlotte Hospital the previous November—plus 'Two Minutes Silence', a self-explanatory concept stolen from John Cage.

• • • **MARCH 25 TO 31, 1969: *FILMING Honeymoon; recording* 'Amsterdam'/ 'Radio Peace'/'Jerusalem'/'Hava Nagila'/'I Want You (She's So Heavy).'**

With both halves of the Lennon-Ono partnership having secured divorces from their bewildered spouses, the couple were free to marry—spurred, no doubt, by the wedding of their chief Beatle rivals, Paul McCartney and Linda Eastman, a fortnight earlier. All that remained was to find a country that would marry them immediately. They flew to Paris on March 16, but were unable to set up the instant ceremony they desired. So on March 20 they flew briefly in to the British territory of Gibraltar, where they were married in a short ceremony, signed the register and had the appropriate photos taken for transmission round the world. They then returned to Paris that afternoon, where a couple of days later they met painter Salvador Dali; and then on June 25 they began a bed-in for world peace at the Amsterdam Hilton Hotel.

So commenced 10 months of frenetic activity, promoting the concept of peace by whatever means were available. Setting their individual careers aside, the couple combined Lennon's international reputation and Yoko's conceptual sense to create a multi-media, barrier-free peace event, which saw them plastering the capital cities of the world with posters; releasing peace anthems; giving interviews to anyone who would listen, and many who wouldn't; sending acorns to world leaders; and arousing the fury (or at best amusement) of the establishment from London to Los Angeles.

As reporters gathered outside their room at the Hilton, convinced they were about to witness the consummation of the Lennons' marriage, John and Yoko prepared for a siege—seven days of incessant media attention, almost all of it filmed and recorded by the Lennons' ever-present assistants. The stage had moved from the couple's work to their lives: in effect, their lives were their art, and so deserved to be preserved for posterity on film and tape. 1969 remains the Lennons' most public year: and there is more media documentation of their activities during that time than exists for any other public figure. The complication was that John and Yoko soon began to regard themselves as works of art in their own right; they ignored their bullshit detectors, and rode head-first into a tirade of media mockery and public indifference. Ask them, and you would probably have found that their every move in 1969 deserved to be classed as art. Posterity can afford to be a little more choosy.

About an hour of highlights from the bed-in encounters were edited into a movie, entitled *Honeymoon*—shot with sync sound, and hand-held cameras. The Lennons did none of the photography, simply directing their crew to catch everything that happened on celluloid, and then sitting in on the final editing. As a documentary, it was slightly shambolic, but it caught the flavour of the moment. The same source produced one side of the couple's 'Wedding Album', a lavish package issued eight months too late in November 1969, and including a photocopy of their marriage certificate, a photo of a slice of wedding cake, even a book of press cuttings about their activities, most of which—an example of the couple's extreme generosity of spirit—were less than complimentary about Lennon and his Japanese bride.

'Amsterdam' was the title given to the 25 minutes of audio vérité recordings included on the 'Wedding Album'. The suite began with Yoko's improvisation 'John John (Let's Hope For Peace),' sung acappella like a Japanese mass; continued with a reasonably coherent (and naïve) interview about their peace campaign, actually taped in London after their return from Amsterdam; and also featured John ordering tea and brown toast from room service, and meeting the press in bed. There were a few brief seconds of John's 'Goodnight', performed solo; what sounds like the chord sequence for 'Because' featured behind one of Yoko's improvisations; and what could almost be a dry-run for the John Sinclair riff used as the basis for Lennon to sing 'Goodbye Amsterdam'.

Along the way, the Lennons also taped an inane ditty called 'Radio Peace;' impromptu versions of 'Hava Negila' and 'Jerusalem;' and a few bars of 'I Want You', as an illustration of what The Beatles were doing currently.

• • • **APRIL 14, 1969: *THE BEATLES* recording *'The Ballad Of John And Yoko;'*** **filming** *The Ballad Of John And Yoko.*

The wedding, the bed-in and the return to Blighty were documented in this song, written at the start of April, and recorded by a two-man Beatles line-up when Messrs Harrison and Starr were unable to make the session. That left Lennon to handle lead vocals, two lead guitar parts, acoustic guitar and percussive thumps; McCartney, meanwhile, chipped in on drums, bass, piano, maracas and backing vocals.

'The Ballad Of John And Yoko' was couched as a traditional blues, and handled as a piece of rockabilly, with Lennon spitting out the lyrics, and throwing in little stabs of electric lead. The production was sparse and loose–far removed from The Beatles' usual perfection–and there was little to distract attention from the words. They married a narrative account of the Lennons' recent activities, told with an ironic dig at the attitude of the British press, with a self-conscious announcement of imminent martyrdom in the chorus, in which the use of 'Christ' as an interjection caused the record to be banned or bleeped in the American south.

This piece of self-dramatisation–coupled with the Lennons' film clip for the song, which centred entirely on themselves with only fleeting reference to the rest of The Beatles–made the record something of an irrelevance to the group's catalogue. Looking back, it seems like the first Lennon solo release: only the credit stopped contemporary listeners from making the association.

• • • **APRIL 20 TO MAY 6, 1969: *THE BEATLES* recording *'Oh Darling'*/** *'Octopus' Garden'/'Let It Be' (overdubs)/'You Know My Name (Look Up The Number)'/'Something'/'You Never Give Me Your Money.'*

While Lennon used The Beatles as his backing group, McCartney too transformed them into a vehicle for his own work. Though 'Abbey Road', taped over many months of infrequent sessions, proved to be one of The Beatles' slickest albums, it aroused little interest from Lennon. He clocked in when required, or more often than not, though as ever he managed to avoid performing on too many of George Harrison's compositions. But he gave little of any lasting value away. His sole contribution to this batch of sessions, then, was finally recording the lead vocals (shared with McCartney) to 'You Know My Name', the jokey piece of rubber soul first attempted back in 1967. McCartney looked back on this as his favourite Beatles session: it certainly sounds as if they were having fun, with Lennon twisting his voice into an array of Peter Sellers-like characterisations, in response to McCartney's night-club crooning, while roadie Mal Evans shook gravel in a tray to make up for the absence of Ringo Starr.

• **APRIL 22, 1969:** *RECORDING 'John And Yoko.'*

On April 21, the Lennons announced the formation of their company-within-a-company–Bag Productions Ltd, who henceforth handled John and Yoko's publicity, financing and co-ordination. A day later, in a ceremony on the Apple roof, Lennon changed his name by deed poll: from John Winston Lennon to John Ono Lennon. Yoko was also an Ono Lennon; together they now had nine 'O's in their names, and this was apparently a sign of great fortune.

Flushed with optimism, the couple booked a session at Abbey Road for that evening, and recorded 'John And Yoko'–the track which, with 'Amsterdam', made up the musical section of their 'Wedding Album' package later in the year. Using a microphone shaped like a stethoscope, as used in the top teaching hospitals, the Lennons first recorded a few seconds of each other's heartbeats. These were superimposed on tape, and then made into a loop, which was repeated for 20 minutes or more while John and Yoko called out each other's names across the stereo divide. Their intonation ranged from the passionate to the disinterested, failing even to satisfy those who might have welcomed the Lennons' equivalent of Jane Birkin and Serge Gainsbourg's 'Je T'Aime.' This was fine as a statement of unity and love; but it lacked any objective interest, and its release to the public was an early sign of arrogance.

In the same way that the purity of Yoko's film *Bottoms* had been spoilt by the inclusion of semi-humorous voiceovers, so the beauty of the original statement–the two hearts pounding together to create a womb-like, mysterious pattern of sound–was subverted by the addition of the couple's voices. Having made the transition from 'Baby's Heartbeat' to their own, the experiment wasn't repeated.

• **MAY 25 TO JUNE 1, 1969:** *WRITING, rehearsing and recording 'Give Peace A Chance;' composing 'Come Together' (version one); recording 'KYA Peace Talk;' filming Give Peace A Chance (also known as Bedpeace or Bed-In).*

Bed-in number two was supposed to be in New York, but Lennon's recent drugs conviction meant he wasn't granted an entrance visa–the harbinger of things to come. Having tried an expensive hotel in the Bahamas, the Lennons' party moved to Toronto, and then to Montreal, just across the border from the USA, and close enough to be monitored by countless US radio stations. By comparison, the Amsterdam event had been a dry run for this media explosion. For a week, the Lennons phoned radio stations across North America, and entertained a procession of journalists and counter-culture figures.

Among the latter was Timothy Leary, guru of LSD, and prospective politician on a free-drugs, free-world ticket. Meeting one of the most enthusiastic followers of his acid-crazed manifesto, he commissioned Lennon to write him a campaign tune, entitled 'Come Together'–a project which appealed to the newly egalitarian Lennon. What resulted was a simple chant, in the style of 'Give Peace A Chance', which went: 'Come together and join the party.' That was it: not really enough to shake the castle walls, but it was still a Lennon original. Lennon promised to finish it off and record it, but along the way Leary was imprisoned for drugs offences himself, Lennon transformed 'Come Together' into another song, and the party anthem was forgotten.

Not so 'Give Peace A Chance', a song which Lennon intended as the anthem of the worldwide peace movement, to replace the spiritual 'We Shall Overcome'. He unveiled the basic chorus, with its simple message–'All we are saying is give peace a chance'–during an interview in Toronto on May 25, and during breaks in the bed-in in Montreal he made plans to record the chant in the couple's hotel room. He taped various rehearsal takes in the run-up to the session, and then on May 31 he ordered a four-track tape machine to be delivered to the room, alerted a cabal of friends and supporters, wrote out four makeshift 'verses' on large pieces of white card to be displayed around the room, and waited for the magic to begin.

Room 1742 of the Reine Elizabeth Hotel was eventually filled with around 50 people–among them a sound engineer in charge of the tape deck, and a full camera crew, documenting–of course–the session for posterity. Several takes of the song ensued, with Lennon and comedian Tommy Smothers playing two basic chords on acoustic guitar, while DJ Roger Scott bashed a table to keep time. Lennon led the ensemble through the four verses–each beginning 'Everybody's talking 'bout...' and proceeding with a litany of appropriate names or nouns–before the massed vocalists faded into the distance singing repeated rounds of the chorus, while Lennon shouted out encouragement and asides. As a piece of instant art, it was–as Lennon's final comment had it–'beautiful'. But it wasn't quite innocent: Lennon took the tapes back to London at the start of June, overdubbed Ringo Starr's backbeat to replace the somewhat shaky percussion on the day, and also brought in a choir of session singers to stiffen up the equally erratic harmony vocals. Like the 'Let It Be' project earlier in the year, then, 'Give Peace A Chance' wasn't quite as uncalculated as it seemed.

But it worked: it was a hit record around the world, was adopted as an anthem by anti-Vietnam protestors in Washington, and remains the most potent symbol of the Lennons' quest for peace. It also inaugurated a new concept: The Plastic Ono Band. 'You are all The Plastic Ono Band' read the copy for the single's adverts, backed by a page from the London telephone directory with the names of friends and heroes inserted into the lists at random. Henceforward, The Plastic Ono Band was anyone John cared to work with. And still the world, and The Beatles, thought that everything else would continue as before.

While Lennon was overdubbing 'Give Peace A Chance', Yoko was supervising the editing of the accompanying promotional film–which basically documented the hotel room recording session. It formed a small part of a longer feature, which was never completed, chronicling the entire bed-in: extracts from the full-length *Give Peace A Chance*, such as the infamous encounter with American cartoonist Al Capp, turned up in the *Imagine: John Lennon* documentary nearly two decades later.

- **EARLY JUNE 1969:** *RECORDING* 'Remember Love.'

Establishing a tradition that survived as long as John and Yoko's relationship, the flipside of The Plastic Ono Band's first single showcased Yoko Ono. To date, the public had only been treated to her more extreme vocal stylings: 'Remember Love', recorded at their home studio immediately after they returned from Canada, was by contrast a delicate ballad, with Yoko breathing her simple message of love into the microphone while John once again showed off his acoustic guitar picking–to a series of chords which came close to another of his recent compositions, 'Sun King'.

- **JUNE 17, 1969:** *OH! CALCUTTA!* opens in New York.

Critic and writer Kenneth Tynan was responsible for producing *Oh! Calcutta!* on the New York stage, and then 13 months later in London. The play, a loose aggregation of sketches contributed by many hands, tore at the boundaries of sexual liberation and censorship, with its frank portrayal of roles, positions and language not usually seen and heard in public.

Lennon was one of many notables whom Tynan approached for ideas. As John remembered in 1970: "He just said, 'I'm getting all these different people to write something erotic, will you do it?' So I came up with two lines, which was the masturbation scene. It was a great childhood thing, everybody's been masturbating and trying to think of something sexy, and somebody'd shout 'Winston Churchill' in the middle of it and break down. So I just wrote that down on a paper and told them to put whichever names in that suited the hero, and they did it." In the New York script, also published in book form, Tynan built a sketch around Lennon's idea, substituting none other than the Lone Ranger for Mr Churchill in the role of fantasy-breaker.

In the show's programme, Lennon contributed a brief autobiography: 'Born October 9, 1940. Lived. Met Yoko 1966!' He's also credited on the play's cast album, though he doesn't appear on it.

JULY 1 TO AUGUST 25, 1969: *THE BEATLES* recording 'Maxwell's Silver Hammer'/'Come Together'/'The End'/'Sun King'/'Mean Mr Mustard'/ 'Polythene Pam'/'She Came In Through The Bathroom Window'/'Because.'

This final set of four-man Beatles sessions saw the completion of 'Abbey Road', with most of the work concentrated on the 'medley' which took up the last third of the record. Lennon was suitably damning about the project–"'Abbey Road' was really unfinished songs all stuck together. Everybody praises the album so much, but none of the songs had anything to do with each other, no thread at all, only the fact that we stuck them together." And it's noticeable that for all its musical invention, and cohesiveness of sound, 'Abbey Road' carries little of Lennon's best work.

Most of his songs, in fact, were throwaways–vignettes, two minutes or less of hasty scene-painting with no personal content; and by 1969, if it wasn't personal, then for Lennon it didn't count. That takes care of 'Polythene Pam' and 'Mean Mr Mustard', which had been polished into shape since their first outings in January 1969, but still revealed little of Lennon's true preoccupations. Likewise 'Sun King', which matched the acoustic guitar riff John had already used on 'Everyone Had A Hard Year' and 'Remember Love' to a set of lush Beatle harmonies, straight-facedly intoning nonsense syllables in mock-Spanish.

'Because' produced another superb exhibition of harmonies, triple-tracked by John, Paul and George. John wrote the song after hearing Yoko play Beethoven's 'Moonlight Sonata' on the piano: he asked her to write out the chords backwards and play them, and the guitar riff behind the song was the result. For his words, Lennon dipped back into his bag of optimism left over from the summer of 1967, to produce a pantheistic vision of happiness and oneness: 'Because the world is round/It turns me on...Because the sky is blue/It makes me cry.'

Lennon's only other contribution to 'Abbey Road' was 'Come Together:' not the simplistic campaign chant he'd written for Timothy Leary, but a bluesy boogie which kicked off from the opening lines of Chuck Berry's classic car-chase song, 'You Can't Catch Me' ('Here comes old flat-top/He comes grooving up slowly') into a set of free-association images inspired by his marriage to Yoko. The Berry influence was also felt in the speed of the imagery, with each phrase passing too quickly to be understood at first hearing, the sound as important as the meaning. And Yoko's inspiration remained in the verses ('He got Ono sideboard...he got Bag Production') and more blatantly in the chorus, a celebration of the couple's sexuality ('Come together, right now, over me').

Almost lost in the record's mix was Lennon's whispered injunction, 'shoot me', between each verse–reminiscent of the ad-libs on 'Watching Rainbows' from earlier in the year. Maybe martyrdom still didn't seem that far away in the summer of 1969.

Lennon missed several of the final 'Abbey Road' sessions–for the first week of July, for instance, he and Yoko were on holiday in Scotland, where their car ran off the road and they found themselves in hospital. The last time that all four Beatles gathered in the recording studio was August 20, when John remixed 'I Want You (She's So Heavy)', and helped out while the closing medley was assembled. A couple of sessions later, the album was complete; and within a week Lennon was telling new Beatles manager Allen Klein that he was leaving the group.

• • •   **AUGUST 1969: *FILMING* Self Portrait.**

'Two Virgins' had nothing on this. That controversial album cover had been a statement of innocence through nakedness: two 'born again virgins' rediscovering Eden through each other. *Self Portrait*, by contrast, took self-exposure to its ultimate extreme: 15 minutes of slow-motion footage of John's semi-erect penis, shot (like *Smile*) with high-speed film. The original plan was for the film to capture the process of erection, but Lennon found the presence of a film crew distracting, and Yoko's efforts to strike suitably erotic poses failed to elicit the right response. A copy of *Playboy* succeeded where his wife had not, and the film raced through the camera for a minute or two while Lennon attempted to concentrate on the nature of eroticism. "My prick, that's all you saw for a long time," Lennon explained later. "No movement, but it dribbled at the end. That was accidental."

The motive for the film remains cloudy, however. Was Lennon attempting a further debunking of The Beatles myth, after 'Two Virgins' had proved that he was human, after all? Or was he influenced by the common notion that all underground film is somehow pornographic? Either way, the short picture failed to impress the avant-garde or the public, as its screenings were restricted to private cinema clubs. While their music, and their peace campaigns, were generously aimed at the world, rather than an élite, the Lennons had yet to make the same transition from experimental to populist in their film work.

• **EARLY SEPTEMBER 1969:** *WRITING and recording home demos of 'Cold Turkey.'*

During the bitter final months of 1968, the Lennons' continual use of LSD and marijuana slipped over into heroin. In the late summer of 1969 they decided to make the break, choosing to go 'cold turkey' (experience all the pangs of chemical withdrawal without medical supervision).

Now convinced that art was there to mirror his life, Lennon poured his experience into a song. It was titled 'Cold Turkey,' a naked admission of its inspiration—at least to those familiar with narcotics terminology. In the event, the fact that there was some kind of drugs connection led the BBC and other radio stations to ban the finished record—short change for a song which, as Lennon insisted, was a warning against drug use rather than an encouragement to experiment.

The chorus of the song carried its stark message: 'Cold turkey has got me on the run.' The verses, round a repetitive two-chord pattern, were equally basic, detailing the pain, terror and loneliness of withdrawal as the body craves for the drug and tries to torture the mind into giving way. The physical descriptions are scary enough: what's fascinating is Lennon's mental response: 'I wish I was a baby/I wish I was dead.' That need to return to the womb, to the warmth and security of childhood, was sparked by the same feeling of betrayal that would later inspire 'Mother' and 'My Mummy's Dead.' A hint of the same desire can be found on 'John And Yoko,' where the combined noise of the couple's heartbeats comes close to the womb-sound therapy tapes occasionally prescribed to help the insecure to sleep.

Marc Bolan, then leader of the acoustic duo Tyrannosaurus Rex, always claimed that Lennon had been trying to sound like him on 'Cold Turkey.' That sounded like arrogant blustering, until you heard Lennon's acoustic demos, where Lennon quavered his way through the lyric like a mutant sheep, bleating out his pain over the final chords of the song. Take one was a simple acoustic guitar/vocal rendition; take two double-tracked the vocal, and added the song's addictive lead guitar line, which was duplicated by Eric Clapton on the record. A third home take found Yoko helping proceedings along, adding her own cackles to Lennon's, and then screaming out 'push me John' over the fade, in what was presumably a throwback to one of the darker moments of her own withdrawal.

Lennon took these demos to his colleagues in The Beatles, and proposed they record the song as a single. Knowing very well they would turn it down, he promptly made plans to tape the song himself, as The Plastic Ono Band's second single. He had previously announced his intention of issuing an instrumental called 'Rock Peace' as The P.O.B.'s next project, but the track never seems to have been recorded—if indeed it was ever written.

· · ·   EARLY SEPTEMBER 1969: *FILMING* Apotheosis.

In the first week of September 1969, three of John and Yoko's films—*Two Virgins*, *Smile* and *Honeymoon*—were given their British première at the Edinburgh Film Festival. A week later, *Rape* and *Self Portrait* were shown at the newly opened ICA in London. When the ICA offered the couple further exposure in early November, they set to work to produce another batch of movies.

The concept for *Apotheosis* came from Lennon, not Yoko; like *Self Portrait*, this was John working in a medium to which Yoko had introduced him, rather than merely supporting her efforts, as on *Smile* and *Two Virgins*. From the start, the idea of a helium balloon ascending into the sky was at the heart of John's concept. The ever-willing Nick Knowland agreed to go up in the balloon with a camera and a soundman: his brief was to capture John and Yoko in his lens as the balloon left the ground, then to offer a *cinéma vérité* portrayal, a balloon's-eye-view, of the ground and the sky as the entourage rose through the air.

Setting off from an airfield in Hampshire, Knowland and the balloon rose on schedule, with the camera tracking the Lennons as they slowly vanished from view, then offering a map-like view of the fields and runways below as the balloon reached towards the clouds. Then all was pure white, until the balloon finally broke free into clear sky, and the sun sparkled into the corner of the shot. Knowland continued filming until the balloon was on the ground, but the arrival of the sun was used as the film's climax, a heady relief from the effectively blank screen of the cloud shots, which had occupied almost half of the film's 16 minutes...

Unlike their previous experiments, *Apotheosis* was shot in real time, with the noise of birds and the wind the only accompaniment. Its elemental simplicity gave it a stark, natural beauty; there was none of the forcedness or authorial intervention which had marred the Lennons' earlier efforts. Indeed, Lennon had quite consciously chosen not to break the purity of the single continuous shot which made up the finished film: he had sent Knowland up in a helicopter to take pictures of a similar balloon in flight, which might be cut into his original footage. But the change of perspective tarnished the concept, and the helicopter film was saved for use in *Apotheosis No. 2.*

Chapter 10

SEPTEMBER 1969
TO DECEMBER 1970

· · · · · · · · · · · · · · · · · ·

SEPTEMBER 13, 1969: *THE PLASTIC ONO BAND* perform *'Blue Suede Shoes'/'Money'/'Dizzy Miss Lizzy'/'Yer Blues'/'Cold Turkey'/'Give Peace A Chance'/'Don't Worry Kyoko'/'John John (Let's Hope For Peace)'* at the Toronto Rock 'n' Roll Revival Festival; performance filmed for **Sweet Toronto.**

At the end of August 1969, Toronto promoters Brower Walker announced that the city's Varsity Stadium would be hosting a rock festival starring The Doors, Alice Cooper and Chicago alongside a batch of fifties heroes–Chuck Berry, Jerry Lee Lewis, Gene Vincent, Bo Diddley, Fats Domino and Little Richard. By the first week of September, however, it was obvious that the ticket sales were not going to cover their basic costs. In a desperate attempt to save the event, John Brower contacted John Lennon in London, and asked him to attend as compère. Lennon agreed, but only if he could perform as well. And so it was that a disbelieving Toronto public were told the news that The Plastic Ono Band would be making their first live appearance in their city, not previously known as one of the rock capitals of the world.

The next four days brought a succession of conflicting messages from London, as the Lennons prevaricated over their plans–finally announcing from bed, while the rest of their party were gathered at London Airport, that they had changed their minds. Guitarist Eric Clapton was sent back to twist their arms, and eventually the makeshift Plastic Ono Band were en route to Canada, rehearsing their set at the back of the aircraft on unamplified electric guitars.

Backstage at Varsity Stadium, the Lennons ordered cocaine, John threw up because of his nerves, and tension mounted. The Plastic Onos eventually took the stage in the early evening, and proceeded to deliver a 40-minute set divided into two distinct halves. Lennon began by powering his way through three of the rock classics he and The Beatles had played in clubs in Liverpool and Hamburg at the start of the decade, before delivering an anguished, if slightly shaky, version of 'Yer Blues', which Clapton had performed with Lennon at The Stones' 'Rock 'n' Roll Circus' the previous December. For Clapton, drummer Alan White and bassist Klaus Voorman, however, 'Cold Turkey' was as new as it was to the audience, who heard the only public rendition of the song which kept close to the free-flowing rhythmic arrangement of John's original demos. Finally, John barked his way through a chaotic 'Give Peace A Chance', before announcing: "Now Yoko's going to do her thing, all over you."

As indeed she did. As the band set off on the chord sequence that had already been the basis for John's 'Watching Rainbows' at the start of 1969, Yoko extemporised a message to her estranged young daughter, Kyoko—'Don't Worry Kyoko (Mummy's Only Looking For Her Hand In The Snow)'. ('Find a hand in the snow,' read one of Yoko's 'Three Snow Pieces For Orchestra' in her book *Grapefruit*.) While the band careered onwards, Yoko wailed, cried and howled her obscure message of reassurance. Then, unaccompanied, she called out the words 'Oh John, let's hope for peace' in agonisingly extended breaths, before Lennon and Clapton forced gales of piercing feedback from their guitars, and Alan White unleashed sympathetic fills and rolls across his drumkit. Finally, as Yoko broke into a long series of sharp screams, Lennon moved to shelter his wife from the crowd, placing his guitar against its amplifier. The other musicians followed suit, and as Yoko gave her last scream there was just the infernal hum of feedback cascading from the stage, roaring on and on until Beatles roadie Mal Evans turned off the equipment.

The audience, far from booing as reported in the British press, merely stood in silence, before emerging from their shock to call out for more. Backstage, Lennon announced that this was "1980s music," the wave of the future.

1969 was the year of the eternal document, so you won't be surprised to learn that the event was filmed and recorded. True to the Lennons' tradition of honesty and authenticity, Apple issued a live album of the event entitled 'Live Peace In Toronto 1969', clad in a beautiful sky blue cover broken only by a single white cloud. It came with a calendar for 1970—or, as the Lennons styled it, *Year One A.P. (After Peace)*—and captured the entire event from introduction to finale, omitting only Lennon's rather impatient gibe at the audience's lack of reaction after 'Cold Turkey.'

The film of the event formed the climax to the official movie of the festival, D.A. Pennebaker's *Sweet Toronto*. That wasn't completed until late 1970, by which time Allen Klein and John Lennon insisted The P.O.B.'s performance should be omitted from the film, which was duly issued as *Keep On Rockin'*. Only in 1989 did the entire set appear on home-video, revealing additional highlights of the occasion—Yoko entering a large white bag on stage during 'Blue Suede Shoes', and then having to be pulled out again after 'Dizzy Miss Lizzy' so that Lennon could retrieve his lyric sheet. The film soundtrack also revealed the extent to which Lennon had remixed the original tapes for the LP release: in so doing, he removed most of Yoko's impromptu and rather intrusive squeals and yells, which had continued throughout John's set with the band.

SEPTEMBER 25/28, 1969: *RECORDING 'Cold Turkey.'*

As if the lyrics were not harrowing enough, Lennon set about constructing a musical arrangement that would approximate the anguish that had sparked 'Cold Turkey.' He and Eric Clapton both played the lead guitar part mapped out on his demo, while the rhythm guitar was omitted—breaking the song into jagged fragments of pain behind Lennon's strangled vocals. The effect was like a message from hell, as if intense emotions had been squeezed into a narrow bottle and were about to break loose. The final two minutes of the record merely heightened the atmosphere, with Lennon groaning and screaming his way towards catharsis. The example of Yoko's full-blooded vocalising had obviously not been ignored.

The finished record had all the hallmarks of spontaneity, but it had actually taken 26 takes to perfect the track. A surviving acetate of an early take had Lennon bending and twisting some of his notes in the song's verses; but this approach was abandoned as too refined, too staged. The moment was too extreme to allow the distraction of vocal gymnastics.

OCTOBER 3/6, 1969: *RECORDING 'Don't Worry Kyoko.'*

For the flipside of 'Cold Turkey,' Lennon and his musicians (Clapton, Voorman and Starr) set about transforming Yoko's maternal cry, 'Don't Worry Kyoko', into the "fucking best rock 'n' roll record ever made," as Lennon put it a year later. Yoko began the song with an endless wail, while the guitars broke like a wave behind her, playing the same skin-tight riff over and over as she explored the possibilities of the human voice. Like 'Cold Turkey,' this was communication beyond words: the Lennons were realising that lyricism was too indirect to convey their feelings.

EARLY OCTOBER 1969: *FILMING Apotheosis No. 2.*

Another day, another balloon: this time it was dusk, rather than early morning, and Nick Knowland shot evocative film of the Lennons lit by a flickering bonfire as his balloon left the ground. These shots, a primaeval blend of darkness and flame, were combined with some of the leftover helicopter footage from *Apotheosis* to create a second essay in the genre.

LATE OCTOBER 1969: *FILMING Cold Turkey.*

Like *Give Peace A Chance* and *The Ballad Of John And Yoko*, this was a promotional film, designed for use on TV pop shows as well as in art cinemas. John and Yoko gathered together off-cuts from the Montreal bed-in footage, plus a rough cut of their September gig in Toronto, and cut clips together with speeded-up film of traffic in New York to create a frenetic, exhausting collage that matched the intensity of the music, but made no attempt to run in sync with it. One final image looked to the future: in its rush from image to image, the film paused for a second on the words 'Power To The Workers' typed on a sheet of paper.

NOVEMBER 26, 1969: *RECORDING and remixing 'What's The News Mary Jane;' remixing 'You Know My Name (Look Up The Number)'*

Since early October, the Lennons had suffered a second miscarriage; commissioned critic Tony Palmer to write a biography of John in a fortnight, and then abandoned the idea after he'd finished it; issued their 'Wedding Album;' and used the comparative failure of 'Cold Turkey' in the British charts as one of the motives for returning John's MBE award to Buckingham Palace. As the Queen was considering her response, John and Yoko were at EMI remixing two vintage Beatles cuts, in preparation for issuing them as an immediate Plastic Ono Band single. 'You Know My Name' was cut down from over six minutes to a touch over four; 'What's The New Mary Jane', effectively a Lennon/Ono project to begin with, was doubled in length as the couple added vocal wails, percussion noises and associated madness to the end of what was already one of John's least conservative songs. Two six-minute mixes were prepared, which sounded like a cross between a stoned nursery-rhyme and a remake of 'Revolution 9;' but neither was released, as EMI's awareness that both songs had been recorded by The Beatles meant that they were unwilling to let The Plastic Ono Band issue them on Apple. After acetates were pressed up, the project was abandoned, and 'You Know My Name' ended up on the flipside of the final Beatles single, 'Let It Be.'

• **DECEMBER 4, 1969:** *RECORDING 'Item 1' and 'Item 2.'*

In late November, Lennon announced that the couple were about to record a fourth album of their unfinished music, after 'Two Virgins', 'Life With The Lions' and the 'Wedding Album.' "One side is laughing," John threatened, "the other is whispering." Thankfully, the album was never completed, though the Lennons did record these two tapes of vocal sounds as part of the soundtrack of a BBC TV documentary about their exploits, which also documented the making of *Apotheosis 2*, and John performing 'Everyone Had A Hard Year' in the grounds of his Ascot house.

• **DECEMBER 9, 1969:** *JOHN AND YOKO announce filming of* **Hanratty.**

World peace was not the couple's only concern at the end of 1969. They had been moved by the representations of the family of James Hanratty, who had been hanged early in the sixties for a murder which it was claimed he had never committed. Protests about the execution had continued throughout the decade, and the Lennons announced that their contribution to the campaign would be to make a film about the case, which would finally prove Hanratty's innocence. John and Yoko organised an event at Speakers' Corner in Hyde Park to launch their crusade, but then everything went quiet. It was generally assumed that the couple had lost interest in the case, but in the event a documentary film about the case, financed by John and Yoko, was given one screening at the Crypt, St. Martin's-in-the-Fields, Trafalgar Square. Aside from setting the project in motion, however, the Lennons seem to have had no involvement with the making of the film.

• • • **DECEMBER 15, 1969: *THE PLASTIC ONO BAND* perform 'Cold Turkey'/ 'Don't Worry Kyoko' at the UNICEF benefit concert, the Lyceum, London; John and Yoko launch the 'War Is Over (If You Want It)' poster campaign.**

The Plastic Ono Band's only European concert—later events planned for Birmingham and Berlin were abandoned as the Lennons went into seclusion during spring 1970—saw them topping the bill at a benefit show for the United Nations' children's charity, UNICEF, in London. Transformed into The Plastic Ono Supergroup by the addition to their ranks of various heavy guests, including Delaney And Bonnie's entire band, Keith Moon of The Who and George Harrison, they performed just two songs–'Cold Turkey' and 'Don't Worry Kyoko'. 'Turkey' kept close to the blueprint, with the presence of a full horn section lending weight to the central riff. But 'Don't Worry Kyoko' was extended to over 20 minutes, which Lennon described a year later as "the most fantastic music I've ever heard...20 years ahead of its time."

He had a point. The piece began with Yoko, emerging from her customary white bag, calling out 'John, I love you', before claiming 'You killed Hanratty, you murderers.' Then the band set off–the guitarists taking the original three-chord riff as their base, the brass growling a counter-melody behind. As the 15 musicians locked horns and blew, Yoko screamed and wailed, and the sound took on a life of its own, growing organically towards a climax as Yoko and the brass players supported each other on a tide of pure emotion. At its peak, the music finally gave way beneath the weight of its tension, collapsing into a free-form, apocalyptic section that only ended with everyone on stage pushing their instruments to their limits. As in Toronto, the audience was stunned into silence as the band left the stage.

Enraptured by the experience, the Lennons set plans in motion for the release of another live album, calling in Nicky Hopkins to overdub Billy Preston's piano part, which had been lost in the mix. But in the absence of any other concert recordings to accompany it, the Lyceum tape was left in the can, emerging only in 1972 as one quarter of the 'Some Time In New York City' double album.

On the same day, Lennon and Ono had paid for massive billboards to be erected in the world's major capital cities, bearing the simple, thought-provoking message: 'War is over, if you want it. Happy Christmas from John and Yoko! Only in London were the posters vandalised.

- **DECEMBER 18 TO 20, 1969: *SIGNING* the *'Bag One'* lithographs; recording 'Rap On Ronnie Hawkins'**

Immediately after the Lyceum show, the Lennons had left for Canada to finalise plans for the giant *Toronto Peace Festival*—a multi-media event scheduled for July 1970, on an airfield near Toronto. The concept was grandiose: all the world's major rock stars (The Beatles, The Stones, Dylan, Elvis) would play together, a million people would attend, and the entire event would be staged for free. Meanwhile, John and Yoko would arrive on a hover-ship powered by air: it was that kind of festival. The proposal eventually collapsed in a welter of accusations on all sides, the Lennons being blamed for their naïvety, and in turn declaring that their fellow organisers had betrayed the original concept of the festival.

Staying at the home of rocker Ronnie Hawkins, Lennon also took time to complete work on his *Bag One* lithographs—the result of the introduction to the art-form brought about by Anthony Fawcett back in 1968. The drawings were converted from Lennon's small originals to poster size, organised into limited edition packages, and given to John so he could sign each lithograph. They were then placed inside special *Bag One* folders, and sold to art-minded (and rich) individuals around the world. It might have been more in keeping with Lennon's principles if they'd been issued as postcards instead.

Not that they would have got very far through the mail, as subsequent events demonstrated. The lithographs documented the Lennons' honeymoon—their sexual consummation, not the Amsterdam bed-in. Drawn in bold, simple lines, they depicted the couple making love—with the most graphic illustrations showing Lennon performing oral sex on his bride, in a pose that mixed tenderness, passion and supplication. When the lithographs were exhibited in Britain and America, the forces of law and order intervened, and several of the more erotic items were seized. The combination of John, Yoko and nudity had once again proved too hot for the establishment to handle.

That same weekend, Lennon recorded a short 'rap' which was used as a promotional message for Ronnie Hawkins' new album on Atlantic, and his single, 'Down In The Alley.'

- **JANUARY 27/28, 1970: *RECORDING* 'Instant Karma!'/'Who Has Seen The Wind'**

On the morning of January 27, 1970, John Lennon wrote 'Instant Karma!' around the same three-chord, three-blind-mice sequence as 'All You Need Is Love! Anxious to record and release it immediately, he called a session for that night, and managed to assemble George Harrison, Klaus Voorman and Alan White at short notice. A request also went out to legendary producer Phil Spector, in London to discuss his possible involvement with The Beatles' ailing 'Get Back' project. As an audition, Lennon asked him to produce 'Instant Karma!;' and was sufficiently struck by his contribution to sign him up as Apple A&R man, and producer of his own records for the next two years.

Spector's hallmark was excess—forcing banks of musicians to play simple phrases and chord sequences in unison, till the sheer weight of sound assumed an emotional power that would have evaded a smaller band of instrumentalists. His sound was overpowering, the rage of a soul in torment—the opposite, in fact, of the clean, precise but ultimately rather shallow noise produced by George Martin and The Beatles, and equally well demonstrated by the pincer-thin rhythm section on the Lennon-produced 'Cold Turkey.'

Spector's skills went beyond bombasticism, however, and within minutes of joining the session he had transformed another heavy guitar work-out into an exercise for piano, drums, vocal and not much else. He worked his magic instantly, forcing Lennon's foot down hard on the sustain pedal for the opening piano notes (nicked from Ritchie Barrett's 'Some Other Guy,' a Beatles favourite from the Cavern days), and producing a drum sound that felt like bursts of artillery fire. Halfway through the first verse, he introduced handclaps, and for the chorus a crash cymbal that rang like an alarm bell. John's vocals were smothered in echo, while underneath, clanking pianos played chords, four to the bar, acting as percussion rather than instruments of melody.

Phil's final touch transformed a rabble of vocal chorus—consisting of Allen Klein and a collection of nightbirds from nearby Hatchett's club, rounded up by Billy Preston—into a choir, mixed so that their voices arched over Lennon's lead vocal. 'Instant Karma!' was Lennon's loudest and simplest record yet; and almost all the credit was Spector's.

What of the song, meanwhile? Well, it was open to interpretation. Across the bones of an old-fashioned R&B song, Lennon laid a democratic chorus ('We all shine on, like the moon and the stars and the sun') and a series of verses that debunked the notion that superstars were any more important than the rest of us, and suggested that immediate enlightenment wasn't always to be trusted. Was the message that you could do whatever you wanted? Or that easy solutions didn't always turn out so easy? Lennon wasn't saying.

At the end of the session, John, Yoko and George settled into a corner and taped Yoko's 'Who Has Seen The Wind!' Like 'Remember Love', this showcased the child-like, innocent Yoko, not the titan wailing in the face of the storm. The song was a message of love, linked to Yoko's belief that we are all wind, all clouds in the sky, drifting in search of a meaning. A greater contrast to 'Karma' was hard to imagine.

• • •   **EARLY FEBRUARY 1970: *WRITES* introduction to *Grapefruit*.**

The comparative success of this revamped edition of Yoko's anthology owed much to her marriage to a Beatle, of course, who duly obliged with a five-second sketch of the author, and a fulsome introduction: 'Hi! My name is John Lennon. I'd like you to meet Yoko Ono.'

Included in this updated edition were the full instructions for Yoko's *13 Days Do-It-Yourself Dance Festival* from 1967; and her *Sky Event For John Lennon* from the following spring. Various pieces also planted the seeds for song lyrics yet to be unveiled.

- **FEBRUARY 11, 1970:** *PERFORMS* 'Instant Karma!' *on Top Of The Pops*.

Five days after the single was issued, Lennon made a rare promotional appearance on British television, performing 'Instant Karma!' in a pre-recorded slot for the BBC's pop singles show. Lennon played piano and sang a fresh lead vocal over a backing tape, while Messrs White, Voorman and Evans mimed appropriately, and Yoko sat blindfolded on a chair, holding up slogans like 'Smile', 'Peace' and 'Hope.' Lennon wore an armband proclaiming 'People for Peace.' Within a fortnight, however, the Lennons had pulled out of the *Toronto Peace Festival*, and their campaign for world peace was quietly retired.

- **MARCH 6, 1970:** *WRITES* 'Have We All Forgotten What Vibes Are?'

Given the chance to comment on the collapse of the *Toronto Peace Festival*, Lennon sat down and hammered out this 2,500-word retort—published in *Rolling Stone* on April 16—to the line which co-organiser John Brower had been selling the underground press (that the Lennons had betrayed the concept of the festival and were more interested in cash than conscience). Like his other letters to the press, 'Have We All Forgotten What Vibes Are?' burns with a righteous anger, detailing Brower's alleged campaign against Lennon's manager, Allen Klein, and the rationale behind John and Yoko's wish that Toronto should remain a free festival.

The couple's credo surfaces only at the end: 'Someone said: "Do we need a festival?" Yoko and I still think we need it—not just to show that we can gather peacefully and groove to rock bands, but to change the balance of energy power. Can you imagine what we could do together in the one spot—thinking, singing and praying for peace—one million souls apart from any TV link-ups, etc. to the rest of the planet. If we came together for one reason, we could make it together!'

This plea for unity, for power through collective action, was a clear signpost towards the Lennons' political radicalisation and belief in mass actions of revolt. For the moment, the end was still idealistic. But John was aware that the tide of the struggle was turning against him: 'We need help. It is out of our control. All we have is our name. We are sorry for the confusion, it's bigger than both of us. We are doing our best for all our sakes—we still believe. Pray for us.'

Within a week, the Lennons had enrolled in Arthur Janov's primal therapy clinic in California, convinced that the mess inside their heads could only be cleaned out from within.

• • • **MARCH 1970: *RECORDING* Grapefruit readings.**

Whilst in California waiting for Janov's therapy to begin, John and Yoko recorded around 30 minutes of readings from Yoko's newly-published edition of *Grapefruit*, designed to be made into a promotional record and played on radio stations in the States. Thankfully, these rather embarrassing spoken word recordings, with both the Lennons doing their best to undermine the sense of Yoko's written words, were never issued to the media.

• • • **APRIL 11 TO JUNE 12, 1970: *PRESENTING* Fluxfest.**

Yoko had been a leading member of the Fluxus movement in New York art for many years: this represented her most public gesture of support after her marriage to John. In the early months of 1970, the couple prepared three separate schedules for *Fluxfest*, a series of events, exhibitions and displays centred around the Canal Street 'store' of Joe Jones–a fellow Fluxus member, and the creator of the Tone Deaf Music Co, whose instruments supported Yoko on some film soundtrack recordings in 1971.

The festival was set to begin on April 11 with a John and Yoko impersonators gathering, who would be fed from a menu consisting entirely of grapefruit variations. The event would launch an exhibition called 'Do-It-Yourself by John and Yoko', John's contributions to which included 'Two Eggs by John Lennon', which was exactly what it said. The following week, John contributed a couple of New York Port Authority tickets to 'Tickets by John and Yoko' and *Fluxtours*. Week three of Fluxfest saw the staging of 'Measure by John and Yoko', which involved gathering statistics about the weight and height of the visitors to the site.

The first week of May saw the unveiling of 'Blue Room by John and Yoko', a collage to which John's major contributions were 'Three Spoons by John Lennon' (consisting, naturally enough, of three spoons) and 'Needle by John Lennon'. 'Weight and Water by John and Yoko', staged between May 9 and 15, involved the flooding of the exhibition room, and the casual positioning of sponges, some dry, some wet. 'Capsule by John and Yoko' occupied the sixth week of the festival; the seventh heralded 'Portrait Of John Lennon As A Young Cloud', an exhibit prepared by Yoko which consisted of a wall with 100 identical drawers built into it, all of which were empty except for one which contained 'John's smile'.

'The Store by John and Yoko' brought back memories of the You Are Here show in 1968, with its collection of various change machines from New York stores and stations. Finally, the Lennons suggested that the last week of the Fluxfest be given over to 'Exam by John and Yoko' a test to discover how well their public had understood their work.

The Fluxus group were as concerned with concept as they were with the concrete, so although there is no evidence that any of these events took place, that scarcely matters. To Fluxus, the important act was the imagination that meant that the events could have occurred. Whether they did or not was strictly irrelevant—as indeed was the whole festival.

• **AUGUST TO SEPTEMBER 1970:** *RECORDING home demos of 'God'/'I Found Out'/'Love'/'My Mummy's Dead'/'Look At Me'/'Well Well Well'/ 'When A Boy Meets A Girl.'*

Though Lennon later dismissed Arthur Janov as little more than a charlatan, the four months which he and Yoko spent undergoing the doctor's radical Primal Scream therapy in California and London altered the course of his life. Lennon had dipped into Janov's book, *The Primal Scream*, empathising with the personal accounts of patients who had discovered the roots of their neurosis in childhood pain, and through Janov's analysis and 'treatment' had freed themselves from decades of inhibition and guilt.

The principle was straightforward enough. Janov believed that the neurosis which modern Western man had accepted as his lot—the alienation from society, the difficulty in forging personal relationships, the constant anxiety of social existence—had been sparked by feelings of rejection and unhappiness in infancy or childhood. Janov's therapy attempted to peel away the layers of neurosis, slowly dragging the subject into his past, stripping bare the events which he had successfully hidden from himself and the world, and finally—by unleashing a primal scream of anguish and need for parental approval and love—reaching the initial moment of rejection. The scream, torn from the depths of the body and reducing the subject to the role of a helpless baby, would cleanse the mind, leaving it open to approach relationships and society in a more rational manner, and to face up to the reality of pain and the possibility of relief.

The aim, then, was catharsis—the violent achievement of inner peace through the unremitting confrontation of pain. To Lennon, the theory seemed sound enough: twice orphaned, to his mind abandoned as a child, he had little problem in identifying the source of his everyday hurt in the loss or absence of a parent. The pain which had driven him to explore himself and the infinite in meditation, in drugs, even in the contemplation of God, which had forced him to find refuge in personal violence or self-destructiveness: it was this pain which he hoped to destroy, through primal therapy.

For many weeks, Lennon took the tablets as prescribed—though drugs were one of the many staples which he was forced to abandon during the course of the therapy. He screamed helplessly like a child, raving on the floor of his room while Janov pulled him deeper and deeper into the darkest corners of his past, to confront the mother who had died, the father who had abandoned him. And in the morning he felt fragile but somehow cleansed, in touch with himself for the first time since he had left Liverpool, able to face up to his own identity rather than hiding behind the image that he and the media had conspired to invent in its place. And after months when he had scarcely written a song, Primal Therapy inspired an outpouring of new material—almost all of it directly linked to the experiences of the past few weeks. Taken together, the new songs effectively offered a précis of Janov's theories, and of the complex liberation which they had produced in Lennon's life and mind.

'I Found Out' was the most direct of these songs. Lennon cut a pair of sparse demos in August 1970, backed only by his primaeval, heavily-echoed electric guitar, which moaned like a voodoo behind his biting vocals. What began as a complaint against the 'freaks on the phone', constantly calling him 'brother' and wanting little slices of his soul, turned into an epic of self-discovery—railing against drugs, religion, sex, the great distractions on the quest for reality. And dropped into the verses were fragments of Janovism: 'Now that I found out I know I can cry... Can't do you no harm to feel your own pain.'

With the confusions of the past stripped away, Lennon was reduced to bare essentials. At home he turned the nursery rhyme 'Three Blind Mice' into a chilling vignette called 'My Mummy's Dead', one of the two takes of which made it onto the 'Plastic Ono Band' album. The title told the story: 'I can't explain, so much pain/I could never show it/My mummy's dead.' Delivered in a voice that came from beyond despair, the song was honest to the point of being difficult to take.

On the same home tape as 'My Mummy's Dead', Lennon revived 'Look At Me', one of the last of his Indian songs from spring 1968 to be recorded. The acoustic demo kept close to the two-year-old original version, and the arrangement was retained intact on the final, released take.

'Look At Me' offered a note of optimism within the exploration of despair. 'Love', another song first taped at home in July/August 1970, used the simplicity and uncluttered approach of the primal therapy songs to offer a stark, beautiful description of his relationship with Yoko. The lyric, set at this stage to a lightly amplified electric guitar, offered closed couplets that were simple and profound at the same time: 'Love is real/ Real is love/Love is feeling/Feeling Love.'

Of the initial batch of post-therapy songs, only 'Well Well Well' lacked that directness of spirit. The chorus, which simply repeated the title, was an ironic comment on the verses, which offered snapshots of the Lennons at work in the sexual revolution, while one couplet deleted from the final lyric suggested John hadn't lost his sense of humour: 'Because she's looking so much thinner/She looked so beautiful I could wee.' Like all these summer-'70 recordings, this was an entirely solo demo, accompanied by an ethnic blues guitar.

Of the three songs at the heart of the 'Plastic Ono Band' album, 'Mother,' 'Working Class Hero' and 'God', only the last was attempted during these summer sessions. It began life on acoustic guitar, with one basic verse: 'God is a concept by which we measure our pain.' This was a bleak view of the spirit life, unlocked by Janov's therapy, and suggested that Lennon was now far removed from the optimist who had looked for spiritual guidance from the Maharishi or the Buddha. Repeating this verse twice at speed, Lennon then leapt into a litany of false idols, each one greeted with the declaration, 'I don't believe in...' With gods, gurus and pop stars attracting Lennon's denunciation, the litany ended with a denial of 'Beatles', before John announced: 'I just believe in me, and that's reality.' (On the finished record, he opened his horizons of belief far enough to include Yoko.)

At this stage, the song went no further, merely ploughing back into the verse and again through the litany. As the list proceeded, Lennon thrashed his guitar in anger, turning his disavowal of the past into a cathartic outburst of emotion. Not everything was so serious, however: Lennon opened one of his takes with a bizarre monologue, which sounded like a refugee from an early sixties doo-wop record, announcing 'I had a message from above...'

One final song cut that summer didn't make the album, and was probably never finished. 'When A Boy Meets A Girl' was a rather desultory tale of love, filled with lyrical clichés–'If I'd lost you now, baby I'd be sorry'–that seemed closer to the teenage heartache songs of 1963 than the truth-seeking of 1970. Its main attraction was its descending minor chord sequence, played on acoustic guitar, which would nonetheless have been too pretty for the album to follow.

SEPTEMBER 26 TO OCTOBER 5, 1970: *RECORDING* 'Mother'/'Hold On'/'I Found Out'/'Working Class Hero'/'Isolation'/'Remember'/'Love'/'Well Well Well'/'Look At Me'/'God'/'Honey Don't'/'Don't Be Cruel'/'Matchbox'/'Why'/ 'Why Not'/'Greenfield Morning I Pushed An Empty Baby Carriage All Over The City'/'Touch Me'/'Paper Shoes'.

'John Lennon: Plastic Ono Band' remains Lennon's most radical musical statement. It stripped bare his deepest emotions, offering himself naked to the gaze of the world in a song cycle that bore testament to the piercing scrutiny of the Primal Scream technique. What Lennon uncovered beneath the trappings of stardom and adulthood were elemental needs, for security and comfort, and a meaning to existence: along the way, he examined the myth of fame, and the cult of working-class authenticity. All this and, with the help of Phil Spector, he made a remarkable-sounding rock record.

Despite only taking part in three days of sessions, primarily to handle the mixing, Spector shared production credits with John and Yoko, who used the period of the sessions to tape Yoko's first solo album as well. Sparseness was the order of the day: both records were cut with a band consisting of Lennon, Starr and Voorman, with Spector and Billy Preston both adding keyboard cameos on Lennon's LP. Spector played piano on 'Love', essentially unchanged from the home demo, except that Lennon's whispered vocal gave the tune an almost unbearable poignancy, a hint that he was singing more from hope than expectation.

Preston's showcase was on 'God', to which he brought a spiritual flavour that was an ironic comment on the philosophical materialism of the lyrics. To the existing song, Lennon had added a coda–a musing on the theme, 'The dream is over.' The dream was the sixties, The Beatles, religion–anything you had used to escape from reality. To ram the point home, John concluded the saga of 'I Am The Walrus' and 'Glass Onion:' 'I was the walrus/But now I'm John.' The underlying message was that you had to do it for yourselves; Lennon wasn't leading any generation into battle.

'Working Class Hero', ironic from its title downwards, crossed that credo with the theme of 'I Found Out' to produce a searing indictment of the way in which society used workers to build its wealth, and then fobbed them off with dull pleasures. 'You're still fucking peasants as far as I can see', was Lennon's reassuring message to his fellow working-class, before sarcastically ending the song: 'If you want to be a hero, then just follow me.' Sadly, some critics took him seriously, and translated this bitter track, inexpertly edited together from two different takes, as more of Lennon's self-glorification.

'Working Class Hero' was John's outward expression of his heightened world vision. 'Mother' performed the same function inside his head, without irony or any attempt at concealment. Lennon was hurt at being abandoned by his parents: 'Mother' told it straight. Spector's touch was to introduce the doomy, distorted church bells that kicked off the track and the album; and to turn Lennon's dry, echo-less original mix into a sea of booming piano sustain and thudding drums, over which Lennon screamed out his desperate pleas for help: 'Mama don't go/Daddy come home.'

'Isolation' spread the web of loneliness to include Yoko, 'Just a boy and a little girl/Trying to change the whole wide world.' And in the middle eight, Lennon double-tracked his piano and vocal, making no attempt to keep his singing in sync, so that his despair echoed from one speaker to another.

'Remember,' cut down from an extended piano work-out, transferred the pain into anger—more bitterness, more betrayal, more belief that promises had not been fulfilled, that the mythical family happiness children are taught at school was never more than an illusion.

Only 'Hold On' offered any hope, and even then it was only the promise of survival, not rescue. 'Hold on John', Lennon sang, before offering the same advice to Yoko, and the world. And as on 'Revolution', 'it's gonna be alright.' The track shimmered with reverb guitar, as if to highlight the shakiness of the man struggling to exist; only Lennon's whispered 'Cocaine' in the guitar solo suggested that he might also be using outside forces to strengthen his hand.

The eerie demos of 'Well Well Well' and 'I Found Out' were turned into full-blooded rock 'n' roll by the three-piece Plastic Ono Band, with Lennon's guitar slicing through the mix like a knife through skin. As ever, it was the clarity and depth of Spector's mix that counted: where Lennon might have ornamented the music, Spector helped it stand proud and clear, its message completely unhindered by prettiness or complication.

With the addition of 'Look At Me' and 'My Mummy's Dead', 'John Lennon: Plastic Ono Band' emerged as a harrowing portrait of the artist in pain, delving deep into his psyche in search of relief, and throwing out shards of hurt in all directions. It remains the ultimate statement of personal expression, parodied and imitated but never equalled. Lennon's problem, however, at least from an artistic point of view, was where he went next. Having laid himself bare in front of the world, what else could be reveal? To the end of his days, Lennon rated this album as his most effective and powerful work, and so it was. But it was also an unrepeatable exercise. Lennon may not have been cleansed or reborn, but while the therapy did its work he was free of artifice and illusion. The flaw in Janov's theory was that after the therapy, the layers of neurosis and self-deceit began to gather again. Lennon never found the strength for a second confrontation.

Assuming that Yoko found her vocal dramatics cathartic, then her neuroses never found time to grow. 'Yoko Ono: Plastic Ono Band', clad in a matching cover to John's album, was her response to her husband's unveiling. Yoko didn't bother with words: if she was in pain, she just screamed, and on 'Why' The Plastic Ono Band raged like titans behind her, Lennon striking sparks out of his guitar, Klaus Voorman and Ringo Starr laying down a tribal beat. As guitar and vocal sparred in bouts of near-hysteria, John and Yoko came close to creating the perfect soundtrack for Primal Therapy—uncontrolled emotion, squeezed onto the tape without any mediation. 'Touch Me' came close to the same amalgam of funk and fear, while 'Why Not' slowed the tempo for an unearthly exercise in spooking out demons. The rest—apart from 'Aos', recorded by Yoko with Ornette Coleman back in February 1968—was Yoko's tape games, emulating a train on 'Paper Shoes', and reworking the theme of her 'City Piece' from *Grapefruit* ('Walk all over the city with an empty baby carriage') on 'Greenfield Morning'.

Along the way, Lennon, Voorman and Starr found time to exercise the same minimalist magic on a medley of favourite rockabilly numbers, which were taped but never released. Carl Perkins' 'Honey Don't' saw Lennon spitting out the lyrics, and fusing the jagged edges of rock 'n' roll guitar with the free-form anarchy of Yoko's music. On Presley's 'Don't Be Cruel', Lennon predated The Cramps by a decade, turning himself into the creature from the swamp by slurring his vocals into one manic phrase. And returning to Perkins with 'Matchbox', he showed off his feelings for roots rockabilly, missing an occasional note in his solo, but making up for technical failures with bags of feel. In the autumn of 1970, everything Lennon played came out raw, sweating and real.

• **DECEMBER 1970: *RECORDING* home demos of 'I'm The Greatest'/'I Promise'/'Make Love Not War'/'How'/'Oh Yoko'/'Sally And Billy'/'Help!'.**

Unable to write music notation, Lennon composed most of his songs from the late sixties onwards on tape. Though he was apt to re-record over the original renditions of songs which he had since learned or taped in the studio, some of these composing tapes survive. One such dates from the aftermath of the 'Plastic Ono Band' sessions, with the exhausted Lennon feeling uncertainly round the piano for familiar chords which somehow seem to evade his grasp. Musically, this is not a Lennon landmark; but it does offer us an early glimpse of four of his most familiar tunes of the next three years.

Just as The Beatles had celebrated the release of 'Sgt. Pepper' in June 1967 by aimlessly recording instrumental jams, so Lennon marked his 'Plastic Ono Band' album by seeking out a new direction for his writing. The confessional mood of that record survived onto 'I Promise', the first of many apologetic odes to Yoko, which were still being written in Lennon's final days at the end of 1980. Yoko had been his only solace in the despair of the primal therapy songs; as such, she had to be respected and obeyed, and 'I Promise' comes as close to self-abasement as anything in Lennon's career. It uses the fifties piano stylings of 'Oh Darling' as its base, with a lyric that looks ahead to a more profound statement of regret, 'Jealous Guy.' For the chorus, however, Lennon harks back to another new song, 'Make Love Not War,' with its hope that 'love is the answer, and you know that it's true.'

'Make Love Not War' could have been an anthem to rival 'Give Peace A Chance' if Lennon had ever finished it. But he never moved beyond the simple repetition of the title, and the shift into the chorus; and the structure was first rejected, then recalled when Lennon turned the same melody into 'Mind Games.'

'I'm The Greatest' underwent a similar transformation. John eventually gave the song to Ringo, noting in an aside that if he'd sung the tune everyone would have complained at his arrogance. But he certainly began writing it for himself, to a loping piano accompaniment, and only a very basic set of lyrics, with none of the iconoclasm of the finished song.

The final version of 'Oh Yoko' in 1971 was a song of joy to his wife, so it's remarkable to hear the first pass at the tune, which was a slow lament, emotionless and insecure, taken at a similar pace to 'Mother.' Another of the 'Imagine' songs to be started during this session was 'How,' which Lennon fell into as he busked his way through The Impressions' spiritual call, 'People Get Ready.' After one take had broken down, Lennon went back to the top of the tune, and played as much as he'd written, over and over again. In this form, the song structure was already intact, with a series of searching questions aimed at himself, emphasised by the definite pauses between lines. And the ghost of 'Mother' still walked, as Lennon improvised: 'How can I go home when home is something I have never had?'

During his interview with Jann Wenner for *Rolling Stone*, Lennon expressed the desire to re-record 'Help!' at the slower tempo in which he'd originally written the song, rather than the hurried take preferred as The Beatles' single release. He devoted a minute or so during this composing tape to trying to perfect a new arrangement, but succeeded only in dragging the first verse through an agonisingly slow haul, and then giving up in disgust when he couldn't work out the piano chords for the chorus.

Finally, 'Sally And Billy' was little more than a fragment, cast somewhere between the unrelenting piano chords of 'Remember' and the jaunty clanking of David Bowie's 'Oh You Pretty Things.' Later that week,

Lennon would tell Jann Wenner how he preferred writing first-person autobiography to third-person fiction. That's probably why 'Sally And Billy,' an ill-focused narrative, was left to one side for five years or more.

• **DECEMBER 1970: *FILMING* Fly/Up Your Legs Forever; recording 'Fly.'**

When the Lennons were offered an evening to exhibit their works at a film festival at the Elgin Theater in New York City at Christmas 1970, they not only gathered together prints of their previous work: they resolved to conceive, film, edit and produce two feature-length movies within a fortnight.

The schedule was duly met, though not without incident. Yoko invented the concept for *Up Your Legs Forever*, a 75-minute series of 'leg shots' in the tradition of her *Film No.4 (Bottoms)* movie. This time the camera swung from the feet to the top of the thighs of the 300-plus denizens of the New York art scene who agreed to perform for the cameras. Each shot ended tantalisingly short of the subject's genitals, a wry joke at the public's expense. The film ended with John and Yoko exposing their naked buttocks, before John recited the credits. The rest of the soundtrack echoed the documentary style of *Bottoms*, capturing dialogue from before and during the filming–though the voices eventually gave way to John playing bottleneck guitar while Yoko improvised a blues song named after the movie. Lennon had little input to the project, beyond financing and supporting Yoko, and taking polaroid pictures of the more attractive auditionees.

Fly was also essentially a Yoko solo project, again with Lennon's whole-hearted support. Like earlier avant-garde movies which had transformed the human body into a mysterious desert of hills and sweeping valleys, *Fly* used the naked female form of an actress, over which crawled a succession of suitably drugged flies. The movie might have been a metaphor, or more likely a playful piece of experimentalism, but its production was blighted by the lack of co-operation shown by the actress, and by the flies, which repeatedly failed to follow Yoko's crystal-clear directions. No matter: the film was edited in time, and clearly pandered to the voyeuristic leanings of the average (male) movie-goer with its concentration on the actress's more private parts. Yoko obviously failed to realise that the true avant-garde would have chosen a less interesting subject: as it was, underground critics accused the Lennons of betraying their concept by pandering to the lowest desires of their audience.

Though he was credited as co-director and co-editor, Lennon's major contribution to *Fly* was to produce and play on Yoko's soundtrack. As she watched a rough cut of the 50-minute film, she improvised more than 20 minutes of vocal sounds, with Lennon offering a restrained, almost classical accompaniment on backwards electric guitar. Yoko synchronised her bleatings to the erratic movement of the flies, which lent the whole proceedings an undeniably comic air.

Chapter 11

JANUARY 1971 TO
AUGUST 1971

. . . .

·   ·   · **JANUARY 22 TO EARLY FEBRUARY 1971: *RECORDING* '*Power To The People*'/'*Open Your Box*.'**

John and Yoko's political radicalisation was sparked by their conversations with members of the British Trotskyist movement, who had criticised the Lennons in print for their 'bourgeois' approach to the issue of world peace—their belief that change could be achieved without revolution.

Conscious of his own class origins, Lennon moved sharply to reflect the interests of his new friends. 1969 had been dominated by his work for peace; 1970 saw the personal take precedence over the fate of the world. In 1971, the pendulum swung back towards the masses, only this time John and Yoko were spouting the slogans of the left, not the peaceniks.

Lennon was always a populist, and though he willingly joined protest marches and signed petitions, he realised that music was his most effective means of protest. Hence the search for an immediate anthem of the left—and the writing of 'Power To The People.' The song's chorus, which merely repeated the title, left the means and ends unclear, and meant it could be claimed by any group which wanted it. The verses offered little more analysis, beyond the need to get out on the streets in numbers—though the line which urged the politicos not to forget their women was both patronising and more feminist than most of the ultra-left in 1971.

Even in its demo form, 'Power To The People' sounded like a single. Phil Spector produced the finished record, but only after Lennon's own attempts had proved inadequate. In the studio, the song took shape as an R&B lope like The Coasters' 'Searchin', with Lennon banging out piano triplets like Fats Domino during the verses, and Bobby Keyes honking away merrily on sax. Lennon then fleshed out the band with a chorus of female gospel singers, and attempted a final take. But the best he and the band could muster was a ragged, tired rhythm track, with Lennon straining desperately to find the notes as if he'd set the piece in the wrong key.

Lennon must have realised that this version couldn't be released. So he tried again, stripping the band arrangement back down to basics, so that the instrumental track for the finished take sounded like an out-take from the 'Plastic Ono Band' sessions, built around piano, bass and drums. The vocal was still strained, and the sax fills never quite took off, but over the lengthy fade Lennon burst into a series of howls that owed more to primal therapy than political revolution.

Enter Phil Spector. He took Lennon's basic track and reinvented it, adding cavernous echo to the vocal and sax, forcing Bobby Keyes back before the mike to blow his lungs out, and turning the gospel singers from a small group into a choir. And, as a master-stroke, he gathered everyone in the studio together and taped their marching feet, which he used as a backdrop to the opening chorus. It created the sound of a political rally in the recording studio; and with Lennon's heavily echoed lead sounding as if it could have been sung through a megaphone, the record hammered home the spirit of community and revolt John had been searching for. He was later to disown the record, or at least its message, as mere sloganeering, naïve and ill-thought; but he must still have loved the sound, which brought to life the amateurish enthusiasm of one of John's (and Spector's) favourite records, 'Quarter To Three' by Gary U.S. Bonds.

For the flip, Lennon took aside his rhythm section and told them to play it funky. Over a devilishly tight riff, midway between James Brown and reggae, Yoko squealed out 'Open Your Box', an idiosyncratic call for freedom of speech and body. Lennon produced the record, and this time without the need to carry the whole show, he gave Yoko's piece a sound to match the starkness of its conception.

- **EARLY MARCH 1971: *RE-RECORDING* vocal for 'Open Your Box'.**

Hidden in the lyrics to 'Open Your Box' were Yoko's injunctions, 'Open your trousers/Open your skirt/Open your legs'. EMI felt this was obscene, so Yoko apparently re-cut the first two lines with less pejorative words, though the end result sounded identical. In fact, it's quite possible that the Lennons only changed the words conceptually, and that no one at EMI spotted that the first version of 'Open Your Box' was the same as the second.

- **EARLY SUMMER 1971: *COMPLETING* filming of *Erection*; recording** 'Airmale'/'Don't Count The Waves'/'You'.

133

Self Portrait had dealt with one kind of erection; this movie—listed as being 'By John Lennon', though Yoko was credited as co-producer and director—focused on a second. Though it was completed in 1971, its conception actually dated back to the previous summer. Aware that the London International Hotel was about to be built in north Kensington, John asked permission for photographer Iain Macmillan to take regular slide shots of the building site from an identical position. These were then photographed in sequence, as a piece of advanced time-lapse work, to document the erection of the hotel.

For the soundtrack, Yoko utilised her recordings with the Joe Jones Tone Deaf Music Co, an offshoot of the Fluxus group which consisted of a collection of toy percussion instruments that played themselves. Their cacophonous rhythm, coupled with Yoko's vocal exhalations, were an apt commentary on the business of construction. 'Airmale' and 'You' were used in the film; 'Don't Count The Waves' was saved for Yoko's 'Fly' album.

Time-lapse photography was scarcely a novelty in 1971; neither was the concentration on a single developing shot, which had long been a central theme in one strand of the avant-garde cinema. But of all John and Yoko's avowedly experimental movies, *Erection* is the most watchable, if only because it evokes every child's fascination with the workings of a construction site. In an obscure way, the accent on creation rather than destruction harked back to the Lennons' first meeting in 1966, and the 'yes' written on the ceiling that had attracted John when he had expected to be rebuffed.

Purely in visual terms, then, *Erection* has its satisfactions, notably when the shell of the building is suddenly filled out with the substance of the walls, and the physical presence of the construction alters the pattern of light and darkness which the viewer has grown used to from the beginning of the sequence.

The film ends with a nod of the head to Andy Warhol's epic movie about the Empire State Building. Warhol's film depicted the building throughout an entire night: Lennon's ended with the lights in the hotel slowly being extinguished, until the screen is left in darkness.

LATE MAY 1971: *RECORDING* home demos of 'Oh Yoko'/'God Save Us'/ 'Call My Name.'

Having demoed 'Oh Yoko' on piano the previous December as a dirge, Lennon moved the song to guitar for this second attempt, and succeeded in bringing it slowly to life as a celebration of love and marriage. The number was as direct as any of John's compositions from this period, and as optimistic—a picture of happiness without a doubt in sight. This guitar rendition tailed off once Lennon had satisfied himself he had a viable format, and ended with him improvising a piece called 'I Want You Babe,' which borrowed the famous 'awopbopaloobopalopbamboom' hook from Little Richard's fifties rocker, 'Tutti Frutti.' Yoko helped out on spontaneous backing vocals throughout the piece.

'Call My Name', written on piano around the same time, saw Lennon in the position of comforter, offering himself as a solution to anxieties and loneliness. Interestingly, the tune of this fragment was identical to the 'Mind Games' song 'Aisumasen (I'm Sorry)', which portrayed a very different picture of the Lennons' marital balancing act.

'God Save Us', meanwhile, was written to order, for a new political campaign. The editors of the British underground paper *Oz* were facing imprisonment for having distributed a copy of the magazine which contained material allegedly likely to corrupt minors. As a regular *Oz* subscriber, Lennon sprang to their defence. He made immediate plans to record a single to raise funds for their legal fees, and hoped that his intervention in the affair would shift the current of opinion in their favour.

As ever when politics were at stake, Lennon kept the lyrics simple, reeling off a series of threats from which God should do his best to save us, instructing his audience to 'pick your nose and eat it too' (a line that was omitted from the eventual single), and ending up 'God save us from the Queen'. Lennon then took this simple recording, cut on rhythmic acoustic guitar with backing by an anonymous conga player, to the Apple studio, for his pick-up Plastic Ono Band to hear and learn.

· **JUNE 1971: *RECORDING* '*God Save Us*'/'*Do The Oz*.'**

To avoid the public treating 'God Save Us' as his follow-up to 'Power To The People', Lennon arranged for session singer Bill Elliott (later a mainstay of Splinter) to handle vocals on the A-side of the single, which would be issued on Apple under the name of The Elastic Oz Band. First, though, Lennon sang the lead vocals himself, holding onto his notes with a Yoko-like quaver, and encouraging the band to play it rough and raunchy. As a final aside, Lennon ended his list of demands by calling for freedom from defeat, deceit and de queen, which was hardly likely to satisfy anyone distressed by the anti-royalist tone of the original lyric. Elliott then listened to Lennon's vocal in the cans and tried to duplicate it, and with Phil Spector on hand to add the appropriate echo, the track was complete.

Lennon himself handled vocals on the B-side, a gritty mess of funk powered by grungy guitar, wailing sax and the equally tempestuous vocal sounds of Yoko Ono, who screamed her support as Lennon yelled out the title line over and over again.

· **JUNE 6, 1971: *PERFORMING* '*Well (Baby Please Don't Go)*'/'*Jamrag*'/ '*Scumbag*'/'*Au at Fillmore East*.'**

Having finished the *Oz* single, the Lennons flew straight to New York, where they met left-field rocker Frank Zappa, and were promptly invited to appear on stage with his band, The Mothers, at the Fillmore East that night. Both Lennon and Zappa found that they had fallen for the other's media coverage: "I was expecting a grubby maniac with naked women all over the place," Lennon admitted afterwards. "He was expecting a couple of nude freaks." Audience expectations were not disappointed, however, as the Lennons and The Mothers produced one of the odder marriages in rock history.

The Lennons appeared as the evening's encore, John sporting an electric guitar, Yoko in her customary bag. Lennon announced "a song we used to do in the Cavern in Liverpool," and the band broke into The Olympics' 1958 B-side to 'Western Movies', a gritty blues titled 'Well (Baby Please Don't Go)'. The band played through the one-verse structure several times, altering the rhythm accompaniment on each pass; Lennon spat out the words, Yoko howled sympathetically, and Zappa lent on his wah-wah pedal between lines before letting rip for a fluid solo.

The rest of the entertainment was more spontaneous. While The Mothers played one of their standard concert pieces, 'King Kong' from their 'Uncle Meat' soundtrack, Yoko wailed, and then Lennon led the audience in lengthy repetition of the phrase 'Scumbag'. Finally, Yoko took centre-stage, while the band squealed out their support behind her, in a piece that was titled much the way it sounded: 'Au'.

The entire performance duly cropped up on the 'Some Time In New York City' album the following year; for the liner notes, Lennon defaced a copy of The Mothers' own 'Fillmore East' album, cut on the same night. The Mothers' pleasure at appearing on record with the Lennons, however, was no doubt tempered by the fact that John and Yoko took composer credit for all the band's improvised jamming, offering Zappa only co-credit for 'Scumbag'. Of 'King Kong' there was no mention.

JULY 1971: *RECORDING* 'Imagine'/'Crippled Inside'/'Jealous Guy'/'It's So Hard'/'I Don't Wanna Be A Soldier'/'Gimme Some Truth'/'Oh My Love'/'How Do You Sleep'/'How'/'Oh Yoko'/'Well (Baby Please Don't Go)'/'I'm The Greatest'/'San Francisco Bay Blues'/ 'Mind Train'/'Mind Holes'/ 'Midsummer New York'/'O Wind'/'Mrs Lennon'/'Toilet Piece'/'Telephone Piece;' filming **Working Class Hero/Imagine**.

The Lennons had ended 1970 with a pair of albums that stripped away artifice and decoration, and took truth-telling as their credo. John exposed himself in words, Yoko in sound; and the music was as uncompromising as anything in rock. Lennon described 'Imagine' as "'Plastic Ono Band' with sugar coating"—a conscious attempt, then, to sweeten the bitter pill with melody and harmony.

It was the lightness of most of the arrangements, the comforting turns of the melodies, that helped make 'Imagine' Lennon's most popular solo work. The anthemic qualities of the title track have disguised the slightness of some of the album's material, while the relevance of one of the most powerful tracks, 'How Do You Sleep', passed as soon as Lennon's feud with its target, Paul McCartney, died down. The 'Imagine' album is still easy on the ear, though, in a way which 'Plastic Ono Band' could never be. Small wonder that McCartney was among those who felt it was his best work.

From the standpoint of the nineties, what's most remarkable about the album is the fact that it was all but recorded in a week at the Lennons' home studio. John and Yoko then flew to the States for Phil Spector to supervise the overdubbing of strings, and the final vocal takes; then they returned home to shoot the material for their *Imagine* feature film, immediately began editing work, and then knocked off a double album for Yoko as an aside.

But 'Imagine' was not the product of the single burst of energy and need which created the 'Plastic Ono Band' songs. Its earliest composition, the delicate ballad 'Oh My Love', dated back to late 1968. Piano-based on the album, it was nonetheless firmly in the mould of Lennon's 1968/69 guitar picking songs, constructed around familiar ebb-and-flow melodic patterns and sharing the period's Manichean view of the world. Early takes of the song, heard before Spector added his New York sweetening, highlighted the delicate balance of the recording, with finger bells and a triangle supporting the fragile piano chords.

'Gimme Some Truth' had been premièred during the January 1969 Beatles sessions. Since then, Lennon had heightened the song's biting invective, throwing in contemporary references to 'Tricky Dicky' Nixon, provided a memorable three-note guitar riff to hold it together, snarled a tough, sneering lead vocal, and finally forced George Harrison to sum up the whole song with a precise and cutting guitar solo. On the final take, Lennon howled out his message—'All I want is the truth'—until the band ran out of steam, and he pronounced: 'This is the truth.' In New York, Spector persuaded him to fade the track long before then, and so it didn't appear on the record.

'Jealous Guy' was the other vintage song on the 'Imagine' album. In this case, though, only the tune was familiar: Lennon had originally written it in India as 'Child Of Nature', in which form it was still being vaguely considered by The Beatles as late as January 1969. Its new words were another confession of guilt to Yoko—what was Lennon up to in late 1970?—which opened, suitably enough, 'I was dreaming of the past.'

'Jealous Guy' had none of the mawkishness of 'I Promise', however: the lyrics were as sincere and honest as anything on Lennon's previous album, and they offered a disarming glimpse of the macho ex-Beatle discovering feminism through an examination of his own faults. Even before Spector added his New York strings, Lennon had duplicated their part with an organ; 'Jealous Guy' was always meant to be lush. Also added in New York was Lennon's delicate whistle over the final verse, which added another layer of vulnerability to his admission of wrong-doing.

The shift in mood from 'Jealous Guy' to 'How Do You Sleep' on the same record is the final proof of John's mercurial nature. 'Sleep' was a vicious assault on his ex-songwriting partner, which accused, judged and convicted him on counts of dishonesty, lack of talent, hypocrisy and—most heinous of all, it seemed—living with 'straights' (unlike the ultra-avant garde Lennons, of course). When the album came out, Lennon was unusually coy about the song—"I could have been writing about myself," he offered in his defence—but the lyrics pulled no punches. Allen Klein, who had his own good reasons for disliking McCartney, added the sly couplet that rhymed 'yesterday' with 'another day,' but the rest was Lennon's entirely unbalanced swipe at an old, dear friend—which is how (on 'Dear Friend') McCartney chose to reply when he cut *his* next album at the end of 1971.

Once again, it was Spector who gave the piece a lasting artistic life. Early takes of the song had lasted eight minutes or more, with Nicky Hopkins vamping away on electric piano, and George Harrison throwing in a delicious slide solo, apparently unperturbed by Lennon's address to their mutual ex-colleague, 'How do you sleep, you cunt.' With Spector in command, the repeat of the first verse was chopped out, and Phil underscored the attack of the lyrics with the most vicious string sound ever caught on record, which soared over the guitar boogie riffs before screeching to a halt at the end of each chorus.

Spector performed similar magic on 'I Don't Want To Be A Soldier,' a long, doomy rage against military madness and societal expectations. In its original form, 'Soldier' sounded like a hybrid of 'Cold Turkey' and 'Well Well Well'—a raw funk riff churning beneath a muddy mesh of rhythm sound, before Lennon built up towards a catharsis that was only fulfilled when the sax solo came roaring in. Little of that drama survived on the record: in its place, Spector substituted a volcanic echo which makes Lennon sound as if he's performing from beyond the grave.

'It's So Hard' was an equally powerful performance, a conventional blues where the grittiness of the guitar riff which electrified the song was matched by the oriental-flavoured strings. The lyrics took the burden of life-after-primal-therapy and stripped it down to the message of the title line, with Lennon growling out lines like 'you gotta be somebody/you gotta worry' like a native New Yorker. And like Buddy Holly on 'Peggy Sue', Lennon played a guitar part that acted as both rhythm and lead, while the band laid down a minimalist backing.

Throughout the album sessions, Lennon recorded his initial guide vocals while the instrumental tracks were being taped, giving the music a live feel missing from most superstar sessions. Nowhere does that vibe survive in better shape than on 'Crippled Inside', a jaunty piece of rockabilly that gently took the rise out of Lennon's psychodramas on his previous album. With honky-tonk piano and some startling dobro work (the latter from George Harrison), 'Crippled Inside' was Lennon's most relaxed piece of music in years, an effective tribute to the country-blues rock 'n' roll which had inspired him in the fifties.

'Oh Yoko' caught much of the same spirit, with Spector's production giving an unexpected richness to what was essentially a small band recording. Spector also joined Lennon for the falsetto harmony vocals, having performed much the same function a few months earlier on George Harrison's 'My Sweet Lord'. The basic mix of the song was much longer than the final cut, lacking the first harmonica solo and the backing vocals, though Lennon's final play-in-a-day excursion round his harmonica was there from take one.

'How' was the 'Imagine' song which came closest to the purity of the 'Plastic Ono Band' album. Having set the mood on his December 1970 demo, Lennon merely extended the song during the sessions, adding the delicious middle section (which harked back to the self-encouragement of 'Hold On') and letting the lyrics, with their series of unanswered questions, speak for themselves. Spector added some tasteful strings, and some echo on the piano, while Lennon took the opportunity in New York to re-cut his rather hoarse lead vocal.

In terms of sound, 'How' was also a dry run for the 'Imagine' title tr' k itself. On the first day of sessions at the Lennons' Tittenhurst Park Studios, John had taken the band aside and played brief piano renditions of the songs they were going to record. As participants Jim Keltner and Nicky Hopkins both recall, 'Imagine' stood out from the first, both for the power of its lyricism, and the haunting simplicity of its melody.

At this distance, it's hard to separate the song from the myth, which would have us believe that 'Imagine' is Lennon's finest song, his ultimate statement of hope for himself and the world. In fact, the words are far less straightforward than that: 'Imagine no possessions/I wonder if you can', Lennon wrote, fully aware that he was no rich man about to pass through the eye of a needle. The song's blatant denial of a Christian after-life, of any existence beyond today, is also at odds with any Utopian interpretation of the lyrics.

The song's lyrical structure–a series of ideas each calling for imagination–is directly based on Yoko's book *Grapefruit*, which is why in later years Lennon admitted that he should have given Yoko a co-credit on the song, as he did on 'Oh My Love'. In Yoko's art, the concept–the dream, if you like–is as important as the result. Lennon wanted results as well, but he followed Yoko in believing that dreaming of a desired event made the event itself more likely. The wider the dream, the more likely a change in the world: hence 'I hope someday you'll join us/and the world will be as one'.

What's interesting, in the light of 'Power To The People' and the promise of the radical sloganeering of the 'Some Time In New York City' album, is the lack of a political programme in Lennon's imaginings. There's a large gap between 'You say you want a revolution/you better get it on right away' and 'Nothing to kill and die for...Imagine all the people/ Living life in peace'. For the next year, the Lennons wandered between two manifestos–one which talked of violent action to secure change, another which preferred to lie back and dream.

There are countless alternate versions of 'Imagine' in existence, but all of them simply capture the path to the finished arrangement, without shedding any fresh light on the song. Before the strings were added in New York, however, and Spector pumped up the piano echo, 'Imagine' sounded stark and strangely sinister, with the piano, bass and drums left dry on the tape, casting no shadow. Like 'How,' this halfway mix would have fitted onto a soundalike successor to the 'Plastic Ono Band' album; but to increase the audience for his message, Lennon chose to allow Spector his head, coating the basic tracks with a thin veneer of sweetness which bridged the gap between cult acceptance and mass commercial appeal.

Though Lennon never intended to include non-original material on the finished album, he did use the 'Imagine' sessions to record a studio take of 'Well (Baby Please Don't Go)', the Walter Ward song which he'd performed a few weeks earlier with Frank Zappa and The Mothers in New York. Freed from the need to convey a message, Lennon turned in a tight, intense piece of R&B, fuelled by a chugging sax riff, some 'Cold Turkey'-style guitar, and Plastic Ono Band rhythm section. In between the repeated verses, he took control for a free-form guitar solo, its feel more important than the actual notes, before Bobby Keyes rekindled the spirit of The Coasters' records of the fifties with a King Curtis-like sax break. 'Well' was presumably cut as a potential B-side, but it remained unissued.

The only other out-take to have surfaced from the 'Imagine' sessions was a much more spontaneous affair. While the engineers set up for a new song, Lennon broke into an impromptu rendition of Jesse Fuller's vintage 'San Francisco Bay Blues', complete with authentic acoustic blues picking. Maybe Lennon was in training for 'Mind Holes', one of several Yoko Ono tracks that were also taped during and immediately after the 'Imagine' sessions. From the outset, it was obvious that Yoko had enough material for a double album: she and Lennon had already taped 'Fly,' which would fill a side by itself, and another side's worth of soundtrack material with the Joe Jones Tone Deaf Music Co's instruments. Yoko wasn't satisfied with this film music as an album in its own right, so Lennon and the 'Imagine' band relaxed between takes of songs like 'Jealous Guy' and 'It's So Hard' by recording Yoko's compositions.

'Mind Holes' featured layers of Lennon's blues guitar picking, plus a little bottleneck for good measure, with Yoko bleating over the top. 'O Wind' offered similar textures, this time with the percussion work of Jim Gordon, Jim Keltner and Bobby Keyes as backdrop, while Yoko first recited her poetry—'The body is the scar of your mind/The scar turns into a wind of pain'—and then emphasised the point with a burst of shrill vocal noises. As ever, the means may have differed, but the Lennons' philosophy was the same: the simple, *Grapefruit*-style instructions of 'Mind Holes'—'Search for the holes in your feelings—memories—pain/Dream of the holes'—expressed in more basic terms the uncompromising vision of Lennon's 'Plastic Ono Band' songs.

Slowly, however, Yoko was learning to marry her stark artistic notions with the rock technology inherited from her husband. 'Open Your Box' and 'Don't Worry Kyoko' were included on her 'Fly' album as early examples; but the most powerful unison of East and West came on the chilling 'Mind Train', 16 minutes of eerie electric riffing which built up to an inferno of sound, while Yoko dispassionately chanted her lyrics of doom and pain: 'I thought of killing that man...dub dub train passed through my mind...33 windows shining through my mind'. Presumably the 33 windows belonged to the 33 buildings that Yoko had once suggested you should watch being covered with snow in her 'Snow Piece For Solo' or 'Trio No. 2'.

Just as Yoko deserved credit for altering the way in which John saw the world, so in turn John twisted Yoko's music towards more traditional structures. The result of the latter process was 'Midsummer New York', with Yoko struggling to keep tempo with a simple rock 'n' roll 12-bar structure, which proved an effective basis for more tales of fear and loathing in the big city: 'Midsummer New York/My heart shakes in terror.' As on 'Mind Train', it was Lennon who took care of the guitar parts, with a freedom and vigour that he rarely achieved on his own records.

'Mrs Lennon' was chosen as the lead single from 'Fly,' and its gentle, elegiac air must have surprised many who took the trouble to listen. The title of the song was ironic: Yoko hated being described as Mrs Lennon, Beatle wife, rather than as an artist in her own right. And the chilling series of surreal images which filled the song was certainly no straightforward declaration of love. Lennon's Bach-like piano accompaniment only added to the atmosphere of foreboding—shared by many of Yoko's songs, which seem to look forward unconsciously to the dark days of December 1980.

The final new recordings on 'Fly' were proof that the couple had not yet shed their playful vision of the artist's role, however. 'Toilet Piece' consisted of a flushing lavatory; 'Telephone Piece' (which also appeared over the credits of Yoko's documentary short, *One-Woman Show*, about her non-existent art exhibit at New York's Museum of Modern Art) was Yoko answering a phone call. Only a few seconds long, these tracks simultaneously debunked the idea of art as an élitist occupation, and invited the world to look on the Lennons as clowns.

So too the *Imagine* movie, the Lennons' most careful attempt at creating their art on film. Their previous movies had been directed at the avant-garde community, establishing their credentials, as it were. They certainly had little hope or expectation of achieving the surprising commercial success of Yoko's *Film No.4 (Bottoms)*.

The *Imagine* movie was different. Here were John and Yoko creating a visual counterpoint to their music—plus a vehicle which would promote their own new records. Indeed, like *Cold Turkey* and *The Ballad Of John And Yoko*, *Imagine* began simply enough as a promo film clip for John's album title track, shortly to be issued as a single in the USA. From the start, as Lennon revealed when the movie was completed, "The film was a back drop to the sound. The interesting part was putting the picture to the sound, not the other way around." Like modern long-form promo vehicles, which offer a selection of promo clips linked by an elementary story-line, *Imagine* sought to offer a pictorial accompaniment to the 'Imagine' and 'Fly' albums. But at the same time, the Lennons refused to think in terms of lateral plot development. As John explained, "*Imagine* was a discontinuum—a comedy, not a tragedy. It's the epitome of nonsense. It was made in a very playful mood."

Hence the weird assembly of near-documentary footage, highlighted by the famous clip for the song 'Imagine', with Lennon sat alone at his white piano while Yoko opens the shutters separating the darkness of the room from the light of the sun; and pure surrealism, which reached its zenith with the Lennons playing chess with an all-white set, and then proceeding to eat the pieces. "With an all-white chess set," John explained, "you have to convince each other, you have to remember which horse is yours."

Convincing anyone apart from each other was something that the film failed to do, however. Though there were memorable moments–the Lennons boating across the lake in their vast grounds, or drawing their names in the sand seconds before the tide swept them away–the film's determined lack of realism made it more a venture in self-indulgence than an insight into their creative thinking. "We were only playing ourselves on a surrealistic level," Yoko explained, but the 'playing' was never more than that. John recalled in 1972: "When we did *Imagine*, we felt great about it, and were saying, 'This is going to widen the field of film! This is it, this is the seventies.'" Instead, the Lennons failed to find a distributor for the full 85-minute print, and only a cut-down, 55-minute film was screened publicly, omitting most of Yoko's musical segments. Yoko slightly re-edited this version for the eventual home-video release in the mid-eighties.

Ultimately, the *Imagine* film project–which used just 20 per cent of the footage shot during the filming–worked better in small clips, as in the promo films for 'Imagine' and 'Mrs Lennon' circulated at the time, and the more recent compilation clips for posthumous releases like 'Jealous Guy.'

A more fruitful project might have been *Working Class Hero*, Nick Knowland's visual record of the 'Imagine' recording sessions. About 60 hours of film and sync sound were shot during the week of recording, again for use in a full-length documentary film. Not even a rough cut was prepared from this footage, however, as the Lennons chose to pursue the conceptual *Imagine* movie instead. But the *Working Class Hero* film did provide the basis for *Imagine: John Lennon*, the 1988 biopic.

Chapter 12

SEPTEMBER 1971
TO APRIL 1973

. . . .

EARLY SEPTEMBER 1971: *RECORDING* home demos of '*JJ*'/'Shoeshine.'

'Imagine' and 'Fly' were the Lennons' farewell to Britain. Having travelled to the States for final preparation of the two albums, they returned home to Tittenhurst Park to prepare another season of their films for the *Art Spectrum* at Alexandra Palace (where the *Top Of The Pops* film clip from January 1972 was shown as *Instant Karma*, alongside *Up Your Legs Forever* and a handful of other promo clips). On August 28, they appeared on the BBC TV programme *Parkinson*, discussing bagism and their predilection for showing themselves in the nude; and six days later they were gone, arriving in New York after a stopover in the Virgin Islands. John Lennon never set foot in Britain again.

The couple made their initial home at the St. Regis Hotel, where they quickly installed their home recording equipment and began to play host to a stream of visiting radicals and artists. Within days of taking up residence at the St. Regis, Lennon had written and recorded two new songs. The couple were both taking large quantities of methadone, as a replacement for heroin; once again, their personal lives were on the line. But John chose not to reflect this in his new music. Instead, 'JJ' was a third-person story-song, an acoustic guitar ditty set to the tune of what would become 'Angela' on their next album. In its initial form, though, the song showed little sign that Lennon had taken note of sexual politics, with its playful tale of, a woman who 'couldn't get laid at all.'

'Shoeshine' was an even simpler piece, set to a traditional acoustic guitar boogie. 'Well I was sitting listening to some rock and roll/I said they don't play music like that no more; it began, before attempting to disprove the point by breaking into Gary Bonds' 'Quarter To Three.' Obviously unfinished, it was most interesting for its use of a couple of lines which turned up in the 1973 LP cut, 'Meat City.'

• • • **SEPTEMBER 1971:** *FILMING Clock*; recording 'Maybe Baby'/'Rave On'/ 'Not Fade Away'/'Heartbeat'/'Peggy Sue Got Married'/'Peggy Sue'/'Send Me Some Lovin''/'New York City'/'Mailman Bring Me No More Blues'/'Honey Don't'/'Glad All Over'/'Lend Me Your Comb.'

Even with many hours of *Imagine* footage still to be edited, the Lennons carried on filming. *Clock* was shot in their St. Regis Hotel room: its visual content marked the passage of an hour of time on a clock on the hotel wall. No doubt this was an oblique comment on the transitory nature of time; but what made this movie bearable was its soundtrack, which consisted of Yoko making phone calls in search of exhibits for her upcoming art show at the Everson Gallery, while John played solo acoustic versions of some of his favourite fifties rock songs—mostly, as the list above reveals, by Buddy Holly and Carl Perkins. Lennon kept fairly close to the original models, and even remembered most of the words; but he took the opportunity to invest his vocals with a devilish quaver that was obviously inspired by the example of his wife.

The most revealing minutes from the soundtrack document the first version of 'New York City,' which evolved into a powerhouse rocker on the couple's next album. Though the rockaboogie rhythm was already intact, this early take had completely different lyrics to the final version, though Lennon's slurred delivery suggests he was busking it rather than reeling off a fixed set of verses. The one link to the record is the chorus line—'Que Pasa New York.'

• • • **OCTOBER 9, 1971:** *THIS IS NOT HERE* exhibition opens; records birthday party jam session; writes 'Attica State.'

For 19 days in October 1971, the prestigious Everson Art Museum in Syracuse, upstate New York, played host to Yoko Ono's most comprehensive retrospective exhibition. The show had only been commissioned in the week that the couple left England, so with less than a month to prepare, Yoko invited John to participate as 'guest artist', and also solicited exhibits from her friends in the art and music communities.

The Lennons held a press conference on the eve of the opening, excerpts of which were later included on the LP series 'The History Of Syracuse Music.' And film clips of the event were also included on a documentary, named after the exhibition, screened on US television on May 11, 1972.

Although *This Is Not Here* (a slogan which the Lennons had displayed on a sign in front of their Tittenhurst Park home in England) mostly consisted of Yoko's earlier work, there was some new material on show. *Clock* was screened continually in the foyer; inside, there was a room devoted to 'Water Pieces' (objects contributed by Yoko's friends), all of which were designed to be filled with water. John had made a small fish tank, inside which was a pink sponge, labelled 'Napoleon's Bladder.'

That night—Lennon's 31st birthday—the couple stayed up late to party. Being John and Yoko, the event was recorded, capturing for posterity the dubious delights of a stellar assembly (including Phil Spector, Klaus Voorman, Jim Keltner, Ringo and Maureen Starkey and Allen Ginsberg) performing drunken renditions of favourite rock oldies, folk songs like 'Goodnight Irene', more recent Lennon classics like 'Imagine' (delivered in a painfully weedy voice by Spector when John refused to join in the fun) and even Paul McCartney's 'Yesterday.'

Earlier in the evening, before too much drink had been consumed, Lennon had composed a new song—'Attica State', a blatant political protest about the killings in a New York State jail. As a chant for demonstrations, the chorus had its moments; but as an epic of radical songwriting, it showed that Lennon still had much to learn before he would rival more experienced social commentators like Phil Ochs. By declaring 'Rockefeller killed the prisoners/That is what the people feel', John also showed an alarming tendency to equate 'the people' with himself—a perennial folly of political activists the world over.

- **AUTUMN 1971: *FILMING* Freedom films.**

Invited to contribute work to the year-end *Chicago Film Festival*, John and Yoko each shot a 60-second illustration of *Freedom*. John scratched the word onto the film itself, leaving it to flicker on the screen for a minute and then die. Yoko was more ironic: to the accompaniment of two repeated notes from John's electronic keyboard, she shot a brief sequence of herself trying to remove her bra—and failing. Her footage neatly undermined its title, and the naïve optimism of the Lennons' political associates.

- **EARLY OCTOBER 1971: *RECORDING* home demo of 'Happy Xmas (War Is Over).'**

'War is over (if you want it)' was the slogan that John and Yoko sent round the world in their late 1969 poster campaign for peace. The same phrase became the title of their 1971 Christmas event—a seasonal record, written at the same time as 'Attica State'. The original acoustic demo of 'Happy Xmas' boasted few words, but the structure was in place, with John struggling manfully to hit the high notes in the middle section. Underpinning the song were guitar chords playing the riff which became the counter-melody, though at this stage John had yet to set his two-year-old slogan to music.

OCTOBER 28/29, 1971: *RECORDING* 'Happy Xmas (War Is Over)'/'Listen, The Snow Is Falling.'

145

Richard Williams of the British music paper *Melody Maker*, preparing a biography of Phil Spector, was invited to attend these sessions–which are thus documented more fully than most. He noted that Lennon spent the morning of October 28 writing, and then destroying, lyrics for a song about Bo Diddley and Chuck Berry: this may have been a fuller version of 'Shoeshine' from the previous month, another early draft of 'New York City,' or perhaps an answer song to Elephant Memory's 'Chuck And Bo'.

The lyrics to 'Happy Xmas' were completed before the session; rather than pursuing any individual theme from the Lennons' campaigns, they acted as a catch-all request for universal harmony. Only the opening lines, with Lennon asking himself, 'So this is Christmas/And what have you done?' took the song out of the mainstream.

In Phil Spector, Lennon had found a past-master at making Christmas records: his 'A Christmas Gift To You' album from 1963 remains the peak of the genre. For the Lennons, he brought out his full coterie of effects, using sleigh-bells and celestes to capture the seasonal feel, and bringing in the children of the Harlem Community Choir to sing the final choruses. Yoko, meanwhile, took over the song's middle section when Spector realised that Lennon's voice couldn't stretch that far.

'Happy Xmas' was at once a surprisingly conventional Lennon record, and an altogether more thoughtful piece of work than the average seasonal offering. Yoko's flipside, written early in 1968 and premièred briefly on 'Song For John' at the end of that year, was equally memorable: out came the tapes of feet trudging through the snow to top and tail the song, while Lennon supported Yoko's fragile, gentle vocals with some melodic reverb guitar.

* * * * ***NOVEMBER 12, 1971: RECORDING** demos of 'Luck Of The Irish'/'Attica State'.*

Two months into their residence in New York, the Lennons had already found their feet in the city's radical community, as activists like Abbie Hoffman and Jerry Rubin latched on to the power of their media profile. 'Attica State' was an early result, with Lennon choosing to comment on events he knew little about. Having written the song in early October, he and Yoko cut home demos a month later. The first take broke down immediately, so they went back and wiped it, only for their second attempt to fail in the same place, as Lennon missed his cue for the chorus. The third pass was more successful, and revealed the original format for the piece–Lennon and Yoko alternating solo lines, and then singing in unison (or as close as Yoko could muster) in the chorus.

Premièred on the same day was a song about a political issue slightly closer to John's experience. Like most of the British left, Lennon had been quick to support the campaigns of the Irish Republican Army against what they saw as the colonialist British state. 'Luck Of The Irish' was John's general response to the problem; later 'Sunday Bloody Sunday' would chart his reactions to more specific events. The song was spurred by a protest march in London which the couple had led in August, and saw John sympathising with the oppressed Irish in their struggle against 'a thousand years of torture and hunger' and 'the British brigands'. For all its melodic charm, the song was always an outsider's view, and its release angered many people in Britain. In its earliest version, it was self-consciously a folk song, written as if it had been passed down the generations. Gradually, the lyrics evolved, as John first whistled and then wrote words for Yoko to sing in the middle section, a parade of idealistic images of Irish beauty to set against the harshness of John's political lament. This November 1971 demo tape actually caught a rather unharmonious mood in the Lennons' apartment, with the first take being abandoned as John chided Yoko for not paying attention; but the second run, backed by solo acoustic guitar, was a blueprint for the full studio take the following spring. This original version, however, was given to the makers of the documentary *The Irish Tapes*, which John and Yoko were financing.

LATE NOVEMBER/DECEMBER 1971: *RECORDING home demos of 'New York City'/'Woman Is The Nigger Of The World'/'Bring On The Lucie/'John Sinclair'/'People'/'Call My Name'.*

Warming to his new stance as the balladeer of the barricades, Lennon leapt to document the changing US political map in song. John Sinclair was his first priority—a campaign anthem for the jailed White Panther and rock manager (of The MC5), serving time in Detroit for possession of a small amount of marijuana. The Lennons had already agreed to headline a benefit at Ann Arbor's Crisler Arena on December 10: a fortnight or so earlier, John completed the song, a bluesy, steel-guitar stomp which—true to his new ideals—told the story of Sinclair's imprisonment in simple verses. He hammered home the chorus line by repeating 'gotta' some 15 times before finishing the line 'set him free'.

On the same day, Lennon made an early pass at another attempted anthem—the song which came to be known as 'Bring On The Lucie'. At this stage, it was simply a three-chord dobro riff, around which Lennon had strung the phrase 'Free the people now.' 'Give Peace A Chance' this was not.

A few days later, Lennon made his first serious attempt at setting 'New York City' on tape. Since previewing the song in *Clock* in September, he had completed the first verse, a Chuck Berry-inspired rock 'n' roll diary of what happened when the Lennons hit New York. The second verse was still improvised, however, and its opening words shed some light on its conception, with Lennon opening up 'Well, I was shooting up speed'.

As well as updating 'New York City,' Lennon had also spent time rewriting 'JJ'. He loved the melody, but couldn't find a suitable lyric. The sexist description of 'JJ' wasn't it; nor, it transpired, was attempt number two, titled 'People'. Lyrically, this was a rather bland call for peace and understanding, using themes that would be rekindled on 'Only People' in 1973. After this brief acoustic outing, the song was again rejected.

'Call My Name' dated back to the summer 1971 sessions which also produced the earliest version of 'God Save Us'. Second time around, Lennon set the tune on acoustic guitar, and completed the lyric, as an updated take on his 1963 composition, 'All I've Got To Do'. The message here was one of support, offering a shoulder to lean on: 'I'll ease your pain, girl/All you got to do is call my name'. But the song's personal politics didn't suit the upcoming album, and so 'Call My Name' was left to be gutted and reshaped into 'Aisumasen' for 1973's 'Mind Games'.

The most important song to come from this demo session also had a lengthy gestation. "Woman is the nigger of the world," Yoko told the editors of *Nova* in a 1968 interview. Three years later, the would-be feminist John Lennon made that the title of yet another anthem. Cut first in their hotel room, then on more professional equipment in their first New York apartment, 'Woman Is The Nigger Of The World' shaped up as a savage portrayal of man's inhumanity to woman, equating the plight of the female sex with that of American blacks. The song's finger-pointing lyrics sat uneasily in Lennon's mouth, but were evidence of the enormous impact Yoko had had on his thinking. All he needed now was to put his own ideals into practice.

• • • • **DECEMBER 10, 1971: *PERFORMING* '**Attica State'/'Luck Of The Irish'/ 'Sisters O Sisters'/'John Sinclair' at John Sinclair benefit, a performance filmed for **Ten For Two**.

15,000 people filled the Crisler Arena in Ann Arbor, Michigan, lured as much by the prospect of seeing the Lennons and Stevie Wonder as by the virtue of the cause for which this was a benefit—John Sinclair's appeal fund. The entire concert was filmed, at the Lennons' expense, on 16mm, and a rough cut of the movie was shown to the couple under the title *Ten For Two*—taken from one of the key lines in Lennon's 'John Sinclair' song. But the movie was never released.

The Lennons took the stage in the early hours of the morning, by which time the audience had worked themselves into a frenzy of anticipation, expecting the reformation of The Beatles at the very least. Instead, they were given John, Yoko, guitarists Leslie Bacon and David Peel, and percussionist politico Jerry Rubin. The quintet had rehearsed just four songs, all of them new to the audience, some of them, to judge by the rather amusing film of the event, new to the band.

'Attica State' was symptomatic of the problem. Trying to fill an entire arena with acoustic guitars would have been trouble enough; singing the song when your wife is consistently half a beat out-of-step was nearly impossible. 'Luck Of The Irish' was slightly smoother, though only after Lennon's guitar-strap had broken, along with his temper. Then came Yoko's solo, on her new song, 'Sisters O Sisters', a feminist call for unity. Finally, John eased the combo through a surprisingly tight rendition of 'John Sinclair,' and the mini-concert was over. The audience were apparently disappointed by its brevity, but it served its purpose: within a couple of days, Sinclair was free.

SEPTEMBER 1971 TO APRIL 1973

- **DECEMBER 17, 1971:** *PERFORMING* 'Attica State'/'Sisters O Sisters'/
'Imagine' at the Attica families benefit.

A few days after Ann Arbor, the Lennons appeared as an acoustic duo at a concert held in Harlem at the legendary Apollo Theatre, showcase of black music. They were there to raise funds for the dependants of those killed in the Attica State prison riots–the event which had sparked John to write a song in October. They repeated two of their selections from the Ann Arbor show, before John told the audience: "I'm putting an electric band together, but it's not ready yet, so I'll just have to busk it." There followed a stark, beautiful version of 'Imagine', backed only by acoustic guitar; 'Imagine no possessions–try it', Lennon sang, the sentiments unfettered by any musical ornamentation.

- **JANUARY 1972:** *RECORDING home demos of* 'Pill'/'He Got The Blues'.

Throughout their frenetic relationship, John and Yoko had never been far removed from drugs. Only during the Janov-inspired cleansing of 1970 had illicit chemicals been forsaken entirely; and by the end of the year John was apparently using heroin again. After the avowedly acid-drenched visions of 1966/67, however, and the confessional 'Cold Turkey,' little of his drug experience showed up in his songs. An acoustic number called 'Pill' might seem to be the exception, but the reality is a little disappointing. It consists of one repeated line, set to a chunky guitar riff: 'You need a special pill to keep you on the line'. John bent the last word round a sequence of tight melodic curves to make the piece more interesting, but he never took it any further.

Likewise 'He Got The Blues', a thinly-veiled piece of self-pitying autobiography, that begins 'Johnny was a poor boy...he did the best he can', and meanders nowhere in particular. 'Johnny' was himself, of course, and also the hero of Chuck Berry's 'Johnny B. Goode;' but his adventures were never completed.

- **JANUARY 13, 1972:** *PERFORMING* 'John Sinclair'/'It's So Hard'/'Luck Of The Irish'/'Sisters O Sisters'/'Attica State' on **The David Frost Show**.

In the first of a series of chat-show appearances in 1972, the Lennons gave their first public performance with their new support crew, Elephant's Memory–a New York bar band who had contributed to the soundtrack of *Midnight Cowboy*. Lennon loved their raunchy approach to rock 'n' roll, and their radical street feel, and for the next eight months they became his constant back-up, as he made another studio album, and planned his return to the road.

For *The David Frost Show*, Lennon previewed four of the songs from the next album, all of which had been given acoustic renditions in his December 1971 benefit gigs. 'Attica State' and 'Luck Of The Irish' scarcely made use of the band: the partnership only caught fire on an electrifying take of Lennon's 'Imagine' LP blues, 'It's So Hard'. On 'Luck

149

Of The Irish' meanwhile, John was still rewriting the lyrics: for the moment, it was 'the kids, the church and the IRA' who were to blame, 'as the bastards commit genocide.' The church was let off the hook when the Lennons finally taped the song in the studio.

LATE JANUARY/FEBRUARY 1972: PRODUCING 'I'm A Runaway'/ 'Everybody's Smoking Marijuana'/'F Is Not A Dirty Word'/'The Hippie From New York City'/'McDonald's Farm'/'The Ballad Of New York City— John Lennon And Yoko Ono'/'The Ballad Of Bob Dylan'/'The Chicago Conspiracy'/'The Hip Generation'/'I'm Gonna Start Another Riot'/'The Birth Control Blues'/'The Pope Smokes Dope' by David Peel.

Yippie street-singer David Peel was one of the first members of the New York underground that the Lennons met, and his madcap live performances immediately appealed to the free spirit in John. Peel accompanied the couple to their Ann Arbor benefit, and like Jerry Rubin was a constant part of the Lennons' entourage during the early weeks of 1972. Around that time, John and Yoko produced an album for him, and issued it on Apple in April—a successor to his two earlier efforts on Elektra.

In fact, producing Peel was scarcely a chore. He performed with, at most, three other musicians, calling in a choir of friends off the street for his choruses. At a time when Lennon himself was writing slogans rather than songs, Peel's populism was bound to raise his enthusiasm. In retrospect, only a couple of the tracks have outlived their contemporary relevance: 'The Pope Smokes Dope' and 'The Ballad Of New York City— John Lennon And Yoko Ono' both look forward to the basic structures of the late seventies new wave, marrying chanted lyrics to simple, uncluttered music. John added dobro to both tunes, while he and Yoko also showed up in the mass choruses.

FEBRUARY 5, 1972: PERFORMING 'Luck Of The Irish' at Civil Rights demo.

Outside the 44th Street offices of the British national airline, BOAC, the Lennons made their first protest about the events on the streets of Northern Ireland the previous weekend, when soldiers shot dead 13 civilians on what became known as 'Bloody Sunday.' John had already begun work on a song to mark his disgust; at this demo, however, he and Yoko performed 'Luck Of The Irish' before rushing back to their Bank Street apartment to dictate a press release for the city's news media—none of whom were in any great hurry to use it.

FEBRUARY 14 TO 18, 1972: CO-HOSTING The Mike Douglas Show: performing 'Woman Is The Nigger Of The World'/'Luck Of The Irish'/ 'Imagine'/'Sakura'/'Johnny B. Goode'/'Memphis'/'Attica State'/'It's So Hard'/'Sisters O Sisters'/'Midsummer New York.'

Afternoon talk shows were never the same after this exercise in cross-cultural fertilisation, which saw the Lennons co-hosting the extremely popular *Mike Douglas Show* with a man not known for his artistic or political radicalism. All three hosts were able to choose guests for the five shows: the Lennons selected a series of underground figures and politicos, plus John's hero, Chuck Berry; Mike Douglas answered with a more sedate mixture of entertainers and charity workers.

The encounters between Bobby Seale and Jerry Rubin on one hand, and Mike Douglas on the other, rank among the classic moments of television comedy—Douglas visibly freaked by the reputation of his guests, Rubin and Seale unable to come to terms with selling their message to mass America. The Lennons bridged the gap, diluting some of the more radical statements, or making them more accessible to the audience, and also performing much of the material which they were about to record with Elephant's Memory for 'Some Time In New York City.'

Musical highlights included Yoko missing her cue after the guitar solo on 'Midsummer New York,' and apologising to the band; Yoko again performing a Japanese folk-song, 'Sakura;' and Lennon and the Elephant's Memory band joining forces for a majestic version of 'Woman Is The Nigger Of The World.' What ought to have been a highlight, but wasn't, was the meeting between Lennon and Chuck Berry. The pair performed two of Chuck's classic hits, but spent most of 'Johnny B. Goode' each trying to sing harmony to the other's lead, while on 'Memphis' they were a little distracted by Yoko screaming on the other side of the stage. Berry was not amused.

• **MARCH 1 TO 20, 1972: *RECORDING*** 'Woman Is The Nigger Of The World'/ 'Sisters O Sisters'/'Attica State'/'John Sinclair'/'Born In A Prison'/'We're All Water'/'New York City'/'Sunday Bloody Sunday'/'Luck Of The Irish'/ 'Angela'/'Down In The Caribbean'/'Not Fade Away'/'Send Me Some Lovin''/ 'Don't Be Cruel'/'Hound Dog'/'Ain't That A Shame.'

For the third consecutive album, John called in Phil Spector to act as production co-ordinator—controlling the quality and mixing of the sound, rather than the entire session as was his normal practice. Most of these songs and arrangements were set before the album was started: Spector's job was to take the political pills, and sugar them for American radio.

Spector's work aside, though, there was little hint of compromise on this package. It emerged eventually as a double set, with the December 1969 Lyceum and June 1971 Fillmore East recordings thrown together as an album entitled 'Live Jam.' The set was presented as a newspaper, an up-to-the-minute comment on the news of the day, seen through the eyes of a radical couple who had been moving in even more radical company. The artwork displayed such delights as a drawing of an oriental woman being stabbed in the stomach; and, in lighter mood, the heads of Richard Nixon and Mao Tse-Tung pasted on top of naked, dancing bodies. (The latter was censored in many American stores.) The lyrics, with their bold message of revolution and rebellion, occupied most of the front and back cover, however: this time, no one could ignore the Lennons' intentions, except by leaving the record in the stores, which is the way it turned out.

'Some Time In New York City'–its very title heightened the diary-like nature of the project–gathered together all of the Lennons' recent forays into politics, like their protests about Attica State and John Sinclair, the birth of John's feminism on 'Woman Is The Nigger Of The World', Yoko's call for women's solidarity, 'Sisters O Sisters', and John's sad tale about 'The Luck Of The Irish'. Two songs last seen in incomplete form were also present. 'New York City' was now a fully-fledged story-song, a series of snapshots of the Lennons in radical New York, replying to the call of the city's harbour: 'The Statue of Liberty said come!'

At the heart of the song was John's liberation at having escaped England, with its petty morality and racist attitude towards Yoko, and its refusal to see beyond the myth of The Beatles in approaching John's more recent work. New York City, a melting pot of races and ideas, had taken the Lennons to its heart: the song was Lennon's vote of thanks.

Elsewhere, 'JJ' had become 'People', and then in turn 'Angela'. This rapid shift of subject-matter rather diminishes the emotional force of the song, a call of sympathy to Angela Davis, a Black Panther supporter on trial for kidnapping and murder. Though the message to Ms Davis was heartfelt enough, its lyrical content left a little to be desired; only speed-writing can have produced a couplet like, 'They gave you coffee, they gave you tea/They gave you everything but the jailhouse key.' But in Yoko's line, 'There's a wind that never dies' (first included in her 1966 message 'To The Wesleyan People'), the album found one of its rare links to the couple's work before they discovered politics.

Yoko also contributed 'Born In A Prison', a thoughtful ballad about the barriers that afflict, and make up, society. While Lennon had stripped away any metaphors or personal concerns from his new songs, Yoko was still approaching problems with poetry. On 'We're All Water,' she simply rewrote her 1967 poem 'Water Talk', which had read: 'You are water/I'm water/We're all water in different containers/That's why it's so easy to meet/Someday we'll evaporate together.' Substitute 'rivers' for 'containers', and you have the chorus of the song, to which Yoko added a series of amusing verses about the essential lack of difference between, for instance, Chairman Mao and Richard Nixon.

The album's most recent song was 'Sunday Bloody Sunday,' a fiery rant about the Derry killings of late January, with Lennon acting as spokesman for the Irish people: 'All you Anglo-pigs and Scotties/Trying to colonise the North/You wave your bloody Union Jacks/But you know what they're worth.' Sloganeering, no matter how sincere, rarely wins battles, however, and the Lennons gradually abandoned their support of the IRA in the wake of terrorist attacks on civilian targets.

Much of the album was, it has to be said, simply crass; but it was saved by the sheer power and excitement of the music. The difference was partly Spector's production, which turned 'Sunday Bloody Sunday' into a swamp-rock inferno, 'The Luck Of The Irish' into a gentle, lush ballad and 'New York City' into a powerhouse rocker that The Rolling Stones would have killed for. And partly it was the sparks struck in the studio between Lennon, always a man for the spontaneous rather than the precise, and Elephant's Memory, who wouldn't have recognised precision if it had offered them a record contract.

Quite how anarchic was the band's attitude to musical form was proved by a series of out-takes cut during the sessions—late-night romps through favourite fifties rockers, which even enticed Phil Spector out from behind the production desk to shake a hand. "Phil, you're in the wrong room," Lennon sighed as a particularly chaotic jam around 'Not Fade Away' fell to pieces. Several Fats Domino and Elvis Presley standards also bit the dust, with Elephant's Memory offering lively but completely uncoordinated support. Yoko made her presence felt on 'Don't Be Cruel' in inimitable fashion, spurring John to ask "What are you doing there?" "Can you hear me?" Yoko replied innocently, to be greeted by the husbandly message: "You're louder than me, so shut up!" But that didn't stop her screaming her way through 'Hound Dog,' while the band struggled to keep track of the song's three chords.

During the rock oldies, John broke briefly into 'Down In The Caribbean,' a strange Latino shuffle that prefigured Ringo's 'No No Song' by a couple of years. But such delights were the exception during these sessions, the pinnacle of the Lennons' brief career as political commentators and organisers.

- **EARLY APRIL 1972: *SUNDANCE* publishes** '*Imagine: It's Never Too Late To Start From The Start.'*

Late in 1971, Lennon was invited to take part in a charity auction to raise funds for the launching of *Sundance*, a radical journal concerned with the meeting between politics and art. Editor Craig Pyes subsequently asked him and Yoko to contribute to the magazine's first issue. In fact, the Lennons agreed to host a regular column in *Sundance*, headed—what else?—'Imagine.'

Their initial column was written in the early weeks of 1972, and then included in the magazine's first issue in April. It had been written around the same time as Yoko had composed a piece for the *New York Times* on 'The Feminization Of Society:' the *Sundance* feature shared a similar tone, so it's safe to assume that it was Yoko who actually wrote it, with John merely submitting ideas. Like her evocative song, 'What A Bastard The World Is,' the article pointed out the difference for the average working-woman between her gut acceptance of the principles of radical feminism, and the difficulty she had incorporating them into her own life. From a writer who usually favoured the conceptual rather than the specific, this was a rare show of insight and sympathy, which went far beyond John's slightly crass rhetoric in 'Woman Is The Nigger Of The World.' John's major contribution to the *Sundance* spread was a series of pencil drawings, off-the-cuff sketches of women engaged in daily life.

- **SPRING 1972: *COMPOSES* limerick for** *The Gay Liberation Book.*

153

Sexual liberation being the message of the moment, John didn't hesitate when asked to contribute to an anthology of homosexual writings. His offering was a limerick–'Why make it so sad to be gay?/ Doing your own thing is OK/Our bodies are our own/So leave us alone/Go play with yourself–today.' There was even a drawing of a nude male perched carefree on a cloud to match.

• • • **APRIL/MAY 1972: *PRODUCING*** *'Liberation Special'/'Baddest Of The Mean'/'Cryin' Blacksheep Blues'/'Chuck And Bo'/'Gypsy Wolf'/'Madness'/ 'Life'/'Wind Ridge'/'Power Boogie'/'Local Plastic Ono Band' for Elephant's Memory.*

The New York rock 'n' roll of Elephant's Memory had made them an ideal back-up band for the equally earthy songs on 'Some Time In New York City.' To return the favour, John and Yoko signed them up to Apple and produced an album for them, a heady mix of raunchy rock, R&B, and the street-ass feel which had attracted Lennon in the first place.

As ever in the production chair, Lennon simply recorded the sound the band made, doing nothing to embellish it beyond adding a little guitar to 'Power Boogie' and 'Cryin' Blacksheep Blues', percussion to 'Chuck And Bo' and electric piano to 'Wind Ridge'. In addition, he and Yoko turned up in the vocal chorus on most songs, Yoko doing her best child-like singalong over the fade of 'Local Plastic Ono Band', while both halves of the couple had a solo line on the stompin' 'Power Boogie', the album's strongest track. Much of the rest was standard bar-room fare: the Elephants boasted a superb sax player in Stan Bronstein, but no vocalist to match him, and for the most part they sounded like a down-market version of the J. Geils Band, or a less vicious MCS. By 1972 standards, though, the 'Elephant's Memory' album was no slouch, and it did cement the band's image as, indeed, the Local Plastic Ono Band.

• • • **MAY 1972: *EDITING*** *Ten For Two.*

The movie of the John Sinclair benefit was never released, and the Lennons' completion of the film seems more like a gesture of dismissal than a step towards making it public. After 'Some Time In New York City,' in fact, the Lennons felt the heat of John's deportation case–fuelled on the surface by his drugs conviction in Britain back in 1968, but covertly inspired by the Republican Party's fear that Lennon might lead political demonstrations against their national convention. The rumour had been sparked by the posturing of some of their radical friends, who had already set Lennon up as their figurehead. What's certain, though, is that John was intending to take Elephant's Memory on the road, together with Jim Keltner and Phil Spector, employing David Peel as an advance party to drum up support in each new town. The tour was roughly scheduled for mid-summer, and would no doubt have been an amalgam of music, politics and play-politics, an underground cabaret for the anti-Vietnam movement. When the lawyers began making threatening noises, however,

John and Yoko quietly drew back from the fray, and the Convention and the Republicans were left in relative peace.

• **MAY 11, 1972: *PERFORMING* 'Woman Is The Nigger Of The World'/'We're All Water' on *The Dick Cavett Show*.**

In retrospect, the major event on this evening talk-show appearance was Lennon's claim that he was under government surveillance as a result of his unresolved immigration case. At the time, that was dismissed as laughable paranoia, "The ravings of a clown," as Phil Ochs said in another context. The controversy in May 1972 was about the title of 'Woman Is The Nigger Of The World', and the offence it might or might not cause to the black community. Cavett was forced by the network to recite a mild disclaimer before the Lennons performed the song, though Yoko's full-blooded rendition of the mighty 'We're All Water' needed no such apologies. This show brought the Lennons' current sequence of TV appearances to a close; subsequent performances would be less controversial.

• **JULY 1972: *SUNDANCE* publishes 'Imagine'.**

The Lennons' second column in *Sundance*, again primarily written by Yoko, was a defence of the new, political element in their work on 'Some Time In New York City.' The article planted songs like 'Sunday Bloody Sunday' firmly in the tradition of their past work—a logical extension of the truth-telling about the world that had begun rather obliquely in *In His Own Write*, and then led John to compose Beatles songs from the heart rather than the textbook; and which had persuaded Yoko to satirise the concerns of the artistic and business establishments in some of her *Grapefruit* pieces, and then to write about her pain as a woman on 'Mrs Lennon' and 'Midsummer New York.'
Yoko again contributed to the third *Sundance*, this time without any obvious help from John. Thereafter the magazine joined a proud tradition of radical journalism by folding within a year.

• **AUGUST 18 TO 26, 1972: *REHEARSING* with Elephant's Memory for 'One To One' concert; recordings made during rehearsals include 'Instant Karma'/'Give Peace A Chance'/'Cold Turkey'/'Hound Dog'/'Long Tall Sally'/ 'New York City'/'It's So Hard'/'Woman Is The Nigger Of The World'/'Well Well Well'/'Come Together'/'Honky Tonk'/'Mind Train'/'We're All Water'/ 'Move On Fast'/'Sisters O Sisters'/'Unchained Melody'/'Born In A Prison'/ 'Mother'/'Open Your Box'/'Roll Over Beethoven'/various instrumentals and jams/various radio and TV spots; also recording solo performances of 'Well (Baby Please Don't Go)'/'Rock Island Line'/'Maybe Baby' for TV announcement of show.**

TV investigative reporter Geraldo Rivera set the *One To One* concerts in motion, when in his usual flamboyant style he exposed the callous treatment of mentally retarded children at the Willowbrook Hospital in New York State. In late July, Rivera called on the Lennons in California and suggested they help him stage a benefit concert for the kids at the end of August. Even at such short notice, they agreed, and were willing to be filmed with Rivera in the initial announcement of the show. Only when tickets were already on sale did Lennon—as scared as he had been in Toronto three years earlier—attempt to opt out of the show. Rivera pulled him around, and after Yoko's attempt to persuade Paul and Linda McCartney to join them for the performance had failed, the Lennons called in Elephant's Memory and began rehearsing for John's only full-scale concert performance after he left The Beatles.

To be precise, there were actually two performances, as the first sold out as soon as Rivera had screened footage of John performing an acoustic medley of fifties rockers as a taste of what was to come. When the second show was fixed, another set of commercials were filmed and taped, some of them featuring the Lennons and the band chanting the news in unison, others with Rivera making his speech while John and the band kicked into 'New York City' behind him.

The Lennons hired out Butterfly Studios in New York, and then the Fillmore East concert hall, to get the feel of playing in public again. All their rehearsals were taped, but though a tantalising list of songs was attempted, few of the performances lived up to the fantasy. John was petrified of losing his voice before the shows, so he mumbled his way through most of the rehearsals, taking the songs an octave lower than in concert, and only letting himself go on a fiery, intense 'It's So Hard', and a raving assault on 'Long Tall Sally,' every bit the equal of McCartney's performances of the same song. Ironically, that number didn't make the show, where the only non-Lennon/Ono composition heard was 'Hound Dog'.

The rehearsals also saw Lennon changing the word 'nigger' to 'nipple' in a performance of one of his new songs—Freudian habits die hard—and investigating the possibilities of turning 'Give Peace A Chance' into a reggae singalong, something he'd tried rather less successfully at the 1969 Toronto show. Most of the surviving tapes, however, show the musicians practising intros and endings, unable for once to rely on the studio trickery of Phil Spector to fade them gracefully away.

• • •   **AUGUST 30, 1972:** *PERFORMING* 'New York City'/'It's So Hard'/'We're All Water'/'Woman Is The Nigger Of The World'/'Sisters O Sisters'/'Well Well Well'/'Instant Karma'/'Mother'/'Born In A Prison'/'Come Together'/ 'Imagine'/'Cold Turkey'/'Hound Dog'/'Give Peace A Chance'.

At lunchtime on August 30, 1972, thousands of handicapped kids attended the *One To One* festival in Central Park. John and Yoko had already purchased $50,000 of tickets to allow the children to attend the afternoon show at Madison Square Garden, where—after performances from Sha Na Na, Roberta Flack and Stevie Wonder—John, Yoko and Elephant's Memory played for a little over an hour. That evening, they played the same set again: together, the two shows raised $180,000 on the night, plus another $350,000 for the sale of rights to the concert to ABC TV, who screened a cut-down version of the show, nominally produced by John and Yoko's Joko Films company, on December 14. But the live album of the show, which John and Yoko had hoped to have in the shops by Christmas, took some 14 years to materialise–stymied by a combination of exhaustion, conflict and political cowardice on the part of the Lennons, who were afraid that any public act might inflame their precarious immigration position.

The shows themselves were a triumph. Even the hollow mix of the afternoon concert which Yoko prepared for her 1986 video and LP releases, 'John Lennon Live In New York', can't hide the power and ease of the performance. The Lennons and Elephant's Memory caught fire together, stripping the 'Some Time In New York City' songs down to basics, and destroying none of the stark strength of the Plastic Ono Band material with their extra instrumentation. Though the afternoon show was a little rusty in places–"Welcome to the rehearsal," Lennon quipped at one point–it still had a series of climaxes: another gritty run at 'It's So Hard', a no-nonsense, sleek 'Instant Karma', a throat-searing 'Mother,' with Lennon close to primalling on stage, and an equally intense 'Cold Turkey,' as John screamed his way towards public catharsis.

The evening show, chosen by ABC TV for their coverage, was even more striking–the sole Beatles' song, 'Come Together,' a gritty highlight, transformed into a churning cauldron of R&B licks. 'Come together/right now/stop the war,' Lennon cried in the choruses, showing he'd lost none of his radicalism; while on 'Imagine', he altered the lyrics for the first, but not the last, time calling on the audience to imagine 'a brotherhood and sisterhood of man'. Clearly some of that feminist teaching was beginning to stick. The cover of 'Hound Dog' closed the show in rollicking style, with Lennon finding space to shout out, "Elvis, I love ya!" between lines. And the finale, once again, was a drawn-out version of 'Give Peace A Chance', stretched for 10 minutes or more, with the audience clanging the percussion instruments left in front of every seat, and Stevie Wonder scatting a series of answer lyrics to the endless choruses. Legend has it that the audience left the Garden as one, and continued chanting 'Give Peace A Chance' for an hour or so in the streets outside. As the TV coverage showed, it was that kind of show.

• **SEPTEMBER 6, 1972: *PERFORMING* '*Imagine*'/'*Now Or Never*'/'*Give Peace A Chance*' at the *Jerry Lewis Telethon*.**

Just a week after the *One To One* shows, the Lennons and the Elephants were back on stage, performing on a charity telethon staged by comedian Jerry Lewis to raise money for the disabled. Radical critics protested that the Lennons were treating every charitable cause as one, and that the telethon was as much a part of the problem as a solution. John and Yoko believed in the cause, and saw the chance to repair their image in the eyes of the great American public. John again toasted the

157

'brotherhood and sisterhood of man' on 'Imagine', before Yoko premièred 'Now Or Never'—not an Elvis Presley hit, this time, but a new composition which neatly summed up the Ono philosophy: 'Dream you dream alone is only a dream/But dream we dream together is reality.' Finally, Lennon led off another rowdy version of 'Give Peace A Chance'—"This is reggae, baby, like they do it in Jamaica"—and the Lennons' performance was over. They never appeared on stage together again.

· · · **LATE OCTOBER TO EARLY NOVEMBER 1972:** *PRODUCING and recording 'Yangyang'/'Death Of Samantha'/'I Want My Love To Rest Tonight'/'What Did I Do?'/'Have You Seen A Horizon Lately'/ 'Approximately Infinite Universe'/'Peter The Dealer'/'Song For John'/ 'Catman'/'What A Bastard The World Is'/'Waiting For The Sunrise'/'I Felt Like Smashing My Face In A Clear Glass Window'/'Winter Song'/'Kite Song'/'What A Mess'/'Shiranakatta'/'Air Talk'/'I Have A Woman Inside My Soul'/'Move On Fast'/'Now Or Never'/'Is Winter Here To Stay?'/'Looking Over From My Hotel Window'/'Jose Joi Banzai' (parts 1 and 2).*

Neither John Lennon nor Yoko Ono were noted for their willingness to take second place in any artistic endeavour, so their relationship was bound to produce personal collisions as often as cultural ones. While John was the songwriter, Yoko the conceptual artist and film-maker, the marriage could survive: each partner could handle minor incursions into their own territory. When Yoko struck a seam of writing creativity that threatened Lennon's musical dominance, trouble lay ahead.

Since making 'Some Time In New York City' in February 1972, Lennon had made no more records; he hadn't even completed any songs. By contrast, Yoko approached the sessions for her next solo album with enough material for two albums, and then some. What's more, this wasn't the avant-garde soundscape work of yore: Yoko had channelled her feminist beliefs into a series of riveting, intensely personal songs, that at once attacked male domination and showed understanding of the insecurity which lay behind it. By any standards, 'Approximately Infinite Universe' was a remarkable album.

In the studio, Lennon supported his wife as she recorded 'Catman', a playful rallying cry for a bunch of castrating feminists; 'What A Bastard The World Is', with its portrayal of liberation held back by the economic and emotional contract of marriage; and 'What A Mess', a hilarious satire on men's attempts to deny abortion rights to 'their' women. John acted as co-producer of the project, translating some of Yoko's more conceptual requests to the band (Elephant's Memory, on their last Lennon project), and pulling off some remarkable reverb guitar work on 'Move On Fast' and the blues jam, 'Is Winter Here To Stay?'. But this was Yoko's project, a brilliant marriage of the personal and the political, and as thought-provoking a sequence of songs as the feminist movement has ever produced. Lennon had nothing to offer in reply.

· · · **MARCH 1973:** *RECORDING 'I'm The Greatest'.*

At the end of 1972, the Lennons moved into an exclusive apartment in the Dakota Building on New York's Central Park West. Still waging war against US immigration, and with Yoko also fighting a legal battle to win custody of her daughter, Kyoko, the couple were in little mood to perform. Yoko continued to write; John mooched around the house, and snapped at anyone who came too close.

Then in the spring of 1973, an invitation to California beckoned, in the shape of Ringo Starr, then beginning work on his third solo album. He had sent out a request to all three of his former Beatle colleagues for new material; Lennon had little in reserve, so he dug out his rehearsal tapes of 'I'm The Greatest' from 1971, and began to tailor the lyrics towards Ringo, rather than himself.

In the studio, Lennon set Ringo behind the drum-kit, George Harrison on guitar and Klaus Voorman on bass, while he played piano and tried to lay down a basic track and guide vocal. It took about 12 passes in all, most of them false starts, before Lennon was satisfied: after each one, he simply counted the band straight back in, as if frightened to lose the momentum of the moment. 'I was the greatest show on earth', he slurred in his best Bronx accent, working laconically through his tongue-in-cheek history of The Beatles, complete with references to 'Billy Shears' from the 'Pepper' album—later emphasised by producer Richard Perry, who threw in bursts of 'Pepper'-style laughter.

None of Lennon's takes were that spectacular, or involved, but they served their purpose: they gave Perry a basic track to build on, and Ringo a sympathetic voice in the cans as he laid down his lead vocal. Ringo only made one change to John's lyrics, playing down his role by singing 'I was in the greatest shown on earth'.

• **APRIL 1973: *RECORDING* 'She Hits Back'/'Woman Power'/'Men Men Men'.**

Less than five months after completing 'Approximately Infinite Universe', Yoko had amassed enough new songs to begin recording another album. The initial sessions saw Lennon adding guitar to 'She Hits Back' and 'Woman Power,' while on the sly shuffle 'Men Men Men', he heard his wife recite: 'J-O-H-N-N-Y, God's little gift to a woman', knowing full well she was taking the piss. He even made a cameo appearance at the end of the song, as the archetypal henpecked husband responding to his wife's beck and call.

The couple had begun April with a press conference to announce the formation of Nutopia, in the rather unrealistic hope that the United Nations would recognise the existence of this imaginary land and grant the Lennons asylum as its diplomatic representatives. Lennon repeated the manifesto on the inner sleeve of his 'Mind Games' album, but otherwise it was never mentioned again. Meanwhile, the couple's relationship had reached crisis point.

Chapter 13

MAY 1973 TO
AUGUST 1974

. . . .

MAY/JUNE 1973: *RECORDING home demos of 'Intuition'/'I Know (I Know)'/'Rock And Roll People.'*

The Lennons spent the first half of 1973 in virtual retreat from the world, appearing only at a couple of low-key political demonstrations in New York. Yoko finished writing the songs for 'Feeling The Space', and also built up a backlog of material that she would still be dipping into a decade later. And after a year of inactivity, John finally regained some contact with his muse. In late spring, he recorded his first home demos since January 1972, premièring two of the songs he taped later in the year for 'Mind Games', plus another recorded during the same sessions, but left unissued for a further 13 years.

As ever, Lennon's songs were a vivid insight into his state of mind. He no longer burned with the certainties of 1970 or 1972; his life was dominated by the day-to-day struggle of maintaining a relationship in a rarefied atmosphere, cut off from the world. John and Yoko's romance was turning sour, and not for the first time, John pleaded guilty in song. 'I Know (I Know)', built around a more restrained version of the guitar riffs which had once powered mid-sixties Beatles singles, was a rather laboured ballad, which had to strain for its melodic effect. But its lyrics were unashamedly autobiographical, portraying a man forced to come to terms with his own inadequacies, 'only learning, to tell the trees from wood.' 'Today, I love you more than yesterday,' he sang hopefully in the chorus, a slice of the wish-fulfilment which Yoko had always recommended as a remedy for disaster. But the melancholy spirit of the music, and the abject submissiveness of the tone, made the optimism sound misplaced. John cut three near-identical acoustic demos, virtual blueprints for the finished record.

'Intuition' was not quite as complete, Lennon having written the verses and the tune for the chorus, but no hook-line. A jaunty piano tune at this stage, it marked the opposite end of the spiral of optimism, with John having 'confirmed an old suspicion/It's good to be alive.' Again, though, there was a hint that he was saying it was true to make it true.

Both songs shared a hesitancy of purpose that was as clear an insight into Lennon's soul as any confessional interview. But the third song cut during this period was light relief. 'Rock And Roll People' was auditioned like a Bo Diddley work tape, all chunky electric rhythm with knee-slaps for percussion. The boogie tune had playful lyrics to match, a run of nonsense images that could have been borrowed from the pages of *In His Own Write*. Lennon made vague plans to record all three songs later in the summer, and started to wade through his earlier composing tapes in the hope of finding something else worth finishing off.

AUGUST 1973: *RECORDING* '*Mind Games***'/'***Tight A$***'/'***Aisumasen***'/'***One Day At A Time***'/'***Bring On The Lucie***'/'***Intuition***'/'***Out The Blue***'/'***Only People***'/'***I Know (I Know)***'/'***You Are Here***'/'***Meat City***'/'***Rock And Roll People***.'**

The start of the sessions for 'Mind Games' were preceded by a fortnight of hectic pre-production work, in which Lennon wrote several songs from scratch, and pulled three more together from left-over fragments. John then went into the Record Plant East in New York and completed all the final mixes in around a fortnight–two weeks which also marked the beginning of his relationship with his PA, May Pang, and of his 18-month separation from Yoko. She had apparently suggested that John begin an affair with May; then, just as suddenly, he was living with May, Yoko having kicked him out. Stanza one of 'The Ballad Of John And Yoko' was over.

The circumstances might have dragged Lennon's demons to the surface; but he chose to keep them hidden, acting instead like the professional tunesmith he had always tried to avoid becoming, churning out John Lennon songs to meet a contract. So 'Mind Games' was the least inspired of his song collections, the overwhelming mood one of ennui. The title of the album said it all: Lennon was playing at being an artist, where in the past his life and his art had been virtually interchangeable. With the two distanced by his lack of emotional involvement, the music lost its personality. What remained was high-class hackwork, just the kind of fakery with which he and McCartney had filled Beatles albums like 'Help!' when they had been under other kinds of pressure.

'Mind Games' itself was one of the album's more convincing musical moments, based as it was around a hook that dated back to the start of the decade. Lennon had long since abandoned his idea of turning the 'Make Love Not War' riff into another 'Give Peace A Chance', but the tune and a fragment of the original lyrics survived onto the 1973 cut, with

John busking the 1970 chorus over the fade-out. He based the new words on a book called *Mind Games* by Robert Masters and Jean Houston. Like Janov's *The Primal Scream*, this was a guide to mental fulfilment, but through gentle consciousness-raising rather than violent therapy. Lennon effectively précised the book, but though he coaxed a remarkable performance from his band, and made his ascending guitar riff sound like an orchestra, lines like 'Millions of mind guerrillas/Putting their soul power to the karmic wheel' meant that 'Mind Games' never transcended its literary origins. And as an early take of the song revealed, Lennon was willing to try out any vaguely spiritual cliché that would fit, with lines like 'Love is a flower/The flower grows within', 'Love is the answer/ Miracles are slow' and 'Yes is surrender/The messages are whole', nearly making it past quality control.

'Aisumasen (I'm Sorry)' also built on the past—on 'Call My Name' from 1971. Once a message of support to a lover, the song was rewritten as another confession of guilt, tied to an admission that 'All that I know is just what you tell me'. It's not difficult to imagine Lennon watching his marriage slip away, desperately owning up in song to the faults that he couldn't admit in real life.

The two lushest songs on the album, both couched in the kind of string and vocal arrangements more associated with McCartney than Lennon, were 'One Day At A Time' and 'You Are Here'—unashamed paeans of love for Yoko, which draw much of their pathos from the knowledge that she had broken off their relationship by the time the record appeared in the shops. 'One Day At A Time' offered an embarrassingly saccharine picture of the couple's life, but 'You Are Here' was genuinely moving, as warm and poetic a love song as Lennon had ever written.

'Out The Blue' rephrased the question a different way. Before Lennon applied sweetening at the remix stage, the song sounded like a 'Plastic Ono Band' out-take—a heartfelt confession of debt to Yoko, performed with total lack of embellishment, and with two lengthy piano solos to break the tension. Where 'You Are Here' painted the relationship in mellow tones, 'Out The Blue' gave it the importance of life and death: 'All my life's been a long slow knife', Lennon gasped, before announcing proudly: 'Anyway, I survived, long enough to make you my wife'.

The other five songs cut during the sessions divided between political chants and no-nonsense rockers. Into the latter category fell 'Rock And Roll People', which the band attempted many times on August 5, each take turning into a boogie jam before Lennon forced them to a halt with a series of jagged chords on his rhythm guitar. 'Tight A$' was just as much fun, a slick rockabilly confection with throwaway lyrics and an immaculate Lennon vocal. And on 'Meat City' Lennon constructed a wall of guitar noise over which he recited an obscure tale of snake doctors, mountains and rock 'n' roll. And here's another clue for you all: play the tune backwards, and the mysterious voice between verses is heard to say: 'Fuck a pig'.

The album could take any number of rockers like this; they were a welcome antidote to the general air of gloom. Where it faltered was in trying to return to the political passion of 'Power To The People' without the certainty to back it up. 'Bring On The Lucie' had surfaced as a chorus a couple of years earlier: Lennon lacked the production skills to make it into an anthem, as Phil Spector could have done, and the new verses raced from incoherence to melodrama, though the savagery of the imagery suggested that Lennon relished the sight of Nixon and his cronies being caught with their hands on the smoking gun.

'Only People' best summed up Lennon's malaise, however. It was based on one of Yoko's credos: 'Only people can change the world.' But Lennon couldn't find the words to suit such a simplistic sentiment, and somehow 'We don't want no pig brother scene' didn't seem to be the slogan to bring a generation together. From the political equivalent of a bull in a china-shop to a self-parodist in 18 months: that was the journey that 'Mind Games' charted.

· **SEPTEMBER 30, 1973: *REVIEW of The Goon Show Scripts* published in *The New York Times*.**

Spike Milligan's radio scripts for the BBC Light Programme series *The Goon Show* invented a new kind of comedy—anarchic, witty, subverting values and narrative expectations. John Lennon lapped up the radio shows in the fifties, recognised Milligan as a kindred spirit, and so leapt at the opportunity to review the collected scripts for the *New York Times*.

In its way, John's 700-word review was every bit as anarchic as the book—ignoring the conventions whereby one described and analysed the text, and concentrating instead on explaining what the Goons had meant to him. 'Their humour was the only proof that the WORLD was insane,' Lennon recalled, describing it as 'a conspiracy against reality.' And he remembered his own efforts in the same vein, in *The Daily Howl*.

Much of the review ws devoted to the difficulty of writing the review, though: 'I'm supposed to write 800 words but I can't count. I could go on all day about the Goons...but it doesn't seem to be about THE BOOK! I keep thinking how much easier it would be to review it for a British paper. What the hell! I've never REVIEWED anything in my life before. Now I know why critics are 'nasty.'' *The New York Times* added their own parody to the foot of the review: in place of the usual academic credentials, they described its author thus:–'John Lennon, the now and former Beatle, studied capitalization in the Liverpool school system.'

· **OCTOBER/NOVEMBER 1973: *RECORDING* 'Be My Baby'/'Here We Go Again'/'Sweet Little Sixteen'/'You Can't Catch Me'/'Just Because'/'Angel Baby'/'To Know You Is To Love You'/'My Baby Left Me'/'Bony Moronie.'**

"It was such a mess that I can hardly remember what happened. I was away from Yoko and I wanted to come back. When I was drunk, I would just ramble on or scream abuse at her or beg her to come back. I don't know what I was saying or doing half the time."

The infamous lost weekend; another chapter in the John and Yoko myth. John and Yoko did separate in the late summer of 1973, and remain apart until the end of 1974. Lennon did get drunk in Hollywood and New York; his 'Oldies But Goldies' sessions with Phil Spector supposedly in command did collapse in chaos; and John did make a fool of himself often and in public.

But the same lost weekend did eventually bear fruit. 1974 saw him complete two albums, 'Rock 'n' Roll' and 'Walls And Bridges;' produce an album for Harry Nilsson; and collaborate on hit singles for Ringo Starr and Elton John. Compare that output with 1973 ('Mind Games' and 'I'm The Greatest') or 1975 ('Fame' and 'Across The Universe' with David Bowie) and the weekend doesn't seem so lost after all.

The initial weeks of separation did have their moments of mayhem, though, fuelled by the slightly erratic behaviour of the man in whom Lennon was tempted to trust his new project: Phil Spector. Before the sessions collapsed after two months of heavy drinking and very slow progress, Lennon and Spector had battled like kids on the floor of the studio, been thrown out of one recording complex after Spector let off a pistol, attracted every musical drunk in town, and taped nine rather anarchic slices of rock 'n' roll—none of which Lennon considered worthy of release when he approached the tapes in a more sober spirit the following year.

Tired of carrying the responsibility as creator, performer and producer, and aware that 'Mind Games' was several notches short of his best work, Lennon equated the liberation of the bachelor life with the freedom of the singer who has a producer to fall back on. In the past, Lennon had always employed Spector, feeding him only enough rope to allow him to work to John's instructions. On the oldies project, Spector could do what he liked; John would do what he was told.

Oldies were in the air that autumn. Spector had just signed a deal to form his own record company, for the first time since he dissolved Philles Records in 1967. And Warner/Spector's first releases were a mixture of reissues of his best sixties productions, for the likes of The Ronettes and The Crystals, and remakes of sixties tunes featuring Cher and Harry Nilsson.

Cher's version of The Ronettes' 'Baby I Love You' set the pattern—slowed to funereal pace, with a couple of dozen session-men playing the simplest parts in unison, and Cher left all the room in the world to emote over the top. Spector loved it; so did Lennon; and so Phil set about arranging another Ronettes' smash, 'Be My Baby,' and his own début single with The Teddy Bears, 'To Know Her Is To Love Her,' in the same way.

Spector also cut the pace of rockers like 'Sweet Little Sixteen', 'Bony Moronie', 'You Can't Catch Me' and 'My Baby Left Me' by half; and rearranged Rosie And The Originals' naïve teen ballad, 'Angel Baby,' into an extravaganza for brass and drums.

Spector's methods were painstaking, even painful for the musicians, who were forced to wait while the producer added layer upon layer to the mountainous ensemble sound before the tapes even began rolling. When

Phil was finally ready to cut the vocals, deep into the night, Lennon would have drunk a bottle or more of whisky; swaying in the vocal booth, John could hear this cavernous, awesome, emotionally overpowering noise in his headphones, crashing like a tide across the booze and the exhaustion, breaking down all the inhibition that his responsibility as a producer and a musician usually demanded. Like Janov's primal therapy, Spector's vast soundscapes liberated John's voice. What emerged was without ego or pretension: some of it was brilliant, breath-taking; the rest the ravings of the drunken fool Lennon might have been in Liverpool if The Beatles had never made it to London.

Looking back in 1980, Lennon dismissed the Spector tracks out-of-hand; he'd had to overdub new vocals before he could release any of them, and his memories of late 1973 weren't pleasant. But as the 'Menlove Avenue' album in 1986 revealed, the sessions had their moments. 'My Baby Left Me' was transformed from rockabilly to party piece, with Lennon's dry rasp echoed by an amateurish choir of revellers. 'Angel Baby' found John fighting for life amidst a cacophony of instruments, but still invoking the innocent spirit and emotion of the original record. Likewise 'To Know Her Is To Love Her,' with Lennon's vocal pure emotion, almost regardless of the words he's singing.

Finer still was 'Here We Go Again'—a song Lennon had demoed in acoustic form before the sessions, and then given to Spector to arrange. His demo hinted at what was to come, using augmented chords to map out the claustrophobic string build-up on the record. The lyrics were vague but telling, full of images of tiredness and betrayal—'All I wanted was a thank you, ma'am...everyone's an also-ran'. Without revealing the details, 'Here We Go Again' sounded like a bowing before the storm ahead, defiant but doomed. Spector's arrangement conveyed all that and more, and Lennon's vocal ranged from the laconic defeat of the verses to the screaming passion of the final chorus. But the track wasn't a single, and it didn't fit the oldies concept, so it stayed in the can.

Some nights, though, the results weren't quite as coherent. The session they recorded Lloyd Price's 'Just Because', Lennon could scarcely stand, let alone sing, by the time Spector had finished the track. He tried, anyway, despite being distracted by the backing vocalists: "I want to suck your nipples baby," he leered across the opening chords, before falling through the song hopelessly drunk, teetering on the verge of collapse. And across the fade, in the space left for him to compose some pithy monologue, Lennon let a little reality in: "I need some excuse for doing this," he slurred, "I need some relief from my obligations. A little cocaine will set me on my feet." And from there he scatted through a psychotic version of 'Yes Sir That's My Baby' before the music came mercifully to a close and he could be carried home to bed.

The rest wasn't that dramatic, though John must have winced when he heard the rasping vocal on 'You Can't Catch Me', and he obviously felt that the endless repeated choruses and one-note organ riff on 'Sweet Little Sixteen' needed fixing before he could put the track out. 'Be My Baby' had almost nothing wrong with it, however, with Lennon sighing orgasmically as the music built to a crescendo, and then letting himself go in a series of sensuous cries over the fade. On moments like that, the cathartic purpose of the Spector sessions was fulfilled. For the rest, Lennon's catharsis came a year later, when he covered up the evidence of his madness.

APRIL/MAY 1974: *RECORDING* 'Mucho Mungo' demos; producing 'Many Rivers To Cross'/'Subterranean Homesick Blues'/'Don't Forget Me'/'All My Life'/'Old Forgotten Soldier'/'Save The Last Dance For Me'/'Mucho Mungo; Mt. Elba'/'Loop De Loop'/'Black Sails'/'Rock Around The Clock' for Harry Nilsson; producing 'Too Many Cooks' for Mick Jagger.

After the collapse of the Spector sessions at the end of 1973, and Spector's subsequent disappearance after two serious car smashes in early 1974, John spent two or three months simply hanging out in Hollywood, drinking with Harry Nilsson, Ringo Starr and Keith Moon, getting thrown out of night-clubs, making the front page of the LA papers, and trying to fashion a relationship with May Pang while he was still phoning Yoko every day to find out if he could come home.

Towards the end of a whisky bottle, he agreed to produce Harry Nilsson's next album; and so in April, they set up at the Record Plant West and began work on 'Pussy Cats'. Nilsson had written just four songs for the project, so Lennon offered him one of his own, a lightweight ballad called 'Mucho Mungo' which he'd started during the 'Rock 'n' Roll' sessions, with Phil Spector adding a middle section to the basic chorus. Lennon cut three home demos of the tune, and then arrived at an early session ready to teach it to Nilsson; but Harry didn't like Spector's additions, and suggested instead that they segue John's tune into the folk song 'Mt. Elba;' and so it turned out. Along the way, one verse from the pair's first acoustic run-through was dropped, for obvious reasons: 'Sailing on the Good Ship Lollipop/Open up a drug store, nice kind of shop!'

Like the Spector sessions, these dates were peopled by a cast of dozens, with every party animal in town demanding the chance to bang a tambourine. And with John arranging most of the oldies that they picked to fill the album up, much of the finished record had the same air of mayhem as the 'Rock 'n' Roll' tracks. Lennon gave Bob Dylan's 'Subterranean Homesick Blues' a frantic, claustrophobic R&B arrangement, with saxophones honking metallic riffs while a school of drummers pounded out a tattoo. (As a sign of the chaos which informed the entire project, John had to cut together the final take from a dozen or so incoherent efforts.) And Bill Haley's 'Rock Around The Clock' was equally bizarre, ending with the entire band playing in double tempo over the fade. The Spector influence pervaded the album, in fact: why else would John have chosen to slow The Drifters' 'Save The Last Dance For Me' to a painful snail's pace, or turn Jimmy Cliff's spiritual 'Many Rivers To Cross' into a funeral dirge? But even at its most laboured, 'Pussy Cats' had something—a spark of magic, a breath of life, which evaded most superstar collaborations. Or maybe it was simply the booze: as Derek

Taylor said in his liner notes, 'Most of what Harry and John said and did was bloody funny and sometimes terrifying. They have been living a vampire timetable recently...They are madmen in tandem! And the record sounds like it.

Before Lennon took the tapes to New York to restore some sanity to the project, there were some late night jam sessions featuring star guests. At one of them, Lennon produced Mick Jagger singing the Detroit R&B tune, 'Too Many Cooks', with Jack Bruce among the supporting cast; at another, witnessed by May Pang, Paul McCartney joined John for the one and only time since the break-up of The Beatles, performing an impromptu 'Midnight Special' alongside a dozen or so other musicians.

JUNE 1974: RECORDING home demos of 'Goodnight Vienna'/'Surprise Surprise'/'Whatever Gets You Through The Night'/'So Long'/'Move Over Ms L'/'What You Got'.

Taking responsibility for the production of Nilsson's album had shocked Lennon out of his spiral of drinking and drugs. In the early summer of 1974, Ringo Starr invited John to write him some material for his own forthcoming solo album; at the same time, John began assembling songs for his own next project–his first for six years not to be conceived with Yoko. For Ringo, John knocked off a piece of hack-work from the same mould as 'Rock And Roll People'. 'Goodnight Vienna' was based around a Liverpudlian catchphrase, and was little more than an invitation to boogie.

A similar brand of rock traditionalism and scatter-shot imagery produced 'Move Over Ms L'–a title which took a sardonic swipe at the woman who had once referred to herself in song as Mrs Lennon. He cut a quick home demo while May Pang made a phone call, rehearsing boogie riffs on electric guitar and then breaking into falsetto for the chorus. He made a second, more serious pass at the song later in the month, whispering the nonsensical verses over acoustic guitar, and throwing in a quick impression of Yoko for good measure.

'Whatever Gets You Through The Night' was written around the same time–with Lennon documenting the process on tape, beginning with a title-line he'd heard on a TV show about alcoholism. Having found the right rhythm, he experimented with new inversions of the basic chords, and made up some tentative lyrics–'It's whatever turns you on' being one verse that escaped the final version. And at one point, he realised he'd heard the tune somewhere before, and ran it neatly into the opening lines of 'Jealous Guy.'

'Surprise Surprise' was an altogether meatier song–an unashamed paean of love to May Pang, the 'bird of paradise' who had rescued him from the misery of his separation from Yoko. The song began life as an acoustic ballad–Lennon admitted that The Diamonds' fifties doo-wop hit 'Little Darlin'' was an early influence–with some 'Julia'-style chording where the middle section would finally appear. Later home demos accentuated the bluesiness of the song, and suggested that new love might be something of a mixed blessing, as the performances had some of the quiet desperation of the 'Plastic Ono Band' album. And gradually the middle section evolved, as John hit upon the key line: 'I thought I could never be surprised.'

'What You Got' was, at this stage, a Carl Perkins-influenced rockabilly tune, with only the chorus familiar from the final record. The message was basic enough: 'You don't know what you got until you lose it' and on the acoustic demo John simply busked words to fill the spaces before and after the chorus, grabbing the first line of Little Richard's 'Rip It Up' for the start of the middle section.

'So Long' was equally unfinished, though its melody line at least was distinct—identical to the tune which John had written for the string arrangement on Nilsson's 'Many Rivers To Cross.' By the time he cut his second acoustic demo, John was putting together some lyrical ideas—a mixture of dream imagery and romantic discovery, with spaces left for a guitar break-down and a chorus that wasn't yet written. After a couple more weeks, the tune was completed, and ready to be recorded as 'No. 9 Dream.'

• • • **MID-JULY 1974: *REHEARSING* for '*Walls And Bridges*' album.**

For around 10 days, John hosted pre-production sessions for his new album at Sunset Studios and Record Plant East, New York—rehearsing with the band from scratch, so that they would grow into the arrangements, rather than approaching them cold on the first day of full sessions. Some of these rehearsals appeared in edited form on the 1986 collection, 'Menlove Avenue.' Together with the unissued cuts, they illustrate how much work John had put into his new songs since the end of June, completing all the numbers he'd demoed that month, composing several more, and digging up a second collaboration with Nilsson from the 'Pussy Cats' sessions in 'Old Dirt Road.' John supposedly wrote a song called 'Incantation' with Roy Cicala during these rehearsals, but no evidence has surfaced on tape.

What's remarkable about these tapes is not the material; it's the subdued way in which the songs are performed, with the small group arrangements and slightly melancholy feel giving 'Bless You,' 'Scared' and 'Nobody Loves You When You're Down And Out' a poignancy not always captured by the final recordings.

• • • **AUGUST 1974: *RECORDING* '*Going Down On Love*'/'*Whatever Gets You Through The Night*'/'*Old Dirt Road*'/'*What You Got*'/'*Bless You*'/'*Scared*'/ '*No. 9 Dream*'/'*Surprise Surprise*'/'*Steel And Glass*'/'*Beef Jerky*'/'*Nobody Loves You When You're Down And Out*'/'*Ya Ya*'/'*Move Over Ms L*.'**

From the vantage point of 1980, Lennon described 'Walls And Bridges' as "the work of a semi-sick craftsman," by comparison with the supposedly inspirational way in which the 'Double Fantasy' songs were created. In fact, much of 'Double Fantasy' had been the labour of years, not hours: it was 'Walls And Bridges' which was the work of inspiration. What it wasn't, of course, was a John and Yoko collaboration, so it didn't fit the myth. The fact that its best songs were as powerful as anything on 'Double Fantasy,' or 'Imagine', for that matter, was allowed to slip by.

The 'Walls And Bridges' material was as graphic and revealing as anything Lennon had written in the past. There has never been a more mature song of romantic regret than 'Bless You', John's sober message to whoever was holding Yoko in his arms in John's absence. 'Surprise Surprise' reflected the sheer physical joy of his new relationship with May; while 'Scared' and 'Nobody Loves You When You're Down And Out' were the view from the bottom of the bottle, but written from determination rather than despair.

The album had its throwaways, of course: 'Whatever Gets You Through The Night' began as a novelty, and ended as a number one hit single, thanks to the vocal duet with current superstar Elton John. 'What You Got' was transformed into urban R&B, with a feel that echoed the great American records of the early sixties, like 'Watch Your Step' and 'Money.' 'Old Dirt Road', the Nilsson collaboration, was a lazy piece of daydreaming out of the 'I'm Only Sleeping' school, with imagery that was as off-the-wall as anything from Lennon's two books. And 'Beef Jerky,' built around a guitar lick from 'No. 9 Dream', was something no one could have predicted—a John Lennon R&B instrumental, buoyed by churning horn riffs and some jagged lead guitar. 'Move Over Ms L' would have fitted into the same pile, if Lennon hadn't rejected the 'Walls And Bridges' take of the song when the band couldn't catch the simple rock 'n' roll feel it required. So the honour of completing the album went to a minute of piano/drums jamming on Lee Dorsey's 'Ya Ya' with John's 12-year-old son Julian—included on the record as a sop to publisher Morris Levy, who was still pursuing John for royalties on 'Come Together,' which Lennon had been foolish enough to admit had been based on Chuck Berry's 'You Can't Catch Me'.

The rest of the material was more substantial. 'Going Down On Love' never quite worked as a piece of slow funk, but its subtle charm belied the desperation of its lyrics: 'Somebody please, please help me/I think I'm drowning in a sea of hatred'. 'Scared' said it even straighter, an unabashed admission that John couldn't survive without Yoko, though he was still trying to overcome the hatred and jealousy, 'the green-eyed goddamn straight from your heart'. The music burned in support, while Lennon emphasised the lonesome whistle of his song by starting the track with a library tape of a howling wolf at midnight.

'Nobody Loves You When You're Down And Out' was, like 'What You Got', structured around a familiar blues lyric. Lennon supposedly wrote the song for Frank Sinatra, but it sounds more like another gasp from the heart, and the production gave his vocal the rasp of a loser in his final decline. 'I'll scratch your back and you knife mine', Lennon sang, aware that his drunken antics earlier in the year had crippled his public image. Surrender might have been an easy option, a slow descent into hell; these songs showed that Lennon preferred to fight his way out.

THE ART & MUSIC OF JOHN LENNON

But it was the album's three songs of love which offered an insight into Lennon's real state of mind. 'Surprise Surprise', with another tight, twisting guitar riff like the ones he'd once used to support Beatles singles, was a lyrical celebration of love and sex, and an admission that maybe there was life after separation after all. 'She makes me sweat and forget who I am', Lennon sang about his new lover, in a naked declaration of passion he hadn't made in his music since 'Happiness Is A Warm Gun'.

The beautiful fantasy of 'No. 9 Dream' was also inspired by May, who can be heard calling John's name in the chorus. Caught in a haze of love and sleep, Lennon was lost for words, unable to articulate his feelings, not even sure what they were; like 'I'm Only Sleeping', though, the song bares no threat of a nightmare. The invented language John used for the chorus only served to heighten the idyllic flavour of the dream.

Alongside these songs of passion and security, though, Lennon was writing 'Bless You'–a slow, delicate ballad that was part farewell, part promise. Yoko was with someone else–guitarist David Spinozza, as it turned out–but John still cared enough to wish her well. And the middle eight showed that hope of a reunion hadn't died: 'Some people think it's over/now that we've spread our wings/but we know better darling/the hollow ring is only last year's echo'. Love songs are always a form of imaginary letter, and John mightn't have been able to express this wish to Yoko in person; but the fact that the hope survived placed the joy of his songs for May in sharp perspective. May can't have failed to notice the fact.

'Steel And Glass' completed the emotional journey. An obvious successor to 'How Do You Sleep', right down to the viciousness of the string arrangement, it took a hefty sideswipe at former Beatles manager Allen Klein, though John was always too coy to say so. As ever, Lennon expressed betrayal by a father-figure in vicious terms: 'Steel And Glass' stands alongside 'The Maharishi Song' as a character assassination, with John sneering lines like 'You leave your smell like an alley cat'. From the adult attitudes of 'Bless You' to this heady vitriol was a long trip across the tightrope of Lennon's emotions.

Autobiographical evidence aside, 'Walls And Bridges' worked simply as a collection of pop songs–more sophisticated than 'Mind Games', and produced with infinitely more verve and imagination. In fact, Lennon never made a richer solo record, nor one which demonstrated such a wide mastery of styles. 'Walls And Bridges' mightn't have been his strongest album, or his most durable; but it did represent his last entire album of new songs, and also the last time–almost–that his music would reflect the contemporary world around him. It hinted at a new maturity of sound to come, taking in elements of the black music mainstream just as The Beatles had done a decade earlier. But things didn't quite work out that way.

• • • **LATE AUGUST 1974: *RECORDING* **'*Only You*'/'*Goodnight Vienna*' *with Ringo Starr; recording* '*One Day At A Time*'/'*Lucy In The Sky With Diamonds*' *with Elton John.*

1 7 0

Immediately after completing 'Walls And Bridges', Lennon and May Pang jetted to California, where they recorded two tracks for Ringo Starr's 'Goodnight Vienna' album, before moving on to Caribou Ranch to repay Elton John's favour in singing on two of John's new tracks.

As with 'I'm The Greatest' the previous year, Lennon controlled Ringo's sessions, cutting a rough lead vocal for Ringo to copy. John's version of 'Goodnight Vienna' was wilder than Ringo's, but still simple enough for the drummer to track; while on 'Only You' it was John who suggested covering the old Platters hit, and who not only laid down the rhythmic acoustic guitar accompaniment but also demoed the lead vocal.

That chore over, Lennon joined Elton John in covering 'Lucy In The Sky With Diamonds', singing harmony vocals and adding some guitar. Elton also tackled Lennon's 'Mind Games' composition, 'One Day At A Time', with John apparently playing guitar, though it's impossible to pick him out.

Chapter 14

O C T O B E R   1 9 7 4
T O   L A T E   1 9 7 8

· ·

OCTOBER 21 TO 25, 1974: *RECORDING* 'Be-Bop-A-Lula'/'Stand By Me'/ 'Rip It Up'/'Ready Teddy'/'Ain't That A Shame'/'Do You Wanna Dance'/ 'Slippin' And Slidin''/'Peggy Sue'/'Bring It On Home To Me'/'Send Me Some Lovin''/'Ya Ya'/'Move Over Ms L; recording new lead vocals on 'Sweet Little Sixteen'/'Just Because'/'Be My Baby'/'You Can't Catch Me;' recording rehearsal takes of 'That'll Be The Day'/'Do You Wanna Dance'/'Stand By Me'/'Bring It On Home To Me'/'Peggy Sue'/'Rip It Up'/'Ready Teddy'/'Thirty Days'/'Slippin' And Slidin''/'Ya Ya'/'Rumble'/'Ain't That A Shame'/'Send Me Some Lovin''/'Be-Bop-A-Lula'/'C'mon Everybody.'*

Listening to the Spector 'Rock 'n' Roll' tapes, which had been returned to him that summer, Lennon realised that it would be virtually impossible to mould them into an album—unless, as with 'Get Back' five years earlier, he was trying to kiss goodbye to a stage of his career. Perhaps he was, in retrospect; but he was still a pro, and so he pulled together the same basic group of musicians with whom he'd cut 'Walls And Bridges', spent two days rehearsing, and then another three knocking off enough tracks to fill an album.

The rehearsals were, as ever, captured on tape. They sound rough and ready, as the band feel their way towards the tight looseness that fifties rock music requires. Lennon also tried out a couple of songs that didn't make the final cut–a ragged 'That'll Be The Day,' with John growling his way through Buddy Holly's lyrics; and a reggae-ish lope round Chuck Berry's 'Thirty Days'. A spirited gallop through Link Wray's instrumental, 'Rumble', even led the band into a brief extract from Led

Zeppelin's song (via Willie Dixon), 'Whole Lotta Love.' The sessions themselves were more coherent, though alternate takes of 'Bring It On Home To Me' and 'Peggy Sue' suggest that the results could have been rawer. With spontaneity the manifesto of the hour, the music was always likely to be erratic; and these recordings divide between rockers that capture the essence of the music and reshape it, and tired imitations of the original arrangements, with Lennon wading through the motions. 'Slippin' And Slidin'' and 'Ain't That A Shame'–the latter with a wonderfully sardonic lead vocal–survived best; while 'Be-Bop-A-Lula' and 'Do You Wanna Dance' never came close to taking flight. Of the rest, an emotional reading of 'Stand By Me' was the stand-out, with John's acoustic playing obviously influenced by his near-identical work on Ringo's 'Only You.'

Finally, John picked out the cream of the Spector crop, and set about remixing and reworking them. 'Sweet Little Sixteen' needed a vocal that didn't rasp; likewise 'You Can't Catch Me.' He left 'Angel Baby' and 'Bony Moronie' as they were; tidied up parts of the vocal on 'Be My Baby;' and in the most overt piece of overdubbing, substituted an entirely new lead line on 'Just Because,' in place of the original drunken sprawl. Where he had once lusted over the backing singers, John added a disarming intro: "Ah, remember this? I must have been 13 when this came out? Or was it 14? Or was it 22? I could have been 12, actually." (Lennon admitted later that recording 'Just Because' had been Spector's suggestion; he'd never heard it before.) And over the fade, John gave away his repair work with his reference to Record Plant East, rather than West; and effectively waved farewell to his recording career. "Everybody here says hi!" he concluded: "Goodbye!"

Not quite, of course: first he had to put the record out. Remember the 'Ya Ya' jam that closed 'Walls And Bridges?' That had been a vain attempt to satisfy the man who now owned Chuck Berry's publishing, Morris Levy. In a further attempt to win him round and avoid a court case, Lennon gave Levy a work-tape of his 'Rock 'n' Roll' album, so that Levy could issue it on his mail-order label. Quite how John expected EMI, Apple and Capitol to react isn't clear: they were collectively furious, however, and rushed through plans for their own competing release. Lennon went along with these as well, and in the resultant court case testified that Levy had broken his word by issuing the record–which begged the question of why John had given him the tapes in the first place.

None of this would have mattered if the two albums hadn't been subtly different. Levy called his 'Roots:' it contained two more cuts than the Apple set, in 'Be My Baby' and 'Angel Baby;' an unedited take of 'You Can't Catch Me;' and marginally longer fades and rougher mixes on most of the remaining tracks. All of which lent credence to the idea that giving Levy the tapes had been a passing whim: when John *really* wanted to release the record, he actually paid some attention to the mix.

Meanwhile, the October 1974 sessions also finally produced a coherent take of 'Move Over Ms L,' John's farewell message to Yoko–which ironically only appeared as the flipside of the 'Stand By Me' single in

173

spring 1975, by which time John and Yoko had been reunited, and Yoko was once again pregnant.

NOVEMBER 28, 1974: *REHEARSING* 'I Saw Her Standing There;' performing 'Whatever Gets You Through The Night'/'Lucy In The Sky With Diamonds'/'I Saw Her Standing There.'

The deal was this: if 'Whatever Gets You Through The Night' made number one, then John had to join Elton John on stage to perform it. Lennon agreed readily, never imagining that his low commercial stock would allow him a solo chart-topper. Remarkably, the single made it all the way in the States, and so on November 28, 1974, a very nervous John Lennon joined Elton's band at Madison Square Garden in New York for his final live concert appearance.

Earlier that day, the musicians had rehearsed their party piece, with a raucous take of The Beatles' 'I Saw Her Standing There' having survived on tape. For the evening's show, they kicked off with Lennon's hit, moved into Elton's latest chart entry, which just happened to be John's 'Lucy In The Sky,' and then completed their segment with 'I Saw Her Standing There,' written, as Lennon announced, "by an old estranged fiancé of mine called Paul." The crowd went berserk: Lennon chewed gum and tried to look unmoved. In the audience, Yoko apparently saw only the loneliness of 'her man.' Backstage the couple met, and according to their myth-making 1980 interviews, the seeds of their reconciliation were sown.

JANUARY 1975: *RECORDING* 'Fame'/'Across The Universe' with David Bowie.

David Bowie had already completed 'Young Americans,' his first exercise in 'plastic soul,' when Lennon finally replied to his invitation to work together. Bowie's plan was to record Lennon's 'Across The Universe' as a mock-dirge; Lennon hated The Beatles' version, and was willing to go along with anything. More significantly, Bowie, Lennon and guitarist Carlos Alomar began jamming, and the result was 'Fame'—Bowie's first US number one single. Built around a James Brown riff, the track featured Lennon calling out the title at regular intervals, while Bowie used tape vari-speed to transform his voice from a Yoko-like squeal to a bassy rumble in the space of a couple of bars. Like the Elton John and Ringo collaborations, 'Fame' suggested that Lennon might profitably increase his work with his musical peers; but all of that came to a halt when he went back to Yoko.

JANUARY 1975: *WRITING* and recording home demo of 'Tennessee;' writing 'Popcorn.'

The last song John was writing before he returned home to the Dakota apartment where Yoko still lived was an ode to playwright Tennessee Williams. The song begins with the line 'Tennessee, oh Tennessee, what you mean to me', so this was obviously not a random tribute; in fact, it seems to have been sparked by a reading of Williams' *A Streetcar Named Desire*, reference to which turned up in a later take of the song. At this stage, the song had little effective structure; but John set down a rough piano take nonetheless, as a basis for future work. He was apparently working on material for his next album, and composed a light, commercial tune called 'Popcorn' around this time; but he doesn't seem to have committed this effort to tape.

MARCH 1975: *RECORDING* 'Stand By Me'/'Slippin' And Slidin''/'Lady Marmalade'.

To accompany a filmed interview he'd held with Bob Harris, host of the BBC's TV rock show, *The Old Grey Whistle Test*, John agreed to shoot promo films for two of the tracks from his newly-released 'Rock 'n' Roll' album. Returning to the Record Plant East in New York, he had his band mime to the appropriate backing tracks, while he taped new lead vocals over the top, throwing in a quick transatlantic 'hello' to his son Julian along the way. At around the same time—maybe even the same afternoon—John was filmed busking his way through a chorus of the Labelle hit 'Lady Marmalade' on his upright piano at the Dakota.

JUNE 13, 1975: *SALUTE TO SIR LEW GRADE* TV show broadcast, including Lennon performing 'Slippin' And Slidin''/'Stand By Me'/ 'Imagine'.

This was a bizarre way for Lennon to end his performing career. In front of an audience of celebrities and socialites, Lennon performed two of his 'Rock 'n' Roll' tracks, plus the perennial 'Imagine', in a move aimed at ending another prolonged legal dispute, this time with the impresario Sir Lew Grade, who effectively owned the Lennon/McCartney songwriting credits through his control of ATV Music. As a slight hint of rebellion, Lennon was accompanied by a band (dubbed 'Etc', as in 'John Lennon Etc.') who wore face masks on the back of their heads, so that no one was quite sure which way they were facing. Lennon was resplendent in a red jumpsuit and shoulder-length hair, looking as if he thought he was somewhere else entirely; but he kept his head amidst the plush surroundings, changing one verse of 'Imagine' to 'Nothing to kill or die for/No immigration too', and answering his own rhetorical statement, 'You may say I'm a dreamer' by shouting 'He's a dreamer' off-mike. He hadn't forgotten his principles, though, and it was still a 'brotherhood and sisterhood of man' that he was trying to imagine.

At the end of his brief set, amidst a succession of night-club acts, Lennon bowed with a flourish, and walked slowly off stage—unaware that with that gesture his public life was effectively over.

EARLY 1976: *RECORDING* 'Mucho Mungo'/'Cookin'' demos.

October 1975 was a month to remember. Lennon celebrated his 35th birthday; his and Yoko's son, Sean, was born the same day. His compilation album 'Shaved Fish' was issued, collecting together his American A-sides and tossing in a fragment of the 'One To One' take of 'Give Peace A Chance' for collectors; and his immigration battle was effectively won, with the announcement that the US government had dropped their efforts to have him deported.

1976 was to bring the completion of his nine-year recording contract with EMI. There had been periodic rumours about a reformation of The Beatles during the mid-seventies; even Lennon was no longer denying them (though Harrison was). Unwilling to begin a new project for EMI/ Capitol, Lennon chose to bide his time; by the time the contract actually expired on January 26, John had already decided not to respond to any of the multi-million dollar offers he had received from the world's leading record companies. For the first time since 1961, he was not under contract. He didn't owe anybody anything; he resolved to devote his time to raising his new son.

Quite how involved he was in that process varies from one account to the next. Lennon recalled in 1980 that he had spent five years as a 'house-husband', rearing Sean while Yoko took care of business downstairs at the Dakota, bamboozling lawyers and selling cows for hundreds of thousands of dollars apiece. Other commentators, notably Albert Goldman, would have us believe that Lennon spent his time divided between drink and drugs; that he was an emotional and physical wreck for much of his final five years; that his relationship with Yoko was a virtual sham, on the verge of disintegration; that the entire 'house-husband' episode was little more than a fairy-tale.

Whom you believe is up to you: maybe some of the evidence to follow will tip the balance one way or the other. What's certain is that by early 1976, Lennon had not yet lost the will to create. His only commitment was to Ringo Starr: for the third album running, Ringo had asked his buddy for a new song, and Lennon obliged with the throwaway 'Cookin' (In The Kitchen Of Love)', which he first demoed at home on the piano. Lennon hadn't quite perfected the chord changes, but the song was already intact—complete with an extra tag-line in the chorus, 'We're gonna have a party (bring your own stuff)'. And for an ending, John went back to his roots, to the same break-down Elvis Presley had used on 'I Got A Woman' on his 1956 début album.

Around the same time, John chose to tape another acoustic demo of a song he'd already cut with Harry Nilsson 18 months earlier. 'Mucho Mungo' was a fantasy escape from reality, and a love song for May, so it makes a surprising choice for recording at the Dakota with Sean crying in the background. Either way, this version hardly differed from the acoustic takes John had cut before the 'Pussy Cats' sessions in the spring of 1974.

• • •   **UNSPECIFIED SESSIONS FROM 1976 TO 1980: *RECORDING* '*Rock Island Line*'/'*John Henry*'/'*Sea Ditties*'/*unnamed blues instrumentals*/'*I'm**

A Man'/'Brown-Eyed Handsome Man'/'Twas A Night Like Ethel Merman'/ 'Beyond The Sea'/'Corrine Corrina'/'News Of The Day From Reuters'/'I Ain't Got Time'

"I didn't even touch a guitar for five years," John claimed during his late 1980 comeback. These undated tapes, and many more besides, prove him wrong. In a sense, their exact origins don't matter, though they probably date from early in his 'retirement'. They exhibit the same semi-serious attitude towards his musical roots as his work with The Beatles, or his jamming during the 'Double Fantasy' sessions. The fifties was Lennon's period; so it's no surprise to hear him busking his way through songs he had played with The Quarry Men, like 'Rock Island Line' (with John chugging away happily on electric guitar, and forgetting the list of cargo the driver had on his train) and 'John Henry,' a traditional blues. In fact, the simplicity of the blues structure pervades most of these tapes, with John closer to the music's feel than to any precise, Eric Clapton-like command of the idiom.

The performances range from a light ramble through 'I Ain't Got Time' on acoustic guitar, to a Dylanesque take on 'Corrine Corrina' and a tongue-in-cheek rendition of Bo Diddley's 'I'm A Man', complete with self-effacing lyrics ('I can't get it up at all').

Equally revealing was a fiery take of Chuck Berry's 1956 single 'Brown-Eyed Handsome Man', taken initially as a blues rather than a rocker, but with John redoubling the tempo for the final choruses just like Jerry Lee Lewis would have done. Along the way, he dropped in and out of Paul McCartney's 'Get Back', obviously forgetting he'd once seen the song as a none-too-subtle message of contempt for Yoko.

Not all the recordings from the late seventies were rock-orientated. One archive tape contains John singing a bizarre piano medley of English music hall favourites, from 'My Old Man's A Dustman' and 'I Do Like To Be Beside The Seaside' to George Formby's 'Chinese Laundry Blues' and 'Leanin' On A Lamp Post'–the whole piece set within a sea shanty, and accompanied by the 'over the points' rhythm from the BBC's fifties TV rock show, *Six-Five Special.*

Another medley found John in continental mood, busking his way through a cod French monologue before delivering 'Beyond The Sea' and 'Blue Moon' in a Gallic accent, and 'Young Love' like a native Cockney. Equally bizarre was 'Twas A Night Like Ethel Merman', which sounded like one of his *In His Own Write* poems set to Scottish music. And in a parodic vein, John also recorded what he thought was a piss-take of Bob Dylan, reciting the 'News Of The Day From Reuters'. As Dylan impressions go, however, Lennon's was a dog, and so was his performance.

APRIL 1976: *RECORDING* *'Cookin''* with Ringo Starr.

In late April 1976, John fulfilled his last professional obligation– helping Ringo Starr record 'Cookin' (In The Kitchen Of Love)' for Ringo's

'Rotogravure' album. Third time around, Ringo's all-star-album formula was wearing thin: so was the quality of the material, Lennon's included. At the session, where John played keyboards and presumably once again laid down a guide vocal for Ringo to follow, everyone did their best to create a party mood; but 'Cookin'' was so slight that it merely emphasised the hollowness of the song. The Lennon/Starr relationship didn't suffer, however: Ringo cut two disco-flavoured albums in the late seventies, but when he returned to rock in 1980, Lennon was only too happy to oblige with the offer of material. You get the feeling that whenever Ringo asked, Lennon would have come up with something.

SPRING/SUMMER 1976: *WRITING Skywriting By Word Of Mouth;* *recording readings from the book.*

With no recording contract, no obligations to any outside party, Lennon was free to create, or not, as he chose. Fifteen years of consistent pressure had taken their toll, however, and he felt uneasy sitting around the Dakota watching the nanny change Sean's nappies. "When I stopped music and started this house-husband business," he told *Playboy* interviewer David Sheff in 1980, "I got frantic in one period that I was supposed to be creating things, so I sat down and wrote about 200 pages of mad stuff—*In His Own Write*-ish. It's there in a box, but it isn't right. Some of it's funny, but it's not right enough."

Lennon's close companion Elliot Mintz recalled that besides this manuscript, titled *Skywriting By Word Of Mouth*, which Lennon showed him in the autumn of 1976, John had also composed a play, and a couple of dozen songs. We'll get to those later; the play, meanwhile, has never been unveiled in public.

But *Skywriting By Word Of Mouth* duly appeared in 1986, in a volume of Lennon's writings compiled by Yoko. It was revealed as a curiously unsatisfying mixture of parody and confession, part frantic word-play, part social satire, part the same kind of ingenious character invention which Lennon would demonstrate on the taped playlets he sent to Mintz later in the seventies. It has been described in some quarters as a novel, but it lacks any kind of unity, formal or informal; if it has a fictional forbear, it's the cluttered, almost opaque work of Thomas Pyncheon, whose novels are inhabited by equally unusual creations engaged in equally random pursuits.

But Pyncheon's books are linked by narrative development, and by moral purpose, no matter how bizarre. The structure of *Skywriting*, by comparison, is determined by Lennon's patience. Just as he had done in the mid-sixties, Lennon wrote out of inspiration, but abandoned the task whenever the initial flow seized up—usually after a thousand words or so, three or four pages of the printed book. As there is no plot to carry, there's also no plot to interrupt; so John could stop wherever he wished, without altering the fundamental impact of his chapter.

Taken sentence by sentence, *Skywriting* is a remarkable achievement: few other comic writers could match the sheer wit and imagination that invests Lennon's word-play, which—unlike his earlier work—is usually funny and more often than not pertinent as well. But the book is almost impossible to read at a sitting—simply because it isn't a book but a collection of unconnected phrases which work just as well in limbo as in context.

More interesting at this distance are the occasional references to John's own life—not just the sly chapter heading, 'Lucy In The Scarf With Diabetics', or the fact that one of the 'stories' has Lennon's alter ego, Dr Winston O'Boogie, as its hero; but also the odd references to historical events which break into the fiction, suggesting that Lennon was using this work as a mixture of placebo and diary. In the piece 'Nobel Peace Prize Awarded To Killer Whale', for instance, a fantasy about a masturbating biologist is interrupted by reminiscences of 'fucking my girlfriend on a gravestone' in Liverpool, and then of the Maharishi's camp in Rishikesh, where 'He made us live in separate huts from our wives... Can't say it was too much of a strain'.

Elsewhere, Lennon looks back to 'Across The Universe', and then gently satirises the way it was composed: 'Words are flowing out like endless rainbow mixed grilling baron von oil field marshall tucker band wagonner rear end zone what you reap van winkle of an eyelid of grass blowers convention centre forward march hair raising the flag of truce is stronger than friction of a second helping'. Not all of *Skywriting* is that rich, but there's the essence of the book in a single sentence—puns cascading from one cliché to the next, free-falling just as the lyric to one of Lennon's most poetic songs had done nearly a decade earlier. This was infinitely more creative than 'Cookin'' or 'Mucho Mungo;' but it didn't lead anywhere, which is no doubt why John abandoned it.

Before he did so, however, he committed a series of readings from his manuscript to tape. The results were stolen from the Dakota shortly after his death, and have not been returned. When they are, Yoko promises that they will be given an official release.

- **SUMMER 1976: *WRITING introduction to Rock 'n' Roll Times.***

Jurgen Vollmer had been one of The Beatles' closest friends in Hamburg in 1961/62; and he took some of the classic early photos of the band, clad in black leather on the stage of the Kaiserkeller, or posed around the streets of Hamburg. When he came to publish a collection of his work, initially only in Germany, he approached Lennon for an introduction. John obliged, with a short recommendation to the effect that Jurgen's photos were the best ever taken of The Beatles. This wasn't just hype: John had already used one of them on the cover of his 'Rock 'n' Roll' album the previous year.

On the subject of photographic collections, John and Yoko had recently announced plans to publish a book called *365 Days Of Sean*—one photo from each day of Sean's first year of life. No doubt the photos exist; the Lennons always documented their lives together. But the book never materialised.

• • • **SUMMER 1976:** *RECORDING 'Many Rivers To Cross;' writing and recording home demos of 'Sally And Billy'/'She Is A Friend Of Dorothy's'/ 'Tennessee.'*

Several months after re-recording 'Mucho Mungo', Lennon felt the need to lay down a solo acoustic version of another 'Pussy Cats' track, 'Many Rivers To Cross.' Taped with the accompaniment of his primitive drum machine, the track kept strictly to the Nilsson arrangement, again begging the question why?

On the same tape, John returned to 'Tennessee', the tribute song he'd begun at the start of 1975. He cut a series of piano demos, each one fuller than the initial fragment taped the previous year. The song now worked in a number of direct references to Tennessee Williams' plays, laced with an air of nostalgic melancholy that was heightened when John later changed the title of the song to 'Memories.'

John also chose to revive an even older song around this time: 'Sally And Billy,' last heard at the end of 1970 when it was little more than a tune and some improvised lyrics. The three piano takes, again backed by a drum machine, that Lennon recorded in 1976 revealed that he'd spent some time filling in the gaps in the narrative. The plot lined up like this: the beautiful, independent and artistic Sally sits in a café reading books; Billy, meanwhile, is a singer who is 'playing with his mind.' Both of them are over the hill, hoping Jesus will intervene and help them decide what they should do with their lives. John might have been hoping the same thing: as it stood, 'Sally And Billy' seems like an unconscious metaphor for John's own lack of purpose.

The most complete song John wrote that summer was 'She Is A Friend Of Dorothy's'—'she's gay,' in New York slang. John taped seven takes of the song, playing staccato notes high on the piano as he introduced the main character, 'hot lips and no shame/all fun and no game.' For the chorus, which made fun of the title line, and threw in a sly reference to 'the Sheik of Arabesque', Lennon speeded-up the tune of 'Aisumasen', rolling his piano chords like a New Orleans bluesman. Though the lyrics required some focus, this was a finished song, both more playful and more melodic than anything he'd written since The Beatles. But like the rest of his 1976 demos, this was work without an end in sight; and though John thought of reviving 'Dorothy' in 1979, he doesn't seem to have done any more work on the song.

• • • **LATE 1977:** *RECORDING home demos of 'Mirror Mirror On The Wall'/'Real Life'/'I Don't Wanna Face It'/'I Watch Your Face'/'One Of The Boys'/'Free As A Bird'/'Whatever Happened To...;' writing 'Emotional Wreck.'*

Lennon was finally awarded his green card—his badge of government approval which marked the end of his immigration battle—in July 1976 after a hearing in which a parade of notables, including Gloria Swanson, Norman Mailer and John Cage, testified on his behalf. The hearing was a formality, but this did not stop the judge from inquiring of John's solicitor–apparently in all seriousness–whether or not he might become a 'state charge' and seek 'national assistance'. "That is most unlikely," he replied before briefly outlining John's assets. After the hearing John was amused to discover that the green card he has sought for so long was actually blue in colour.

Six months later, he felt sufficiently secure in his status to appear at President Carter's inaugural ball at the White House. Thereafter, he made no public appearances until he and Yoko called a press conference in Japan on October 4, 1977, to explain that they were concentrating on child-rearing, not business, and that they wouldn't be resuming their artistic careers until their son was five-years-old, in 1980.

The Lennons were then close to the end of a four-month stay in Japan, captured in the photographic portfolio *A Family Album*. But this apparent idyll was actually a time of some stress for John. Having exhausted the spurt of creativity which had driven him to write *Skywriting By Word Of Mouth*, he found himself drawn into a long period of depression. Lennon may or may not have dealt with this crisis by taking refuge in drugs or physical violence; you'll have to decide that for yourselves. But towards the end of the summer, he did manage to channel that gloom into work, composing a song called 'Mirror Mirror On The Wall' while he was still in Japan, and cutting an acoustic guitar demo of the song which has sadly been destroyed.

Back at the Dakota in October, Lennon reworked the song on piano, and taped five more solo demos. The song was a weary piece of self-examination, almost self-pity: 'I look in the mirror and nobody's there...I keep on staring, is it me?' Its descending chord sequence added to the pervading sadness, and the overall feel was somewhere between 'Scared' and the as-yet unwritten 'Watching The Wheels'. It's a chilling piece of work, even in this unfinished state, and it testifies to the depth of Lennon's crisis in late 1977.

The sheer act of writing about his misery seems to have lightened it, however, and over the next few weeks Lennon composed a sheaf of new songs, almost all of which he taped for posterity–the exception being 'Emotional Wreck', a 'Watching The Wheels' prototype. In itself, this last song is significant. In his promotional interviews for 'Double Fantasy' in 1980, Lennon made great play of the fact that his new songs had arrived almost without invitation. "They were inspired songs," he claimed, "and there were none where I had to sit down and make a dovetail joint." And he dated them precisely, to the Bermuda holiday he took with Sean in June 1980, when he supposedly began to write his first new compositions since 'Walls And Bridges' in 1974.

As Lennon's carefully preserved composing and demo tapes reveal, that was simply a line for the press, something to make 'Double Fantasy' sound like a work of inspiration rather than craftsmanship. In fact, the songs on that album, and on its companion piece, 'Milk And Honey,' evolved over a period of three years or more. And with the exception of 'Woman', and maybe 'Dear Yoko', none of them emerged fully-formed from the chrysalis: they were painstakingly constructed from a series of sessions and rewrites, only assuming their final form after they'd undergone numerous changes of title and lyrics. That doesn't detract from their art, or devalue their emotional impact: it simply means that, like any of his public comments, Lennon's explanation of the roots of 'Double Fantasy' has to be approached with caution.

Besides 'Emotional Wreck', John began work on a song called 'I Don't Wanna Face It' in late 1977. He built the song around a two-chord acoustic guitar riff, and used its fragmentary lyrics to explain to himself—there was no other audience—why he couldn't resume his place in the world. And he also offered a glimpse of why he was sometimes so hard to live with: 'I can dish it out/but I just can't take it'.

'I Watch Your Face' was a far less painful exercise, a hillbilly song which had something of the flavour of Buddy Holly's 'Raining In My Heart', even a hint of a far less likely source, The Applejacks' 'Tell Me When'. And Lennon ended his first demo with a brief suggestion of the intro of another song he had yet to write—'(Just Like) Starting Over.' The song, such as it was, seems to have been inspired by his son: 'While you are sleeping/No one told me life was so worth keeping'. But that was as far as the lyrics were ever taken.

'Real Life' also saw John coming to terms with existence, rather than shying away from its implications. John reworked this tune constantly till the end of his life, frequently stealing part of its structure for another song. This initial take, for instance, has a verse which ended up in 'I'm Stepping Out', and a hint of the eventual chorus to 'Watching The Wheels' along the way. Vamping at the piano, John improvised lyrics—'Picked up the paper/read the Daily News/nothing doing anyway'—before returning to the simple message of the chorus: 'Just gotta let it go/it's real life'. There followed a semi-classical piano interlude, before the take collapsed, with Lennon slapping his own wrist: "Oh rock yer balls, you bum."

'Free As A Bird' took off from a basic doo-wop chord sequence, taking in some of the stately changes of 'Grow Old With Me' as it progressed. This was another tune of great promise, which Lennon either forgot about or didn't bother to return to: despite its incomplete lyrics, it had an air of majesty that deserved further attention. The words explored different ways of conveying the metaphor in the title: quite clearly it was the concept rather than any particular lyrical phrase which had been the initial inspiration, and nothing Lennon sang on this tape quite did the title justice.

Like 'She Is A Friend Of Dorothy's' from the previous year, 'Whatever Happened To...' saw Lennon making a rare excursion into writing in the third-person—creating characters rather than analysing his own. Just two takes of the song exist: the first broke down during the guitar intro, but the second was complete. Lennon had loved the strident rhythm guitar-work of Richie Havens in the late sixties; 'Whatever Happened To...' was in a similar style, with barrages of chords punctuated by dramatic pauses.

'She used to be an artist but she threw away the key ...whatever happened to the woman we once knew:' well, maybe John was writing obliquely about himself after all. Either way, these demo takes were merely documents of work in progress, with John experimenting with chord inversions for maximum impact; but once again he never bothered to return to the song in later sessions.

Finally, 'One Of The Boys' offered a less intense view of the artist at 37. The faintly tropical flavour of this guitar-based tune reflected the humorous acceptance of the lyric; John might be growing older, but 'they say that he's aged very well, he's still one of the boys.' There was a double joke here, of course: 'the boys' was how Beatle aides and fans always referred to the group in the sixties. This mild self-mockery took some achieving in late 1977, but it was a sign that Lennon had written himself back into something approaching good humour. The next step was to find a project into which his restored creative powers could be directed.

• **LATE 1977/EARLY 1978:** *CREATING Mind Movies.*

Elliot Mintz had first interviewed the Lennons in late 1971; then in 1972 he'd lost his job as a DJ when he aired their 'Some Time In New York City' album in its entirety. Six years on, he was one of the couple's few confidants: a trusted aide who doubled as friend and adviser, a role he continues to play for Yoko Ono today. In the late seventies, he was in constant contact with John; and it was Mintz to whom Lennon sent his taped *Mind Movies*, bizarre playlets which John taped at home, mixing dialogue from TV and radio dramas with Lennon's own invented characters, foremost amongst whom were the Great Wok and Maurice Dupont, *Agent Provocateur du jour*. If you're not Mintz or Lennon, these tapes don't have a great deal of relevance; but like the collage art that Lennon was creating around the same time, they were a sign of an imagination with too much freedom on its hands.

• **MID-1978:** *PREPARING material, and writing programme notes, for* **The Ballad Of John And Yoko.**

With Lennon writing a steady stream of new material, one might have expected him to begin work on a follow-up to 'Rock 'n' Roll' and 'Shaved Fish.' Instead, he and Yoko made tentative plans to write a Broadway musical, based on their own relationship, and called—what else?—*The Ballad Of John And Yoko.*

Several of the songs John had already written were set aside for the project, like 'She Is A Friend Of Dorothy's', 'Whatever Happened To...', 'Mirror Mirror On The Wall', 'Free As A Bird', and 'Real Love' (a slightly augmented arrangement of 'Real Life'). Yoko composed 'Every Man Has A Woman Who Loves Him' around the same time; some of her other 'Double Fantasy' material may also date from this period.

The couple don't seem to have considered the problem of writing a script to link their songs; and, of course, they didn't mention the proposed musical in their 1980 interviews, because that would have ruined the illusion that John had spent five years steadfastly ignoring the guitar

183

hung on his bedroom wall. But when Yoko compiled *Skywriting By Word Of Mouth* in 1986, she included what was apparently an essay John had written for the theatre programme, though that seems rather premature.

Whatever, *The Ballad Of John And Yoko* is a remarkable document—written in prose of such clarity that it is difficult to identify it with the creator of *In His Own Write* or *Skywriting*. For once, Lennon was serious: any humour was sardonic.

This autobiographical testament begins with the search for the ultimate woman, and the realisation that he'd found her in Yoko. So the *Ballad* began, 'just in time for me to avoid having to live with my ex-wife's new nose.' Lennon recounts the racism the couple experienced in Britain; the hypocrisy of the British press, and of his fellow Beatles; and then the madness and magic of the bed-ins, the peace campaigns, the 'revolutionary period', the move to New York, and the eventual birth of their first child.

There's no mention of the 1973 separation; precious little of John's musical career; and the essay ends with Lennon admitting: 'I've already 'lost' one family to produce what? 'Sgt. Pepper?' I am blessed with a second chance. Being a Beatle almost cost me my life, and certainly cost me a great deal of my health...I will not make the same mistake twice in one lifetime...If I never 'produce' anything more for public consumption than 'silence', so be it!'

It's a powerful piece of writing, though surely a strange note for a theatre programme; more like an artistic suicide note than a warm-up routine for a Broadway audience. There's more to *The Ballad Of John And Yoko*, perhaps, than meets the eye; but whenever it was written, and why, it puts into clear English the underlying message of the 'house-husband' years: Lennon was tired of living his life to others' expectations.

What's intriguing is the clash between the mature self-confidence of this essay, and the blatant indecisiveness revealed in the songs which date from the same period.

Chapter 15

L A T E   1 9 7 8   T O
D E C E M B E R   1 9 8 0

. . . .

LATE 1978: ***WRITING*** *and recording home demos of 'People'/'Stranger's Room'/'Everybody's Talkin', Nobody's Talkin.''*

According to Yoko's astrologer, John Green, Lennon spent around 15 months after the couple's return from Japan in his bedroom, watching TV and losing weight. According to Yoko, the couple were planning a Broadway musical. According to Lennon's tape boxes, he was writing new songs—three of which have survived, and were reworked for the couple's 'Double Fantasy' sessions in the autumn of 1980.

'People' was merely a reworking of 'Emotional Wreck', which John had begun the previous year—another step on the road to 'Watching The Wheels'. The chorus hadn't yet evolved, but John had hit upon the circular piano riff which underpinned the finished record, and the basic verses—a wry comment on public expectations, an apologia for his lack of activity in recent years.

When he did put his mind to new material, what emerged was in the same tradition as songs like 'Rock And Roll People' and 'Move Over Ms L.' He wrote 'Everybody's Talkin', Nobody's Talkin'' around the same time as 'People', and cut a rough demo on acoustic guitar. When John wrote a new chorus, the song became known as 'Nobody Told Me:' at this juncture, it shared that song's chaotic rush of images, which scattered in the mind as if you'd flipped the channels on TV—as likely an inspiration for the song as any. Without a hookline, the original chorus ran, 'You can't tell no one nothing no way never,' to the same tune as 'Nobody told me there'd be days like these' on the record.

'Stranger's Room' is more obviously a tale from the heart—as confirmed by John's comments on its eventual incarnation, 'I'm Losing You' on 'Double Fantasy.' On his composing tape, Lennon had just one verse, which he repeated over and over again, feeling his way towards the phrasing he wanted.

There was no chorus, as such, merely a lonely lyric of alienation that could have been narrated from another woman's room, on a casual fling away from Yoko. Internal evidence is slight, however; and in the end, the atmosphere of the song was more important than the setting.

LATE 1978 TO EARLY 1979: *DRAWING* self-caricatures.

Most of the cartoons that illustrate *Skywriting By Word Of Mouth* were drawn within a period of months around the end of 1978. They portray the artist as a loner, a dreamer, above and outside the corporeal world—as worthy a metaphor for the times as any of Lennon's lyrics of alienation.

MAY 27, 1979: *PUBLICATION* in London, New York and Tokyo of 'A Love Letter From Yoko And John To People Who Ask Us What, When And Why.'

What When and Why indeed. It was a surprise, to say the least, to open the London *Sunday Times* in May 1979 and find a page devoted to a paid advertisement bearing not an invitation to sample a new Porsche or a fine wine, but a message to their friends and fans from the reclusive Lennons. Stranger still, the message advertised no forthcoming project, not even the hint of a new album or tour. As with their peace campaigns of the late sixties, the message justified itself: this was a worldwide event to rank alongside the poster blitz of December 1969.

Peace was the subject a decade later as well, though this time it was inner and spiritual. John and Yoko were thriving, we were told, in the simple, faintly poetic prose we'd come to recognise as Yoko's. Sean was wonderful; so were the cats; so was the world, if we'd only look to see. Magic could achieve everything: wish and it was yours. The Lennons loved us. And there was a postscript: 'We noticed that three angels were looking over our shoulders while we wrote this.'

Any news of the Lennons was welcome in 1979—a time when, if you believe their detractors, the couple were sliding further apart, and towards the spectre of drug addiction. So was their 'love letter' another piece of wish-fulfilment—the Lennons putting their own theory to the test, hoping that by saying the garden was rosy it would become so? Were they expecting to lead the world towards spiritual renewal, the substitution of hope for pessimism and distrust? And who were the three angels? The other Beatles? The Three Stooges? No one was saying, then or now. The letter went unexplained during their comeback interviews, and remains one of the weirder episodes in the disjointed history of the couple's final years.

• **LATE 1979:** *WRITING and recording home demos of 'My Life'/'Real Love'/'Beautiful Boy'/'I'm Crazy.'*

Throughout the so-called 'house-husband' years, Lennon was unable to resist the lure of the guitar pinned on his bedroom wall. Little of his work during the late seventies was complete, or would have been remotely suitable for release; but his unfinished songs and half-aired melodies were still the major source of inspiration for 'Double Fantasy' in 1980, despite his claims otherwise.

Often the most unpromising material was milked for the finished album. One such example is 'My Life', which Lennon cut once on piano towards the end of 1979, then twice on guitar, the first take breaking down. In its simplest form, Lennon sang the skeleton lyrics in falsetto; the later takes use a lower register, and an acoustic guitar riff which wouldn't have been out of place on a John Denver record. And the words were equally banal, and also rather eerie, in the light of later events: 'This is my life/take it, it's mine to give...do what you will/I dedicate it to you.' They were set around a tune that was close to the opening section of 'Starting Over' a year later; while another line in the song, 'Life is something that happens while you're making plans', was subsequently transferred to another song begun around the same time.

That was 'Beautiful Boy,' a title which alternated with 'Darling Boy' until Lennon combined them both on 'Double Fantasy.' May Pang wrote that she had heard the tune as early as 1974; then again, she also thought that 'Tennessee' grew into 'Watching The Wheels', so she's not an ideal witness. But it's quite likely that in searching for a vehicle for his lullaby to his son, John picked up a finished melody that he'd not used on 'Walls And Bridges'. Either way, the tune was fully formed on John's first double-tracked demo, as were the poignant words, though there were some slight changes to be made: 'Hold my hand before you cross the street', Lennon sang, 'The traffic's slow but you never know who you're gonna meet.'

As early as 1977, Lennon had begun work on 'Real Life', a song which provided words and music for two 1980 recordings, 'I'm Stepping Out' and 'Watching The Wheels'. What was left of the tune turned into 'Real Love', a gentle acoustic ballad for which John cut seven near-identical demos towards the end of 1979. Take six has since been issued on the *Imagine: John Lennon* soundtrack album, and conveys the fragility of this slightly melancholy glimpse of a man removed from the world, yet trying to regain touch with his emotions.

That same distance from everyday existence inspired 'I'm Crazy,' the third title for the song which was now close to becoming 'Watching The Wheels'. The earliest surviving home recording of the song dates from this period, and contains another reference to 'the traffic flow' which John could see from his sixth-floor bedroom window. Cut on piano, the song lacked a pay-off line to the chorus, but the eventual verses were more or less there, and John ad libbed his way through an additional set of lyrics which suggested that he had retained a little of his sense of irony: 'People say I'm stupid/giving my money away/They give me all kinds of names and addresses/designed to save me financially/I tell them that I'm doing fine watching flowers grow/Don't you know that you don't own the whole damn world! Mercifully, perhaps, that was the last we would hear of those particular couplets.

· · · · **EARLY 1980: *WRITING* and recording home demos of 'Serve Yourself'/ 'Don't Be Crazy'/'Girls And Boys'/'Clean-Up Time'/'Watching The Wheels'/ 'The Worst Is Over'/'Beautiful Boy'/medley of 'Beautiful Boy'/'Memories'/ 'Across The River.'**

The dawn of 1980 brought no resolution to the lingering discontent in John Lennon's life. Terrified of returning to rock stardom, but aware that he was frittering his time away at home, he continued to cut demos and write songs at the Dakota, without any specific project in mind.

The previous summer, Bob Dylan had announced his advocacy of evangelical Christianity with a forthright declaration of faith, the 'Slow Train Coming' album. Its key song, for which he won a Grammy, was 'Gotta Serve Somebody'—a tongue-in-cheek piece of gospel which insisted that between the Lord and the Devil there was no space to hide. Lennon's spiritual beliefs did not confine him to any God or prophet; he increasingly accepted the power of the unconscious, as a substitute for political, people-powered change. So the strict moralism of Dylan's album shocked him: "I was very surprised when Bobby boy went that way," he told David Sheff in 1980, "very surprised. But I'm not distressed by the fact that Dylan is doing what Dylan wants to do."

The sense of betrayal was somewhat stronger earlier in the year, when Lennon struck back at Dylan's beliefs—perhaps having seen him perform 'Gotta Serve Somebody' at the Grammy Awards in February. John's riposte was 'Serve Yourself:' a vitriolic attack on those who claimed to have found the meaning of life in God or religion. 'You've got to serve yourself,' Lennon ranted in the chorus, 'Ain't nobody gonna do it for you.' In all, he cut no less than 12 takes of the song, most of them as a piano blues, New Orleans-style, complete with mock-serious monologues about creationism and the power of masturbation. 'There ain't no room service here,' he quipped, before ad-libbing a verse about man's descent from monkeys or visitors from outer space.

A couple of versions of 'Serve Yourself' were recorded with relentless acoustic guitar back-up, however, complete with Lennon working his way through the dictionary of slang between verses. The sheer venom of these takes was unmatched by anything since 'How Do You Sleep', and it added extra bite to his admission that 'there's only one thing missing in this godalmighty stew/and that's your mother'—one last act of Oedipal worship in the midst of a slaughter of prophets and gurus.

None of that temper surfaced in Lennon's other 1980 songs, most of which were directed inwards rather than at outside targets. That spring, 'I'm Crazy' became 'Watching The Wheels:' having worked up the song on piano, Lennon switched to electric guitar for his next demo, playing a boogie rhythm and some apparently random chord changes behind the familiar tune.

Among the other songs Lennon had left incomplete the previous year was 'Beautiful Boy.' In the early months of 1980, he made another attempt, accompanying his electric rhythm guitar with a simple drum machine, and working round and round the changes until the final lyrics came. One take lasted 10 minutes or more: another became a medley, moving from 'Beautiful Boy' to the long-abandoned 'Memories', then into an otherwise unknown song called 'Across The River,' an easy-paced boogie, and back through 'Memories' again.

Lennon continued to work on the song called 'Real Life' or—now—'Girls And Boys' in early 1980, producing a succession of identical guitar demos. Equally prominent in these sessions was a new tune, optimistically called 'Clean-Up Time'. It was an admission that 1979 had been a year of private excess, but that the new decade promised a fresh broom. Several piano demos of the song have survived, each with a vague gospel feel, and soft, almost spoken vocals. 'Show those mothers how to do it', Lennon whispered in the chorus, before satirising the set-up in the Dakota: 'The queen is in the counting home/counting out the money/The king is in the kitchen/making bread and honey.' The similarity to 'Cry Baby Cry' from 1968 can't have been accidental—nor the sly dig at Yoko's reliance on tarot card readers and fortune-tellers: 'The oracle has spoken/we cast the perfect spell'.

'Clean-Up Time' was optimistic, however, and that mood survived, albeit shakily, on 'Don't Be Crazy,' itself a reworking of 'My Life' from the previous year. Using the same structure—what later became the middle of 'Starting Over'—Lennon threw in an adapted line from Buddy Holly's 'It's So Easy' ('Where you're concerned/the lessons have been learned'), and contrasted the general message of bonhomie with a pointed suggestion: 'Why don't they leave us alone/we cannot fill the empty sky for you'.

Gradually that spring, 'Don't Be Crazy' became 'The Worst Is Over,' closer still to the final feel of 'Starting Over.' With his primitive drum machine in support, Lennon was still considering lyrical variations: 'The worst is over now, it's all downhill', he sang, 'relax and take it easy.' Suitably inspired, Yoko turned the same thought into 'Hard Times Are Over.'

- **JUNE 1980: *RECORDING* demos of *'Clean-Up Time'*/*'Beautiful Boy'*/ *'Woman'*/*'I'm Stepping Out'*/*'Watching The Wheels'*/*'Dear Yoko'*/*'I Don't Wanna Face It'*/*'Borrowed Time'*/*'I'm Losing You'* in Bermuda.**

Here's where reality and myth finally take flight. Time and again in his final interviews, Lennon explained how he'd taken Sean on holiday to Bermuda, visited a rock disco, heard the B-52s performing 'Rock Lobster,' and realised that the world had finally caught up with the Lennons' experimental work from a decade earlier. He was fired to compose a series of new songs, cracking an artistic stalemate that had lasted five years or more, and inspiring his wife to write her own songs when she heard John's on the phone in the Dakota.

John certainly went to Bermuda in June 1980; he may even have written some songs there. But, as we've seen, most of the preparatory work had been carried out in New York during his supposed retirement from creative composition. What seems more likely is that during the late spring of 1980, the Lennons had agreed to launch a comeback in the summer. Lennon went to Bermuda for a holiday, but dragged along his guitar, tape deck and drum machine, in the hope of cutting listenable demos of his work in progress. These he may have played down the phone to Yoko; in turn she may have sung her contributions to the project, some of which dated back to the Broadway musical of 1978, others even further ('I'm Moving On', for instance, was first attempted during the 'Feeling The Space' sessions in 1973).

So the Bermuda myth isn't quite gospel. What is certain, however, is that the Lennons entered the 'Double Fantasy' sessions five weeks later with no fewer than 22 songs complete, while more emerged during the recording process. At least four of these were probably written, or at least perfected, in Bermuda.

The Bermuda demos are a remarkably homogeneous batch, sharing some of the acoustic richness of the pre-'White Album' Beatles demos from late May 1968. Another link between them is that they are all solo blueprints for the recording sessions to follow. There was no more rewriting or editing; this is the way Lennon expected his records to sound, albeit with the instrumental spice that session musicians would bring. Most of the cuts had double-tracked vocals and guitars—slightly erratic in places, but still performed with a confidence entirely missing from the tentative Dakota demos of recent years.

Even if the whole exercise was a sham, then the fact that it produced 'Woman' made this a memorable week in Lennon's career. There are no documents of work in progress here: 'Woman' emerges fully-formed, a remarkable tribute to Yoko and to womankind, for recognising 'the little child inside the man'—a rare piece of self-perception. Its clarity of thought also marked it out from the other 'Double Fantasy' material: for once, Lennon was able to pay homage to his wife without falling into self-abasement.

'Dear Yoko' was an obvious continuation of the same theme, though without any of the melodic grandeur. Instead, Lennon updated his favourite Buddy Holly changes, producing a song of simplicity to rank alongside the equally positive 'Oh Yoko' from the 'Imagine' sessions.

'Borrowed Time' assumed an eerie significance in the light of Lennon's murder: to hear him naïvely talking of 'living on borrowed time/without a thought for tomorrow,' and recounting the joys of getting older, took on a tragic mantle after the events of December 1980. Again, the aura of optimism is almost tangible—as if Lennon's spirit had been lightened by the decision to return to work.

Which makes 'I Don't Wanna Face It' all the more ironic. The skeleton of the song dated back to 1977; Lennon performed it in Bermuda as a frantic rocker, boiling over with fear and resentment at being asked to play a public role. It contrasted with another new song, 'I'm Stepping Out', which had been developed from the early lyrics of 'Real Life', again from Lennon's composing sessions in 1977. Far from dreading the public eye, the narrator of this song couldn't wait to get back on the streets and in the clubs. Not all of the song was strictly autobiographical, however: Lennon wrote an extra verse which didn't make the record—'Called up the doctor but he was sick to death/He don't make house calls any more/He gone out dancing just to sweeten up his breath/He left a message on the floor.'

Finally, 'Watching The Wheels'—completed at last after three years of intermittent work. Lennon had patched up the chorus, and given the song a Dylanesque guitar part which didn't survive onto the record. As it stood, the song settled the delicate balance of the new material—divided between nervous acceptance of the real world, and a determination to keep himself secluded from fame. In truth, these Bermuda demos were a giant step towards the world, a commitment that his five years of retirement were drawing to an end. By the time he had assembled the 'Double Fantasy' band in early August, all traces of the tentative, reclusive Lennon were invisible; instead he took on the trappings of his role, as the elder statesman of rock returned to offer an example to his peers.

- **LATE JULY/EARLY AUGUST 1980:** *RECORDING home demos of 'Life Begins At 40'/'Starting Over'/'Forgive Me My Little Flower Princess.'*

Having made the decision to re-enter the commercial world, John and Yoko booked the Hit Factory studios in New York for two months from the beginning of August 1980. They had yet to select an outlet for their new recordings; but the mere act of arranging sessions was enough to unlock another seam of Lennon creativity.

John had already agreed to contribute to Ringo Starr's forthcoming album, which was set for early in the New Year. By November he was ready to offer Ringo four new songs—one of which was 'Life Begins At 40', written as a joint present to himself and Ringo in honour of their birthdays in October and July respectively. 'Age is just a state of mind', John sang in an exaggerated hillbilly drawl, in a song which he introduced as coming from "the Dakota country and western club." Like other songs for Ringo—'Cookin'', 'Goodnight Vienna'—this was merely an extended joke, though none the less amusing for that.

'Starting Over' was altogether more serious in intent. The song acted as a theme for the Lennons' return to the music business, and as a re-statement of their commitment to each other (or, at least, Lennon's to Yoko). Cut around the same time as 'Life Begins At 40', to the same guitar/rhythm-box accompaniment, 'Starting Over' built on the rickety foundations of 'My Life', 'Don't Be Crazy' and 'The Worst Is Over,' combining the strongest melodic elements of all three. Even this close to the 'Double Fantasy' sessions, however, Lennon still hadn't finalised the lyrics. 'Why don't we take off alone/spend a weekend in an old hotel/a little place without a phone/a second honeymoon would do us well', he sang in the middle section without a hint of satire. Another rejected line suggested that he was regaining his powers of self-mythology, however:

191

'The time has come, the walrus said/for you and I to stay in bed.'

No such confidence inspired 'Forgive Me My Little Flower Princess.' Lennon never completed the song to his satisfaction: the studio take cut early during the 'Double Fantasy' sessions was only a reference recording, so John could return and rewrite the lyrics. They needed it: as it stood, this was Lennon back down on his knees in front of Yoko, apologising for 'crushing your delicateness' with his 'utter selfishness.' Strange that a return to creative activity should automatically produce a naked admission of guilt...

•   •   •   **EARLY AUGUST TO LATE SEPTEMBER 1980: *RECORDING* '*Starting Over*'/'*Kiss Kiss Kiss*'/'*Clean-Up Time*'/'*Give Me Something*'/'*I'm Losing You*'/'*I'm Moving On*'/'*Beautiful Boy*'/'*Watching The Wheels*'/'*I'm Your Angel*'/'*Woman*'/'*Beautiful Boys*'/'*Dear Yoko*'/'*Every Man Has A Woman Who Loves Him*'/'*Hard Times Are Over*'/'*Borrowed Time*'/'*Forgive Me My Little Flower Princess*'/'*Nobody Told Me*'/'*I'm Stepping Out*'/'*I Don't Wanna Face It*'/'*Maggie Mae*'/'*Only The Lonely*'/'*Mystery Train*'/'*She's A Woman*'/ '*Rip It Up*'/'*C'mon Everybody*'/'*I'm A Man*'/'*Be-Bop-A-Lula*'/'*Dream Lover*'/ '*Stay.*'**

'Double Fantasy'—the title itself says a lot. The front cover too: was the fantasy the fact that two 40-somethings had defied the odds and willed their relationship to survive; or that they were pretending passion for the cameras? In their publicity interviews, the couple heralded their album as a statement of intent, as a source of inspiration to their generation, a message from beyond the barriers of middle age. And the record was programmed as a dialogue, 'A Heart Play,' as the subtitle had it, between a married couple—alternating songs of love and despair, longing and gentle companionship.

The actual state of the couple's marriage at this point has been questioned by so-called 'insiders,' some of whom claim that John was about to leave Yoko, others that Yoko was tired of life with John. Little of that surfaced during the sessions, or overtly in the songs: the one directly negative piece, Yoko's 'I'm Moving On,' dated back to 1973, a time when the marriage was definitely in disarray. The other tunes had their moments of tension, but only within a determination to resist the forces of time and the great ennui, as Mike Nesmith put it.

One thing is certain: Lennon revelled in the opportunity to play with other musicians. At the suggestion of producer Jack Douglas, and without the initial knowledge of John and Yoko, the entire sessions were recorded from the control booth. The session tapes reveal that from the first, Lennon was in his element—utterly confident, disarmingly articulate about what he wanted from his musicians, encouraging them through the creative process, but still willing to criticise constructively to sting one last take out of a tired group.

On the first morning of sessions at the Hit Factory, Lennon played the band some of his Bermuda demos, and then led them into rough arrangements of several of the songs. 'I'm Stepping Out,' complete with the extra 'doctor' verse, was first to be taped, with Lennon rejoicing over the intro that he "finally gets the kids to bed and gets into his own space," and coaxing Hugh McCracken into the guitar solo by muttering "let's begin the beguine." After a couple more takes, one of which was edited down for the posthumous 'Milk And Honey' album, Lennon began work on 'Borrowed Time'–again not attempting to make a record, merely breaking in the band (though one of these takes was also issued in 1984).

The remainder of the 'Milk And Honey' tracks featuring Lennon and the band were taped during this week, and 'Nobody Told Me', 'Forgive Me My Little Flower Princess' and 'I Don't Wanna Face It' all kept close to the earlier home demos, with a jagged, unrehearsed quality that confirms their ephemeral purpose.

The fact that none of these songs were attempted later during the sessions suggests that the game-plan for 'Double Fantasy'–or 'Fuchsia', as it was originally slated–was laid out in advance. No other Lennon or Ono songs were taped during these two months, either: the only out-takes in existence are either alternate takes, early mixes, or else impromptu jam sessions on rock 'n' roll oldies between takes. One such set of recordings was made during the filming of a promo video for 'Starting Over' at the end of August, and documents the band trying to persuade Lennon to play McCartney's Beatles' B-side, 'She's A Woman'–only for Lennon to outwit them consistently by falling into his own favourite oldies. Another has John busking Roy Orbison's 'Only The Lonely' between takes of 'Starting Over,' and toying with the guitar chords of an as-yet unfinished song, 'Gone From This Place'.

'Double Fantasy' mixed seven of John's songs with seven of Yoko's, and equal care went into the recording of each. In the event, British critics claimed to prefer Yoko's incisive accounts of married life to Lennon's more sentimental offerings, and the no-nonsense ultimatum of 'I'm Moving On', or the directness of 'Beautiful Boys', is far more honest and worldly than Lennon's romantic daydreams on 'Starting Over' or 'Dear Yoko'. 'Beautiful Boys', ostensibly an answer-song to Lennon's own 'Beautiful Boy,' pinned Lennon exactly, with its reference to 'all your little ploys', and its telling summary, 'You got all you can carry/and still feel somehow empty.' This to a man who was telling her 'I'm forever in your debt'.

Elsewhere, Yoko ventured into reggae on the tentative 'Hard Times Are Over;' wandered a little too close to 'Makin' Whoopee' on 'I'm Your Angel;' explored sexual paranoia and desire on the new wave rocker 'Kiss Kiss Kiss', which ended with a violent orgasm, in stereo; and returned to the sterility of relationships on 'Give Me Something'. In reviving 'Every Man has A Woman Who Loves Him' from the proposed Broadway musical, Yoko put her own love into question: 'Why do I roam when I know you're the one/Why do I laugh when I feel like crying'. From her standpoint, this was no romantic fantasy; what's startling, in retrospect, is how far her lyrics are removed from the idealism that supposedly inspired the project.

In his way, Lennon was equally honest–'Starting Over' was a straight-from-the-heart admission of need for his wife, while 'Woman' mixed a tribute to the female sex with his customary confession of failure in his relationship. Look closely, in fact, and you'll find that even the most open-hearted Lennon songs on 'Double Fantasy' were invested with a sense of loss. 'I miss you when you're not here,' he sang on 'Dear Yoko;' 'however distant, don't keep us apart' in 'Woman;' 'why can't we be making love... don't let another day go by' on 'Starting Over.' And then, of course, there was 'I'm Losing You'—in which John placed the loneliness and paranoia of 'Stranger's Room' into context, inspired by his inability to reach Yoko on the phone during his holiday in Bermuda. For once, the song showed him willing to stand his ground, as the music cut close to the savagery of the 10-year-old 'Plastic Ono Band' album: 'I know I hurt you then/But hell that was way back when/Do you still have to carry that cross?'

The inner tension of 'Double Fantasy' suggested that Yoko may have written the album's theme in 'I'm Moving On' back in 1973, with its searing denunciation of Lennon's character: 'You know I'll see you through your jive...You're giving me your window smile...You're getting phony.'

The 'Double Fantasy' songs, then, aren't as one-dimensional as they seem. Their apparent romanticism owes much to the lushness of the production, the care of the arrangements—and the fact that any spark in the original run-throughs was effectively dampened by Lennon's overdubs, as he double-tracked his vocals throughout the album and added unnecessarily soft backing chorales to 'Starting Over' and 'Beautiful Boy.' Elsewhere there were moments of magic, however—the merry-go-round jangle of the chorus of 'Watching The Wheels,' arranged like another 'Plastic Ono Band' out-take; the majesty of the lead vocal on 'Woman;' the warmth of 'Beautiful Boy;' and the snatches of 'found sound' that cropped up across that song, 'I'm Your Angel,' 'Watching The Wheels' and 'Clean-Up Time.'

Overall, though, 'Double Fantasy' is the work of a man feeling his way back into a career—substituting craft and experience where he had once relied upon inspiration. The album began with the tinkle of a wishing bell—a sound that not only mocked the funeral tolls of 'Mother,' but also stood as Lennon's testament of faith in the strength of his relationship, and the return of his creative powers. What makes 'Double Fantasy' finally so affecting is not just hindsight in the wake of tragedy: it's the realisation that in its frailty and occasional lack of direction, it's as authentic a picture of the slightly bewildered Lennon as 'Imagine' had been of an altogether more certain artist nine years earlier.

• • • **NOVEMBER 1980: *RECORDING* home demos of 'Grow Old With Me'/'Gone From This Place'/'Dear John'/'You Saved My Soul.'**

On September 22, John and Yoko signed a one-album deal with Geffen Records. Within days, the couple's first 'comeback' interview was published, in *Newsweek*—the same day that they completed a major interview stint with David Sheff of *Playboy*. A couple of weeks later, they were filmed in Central Park for ABC's *20/20* news show—recordings that cropped up in the promo video for 'Woman,' and were used for the introduction to Yoko's song 'It Happened' early in 1981. In mid-October 'Starting Over' was issued as a single in the States; a week later in Britain too. And a month later, 'Double Fantasy' itself was issued— together with a promo disc that rekindled memories of the 'Wedding Album' by including a short burst of John and Yoko calling out each other's names.

In the midst of this activity and media attention, John began work on his final songs. He and Yoko were already planning their next album, prospective title 'Milk And Honey;' in fact, they told the press in early December that it was almost completed, which certainly wasn't true. And they had already asked their studio band to set aside time in the spring for a major concert tour—a sweep through Japan, Europe and the United States, with at least one American show being satellited live around the rest of the world.

One might have expected, then, that Lennon's final work would reflect his rediscovered superstar status. Instead, this batch of songs, none of which progressed further than home demos, sent out a dubious batch of signals to the troops. 'Grow Old With Me' was, according to Yoko's sleeve-notes on 'Milk And Honey,' written in Bermuda as an answer to her own 'Let Me Count The Ways'—both songs a reference to the couple's apparent obsession with the relationship between the poets Robert Browning and Elizabeth Barrett. Lennon's stately song, based on hymnal piano chords he'd already mined on his demos of 'Memories' and 'Free As A Bird,' certainly began from Browning's poem of the same name, before simplifying the poetic sentiments into one single line: 'God bless our love.'

'Gone From This Place' was equally melodic, though the surviving takes are composing tapes rather than demos. Take one boasted just one line: 'Well I won't be satisfied till I'm gone from this place;' take two embellished it, and hinted at a middle section as well, from which only the ironic whisper 'I don't wanna die' can be distinguished.

Death is also a preoccupation in 'You Saved My Soul,' a remarkably brazen act of self-exposure that surely not even Lennon could have considered for release. Cut with reverbed electric guitar backing, it stars Lennon as a psychological victim, for the last time, indebted to Yoko's strength for pulling him through. The first verse describes how he nearly gave his soul to a TV preacher before Yoko saved him from 'that suicide;' the second takes the metaphor seriously, with its admission that only Yoko's intervention had stopped him from throwing himself out of an apartment window on the West Side of New York—not a million miles from the Dakota, one suspects. In one last irony, John ends this song of spiritual subjection by bursting into a chorus of 'Serve Yourself'— something that 'You Saved My Soul' suggested was still a motion or so away.

It would somehow be fitting if 'Dear John' was actually Lennon's final composition—not just because it deals with his favourite subject, himself, or because like so much of his output in the seventies, it was unfinished.

Its title refers to the letters received by GIs away at the war, from sweethearts who have deserted them at home. Its lyrics, just one repeated verse (apart from a tongue-in-cheek improvisation over the final chords), stand as a more encouraging message than that: 'Don't be hard on yourself, give yourself a break', he sings, before telling himself, 'the race is over, you've won'. Whether the race was to the top of the charts, where 'Double Fantasy' was already headed, or whether it referred to some darker struggle of the soul, we'll never know. Either way, this last piece of self-analysis represented a victory of sorts: at least John didn't attribute all his success at remaining afloat to Yoko.

EARLY DECEMBER 1980: *REMIXING* '*Kiss Kiss Kiss*'/'*Open Your Box*'/ '*Every Man Has A Woman;*' *recording and mixing* '*Walking On Thin Ice*.'

The final week of Lennon's life was as hectic as any seven days from the height of Beatlemania. Day after day he and Yoko submitted themselves to lengthy interrogation from the media: *Rolling Stone*, and several radio stations were all granted lengthy interviews. The couple also posed for several photo sessions with Annie Leibovitz, under commission for *Rolling Stone*—one photo from which, chosen for the front cover of the magazine's tribute issue in early January, showed a naked Lennon curled foetally atop a clothed, distant Ono.

The pose makes uneasy viewing in the wake of Lennon's more self-destructive songs from this period; and in view of the apparent cynicism which led them to be filmed simulating sexual intercourse for a friend's video camera—short clips from which were incorporated into Yoko's videos the following year. If Albert Goldman is to be believed, this session mocked the true state of the Lennons' relationship: even if his speculations were exaggerated, then the *Rolling Stone* shot, with Lennon as child, Ono as his disinterested mother, still seems close to some psychic truth.

In that light, it's appropriate that Lennon's final work in the recording studio saw him planning solo releases by his wife—both a disco-mix promo single which would include club versions of songs from the 'Double Fantasy' set, plus an updated mix of 'Open Your Box' from 1971; and a brilliant new single, 'Walking On Thin Ice'.

Like so many of Yoko's songs, as far back as 'Mrs Lennon' and 'Mind Train', 'Walking On Thin Ice' reeks of impending tragedy—from its title image to the doom-laden fairy-tale she recites in its midst. It was backed as a single by 'It Happened', a song that seemed to be an obvious reference to the murder—until one discovered that Yoko had written and recorded it seven years earlier.

In Lennon's eyes, 'Thin Ice' opened up "a new era of Lennon/Ono music." What's sad is that it's true. For the first time since 'Fly' in 1971, John and Yoko had succeeded in regaining a place in the avant-garde—only this time their experimentation was allied to a precise feel for contemporary tastes, which allowed the record to become Yoko's only hit single in 1981. John's production gave it an eerie, glacial feel; he hammered his electric guitar to echo Yoko's wails of pain with sharp bolts of noise, and gave the track a percussive base that was always shifting under your feet, powered by a riff that suggested that the ice was about to crack.

And so it did, as Lennon fell in the entrance to the Dakota, scattering rough mixes of 'Walking On Thin Ice' on the ground as he sagged under the weight of Mark Chapman's bullets. It was an abrupt, breath-taking ending to a life and a career, neither of which was close to resolution. The timing added to the sense of waste: not just the human loss, of a father, husband and friend, but the awareness that Lennon's future had been precariously in the balance, that 'Walking On Thin Ice' might have heralded an artistic rebirth, or that the tortuous self-analysis of 'You Saved My Soul' might have led Lennon down another dead end. The lack of an orderly climax to the story led many observers to invent one: but the real man was more interesting, and maddening, than that. Rather than succumb to the stereotypes—the saint, the peacenik, the moptop, the victim, the bigot, the aggressor, the junkie—we should celebrate the reality of the work, not as a crusade for world peace or universal harmony, but as one man's struggle to make sense of his life, and the times into which he had been born. In a world where only flux and fate are certain, we can all learn from his battles, his victories, his failures, the delicate balance in his work between life and death.

Appendix 1

I N T E R V I E W S

. . . .

Both as a member of The Beatles and as a solo artist, John Lennon gave literally hundreds of interviews to the media, both the national and local press, specialist music publications, and to television and radio. The Beatles met representatives of regional newspapers throughout their British tours, and also gave scores of interviews to writers in the United States, Australia, Germany and so on. It would be the task of a lifetime (not mine, thank you) to collate and collect them all, and no doubt someone will one day submit a thesis on that very subject. Until then, here is a selective list of major Lennon interviews, broadcast or otherwise, which add flesh to the John and Yoko myth, or to the art and music surveyed in the rest of this book.

• **OCTOBER 27, 1962:** Of all the Beatles interviews issued on record since 1963, this is one of the most fascinating, simply because it is the earliest. It predates the group's national success, coming less than a month after the release of 'Love Me Do'. Taped for hospital radio by Monty Lister in Port Sunlight, it offers no great insight into the group—bar the admission by all four that John Lennon is their leader. But it does capture The Beatles before stardom turned the process of being interviewed into a battle of wits and puns. The interview was included as a flexi-disc in Mark Lewisohn's book, *The Beatles Live!*

• **MARCH 27, 1964:** To mark the publication of Lennon's first book, *In His Own Write*, he appeared on the BBC TV feature programme *Tonight*, reading extracts from the book and being interviewed by Kenneth Allsop. It was on this occasion, as noted elsewhere in this book, that Lennon was asked why he did not turn the verbal imagination obvious in the book to use in his songs—with notable consequences.

• **MARCH 4, 1966:** 'How Does A Beatle Live?' asked Maureen Cleave in an interview published in the *London Evening Standard* on this date–a piece which had far-reaching effects as the source of the infamous 'more popular than Jesus' quote which marred The Beatles' final American tour. In retrospect, however, Cleave's insightful and sympathetic article is more notable for the way in which it pinpoints the hollowness at the heart of Lennon's existence before Yoko–life in the suburbs surrounded by his millionaire playthings, searching for a role and a purpose between Beatles tours.

• **MAY 13, 1968:** In New York to publicise the launch of their Apple company, John Lennon and Paul McCartney came face to face with the cream of the American press. The naïve, simplistic Beatles emerged the losers, having had the gaping holes in their idealistic vision of a 'Western Communism' exposed by the comparatively stringent questioning. Along the way, McCartney exchanged phone numbers with photographer Linda Eastman; John and Paul found the first chink in their joint armour when they disagreed publicly about how Apple would be run; and John announced that he had just begun work on the script for a movie based on his first two books.

• **SEPTEMBER 18, 1968:** As the leaders of the American rock press, *Rolling Stone* magazine had a special relationship with Lennon. His picture, shaven-headed for the *How I Won The War* movie, adorned the front cover of their inaugural issue; and then a year later, Lennon gave his longest and most searching interview to date to Jonathan Cott, a piece which appeared in *Rolling Stone* on November 23, 1968.

Among the subjects under discussion were black power, Jean-Luc Godard, Bob Dylan and Lennon's own creative process. Throughout, Lennon did his best to remain a loyal member of The Beatles, whilst his every statement hinted at his growing distance from his colleagues.

• **APRIL 1, 1969:** Note the date. Among the April fools when John and Yoko were interviewed on the British independent TV channel's discussion show *Today* by boxing commentator Eamonn Andrews, were fellow guests Yehudi Menuhin, Rolf Harris and Jack Benny. Whilst the Lennons expatiated their views on bags, peace and acorns, their fellow guests shuffled their feet in embarrassment, and the audience broke into gentle barracking. For the first time, the Lennons were exposed to the distaste of the British public for their life, their morals and their beliefs.

• **SEPTEMBER 14, 1969:** This is supposedly the date on which John, Yoko and George Harrison were taped in conversation with the Indian mystic Swami Bhaktivedanta–a dialogue published in book form after Lennon's death as *Lennon '69: Search For Liberation*. The conversation is less mystic than mystifying, as Lennon and Harrison seek in vain to understand the complex spiritual beliefs of the Swami, who expounds his own particular interpretation of Krishna consciousness. "We should go to a true master," Lennon notes at one point, "but how are we to tell one from the other?" Another point of interest: on September 14, 1969, the Lennons were actually in Toronto after playing the 'Rock And Roll Revival' show the previous day.

• **DECEMBER 17, 1969:** At the Ontario Science Hall, John and Yoko announced the 'Toronto Peace Festival', a multi-media event to be staged the following summer. They told the Canadian press that they had decided to call 1970 'Year One AP (After Peace)', and promised that their next album would be a record of laughing and whispering. Little came of any of these plans: within weeks, John was writing 'Have We All Forgotten What Vibes Are?', his vitriolic response to the collapse of the Toronto Festival.

• **JANUARY 5, 1970:** Now in Denmark, where they had gone to discuss the Peace Festival and the custody of Yoko's daughter, Kyoko, with her ex-husband Tony Cox, the Lennons held a small-scale press conference to announce that all their future record royalties would be channelled into their peace campaign. Like other contemporary promises, this seems to have been quietly ignored when they made their next record.

• **FEBRUARY 4, 1970:** In a public ceremony at the Black House in London, the Lennons gave their support to the campaign to defend the black rights leader Michael X against murder charges. They swapped a bag containing their hair, which had been cropped short in Denmark, for a pair of blood-stained boxing shorts once worn by Muhammed Ali. The British press chose to ignore the entire episode.

• **SEPTEMBER 22, 1970:** Having completed their programme of Primal Therapy, and with the zeal of the newly converted, the Lennons appeared on *The Dick Cavett Show* in the States with Dr Arthur Janov, to publicise the therapy and its effect.

• **DECEMBER 8, 1970:** The Lennons' lengthy conversation on this date with *Rolling Stone* editor Jann Wenner provided the most momentous interview of John's entire career—spread over two issues of the magazine early in 1971, and subsequently published in book form (without Lennon's permission) as *Lennon Remembers*. Still burning with unleashed emotion after the course of Primal Therapy and the recording of 'John Lennon: Plastic Ono Band', Lennon embarked on a crash course in rewriting Beatles history, lambasting his former colleagues and aides, exposing many long-cherished Beatle myths, and spewing invective in all directions. In its way, this *Rolling Stone* interview is as important a confessional document as the 'Plastic Ono Band' album itself. (It also provided the raw material for National Lampoon's satirical Lennon tribute, *Magical Misery Tour*, which was made up of choice quotes from the interview set to a pastiche of the 'Plastic Ono Band' music.)

• **FEBRUARY 1971:** The British equivalent to the *Lennon Remembers* interview was an equally lengthy conversation between John and Yoko and the political activists Tariq Ali and Robin Blackburn, for the Trotskyist paper *Red Mole*. The political bias of their interlocutors made this less of an interview, more of a dialogue, and Yoko's attempt to shift the focus away from immediate political objectives proved more interesting than Lennon's enthusiastic adoption of left-wing tactics.

• **SEPTEMBER / OCTOBER 1971:** During their research for the book *Apple To The Core*, authors Peter McCabe and Robert D. Schonfeld were granted a series of interviews with the Lennons, newly-ensconced at the St. Regis Hotel in New York. Never intended for separate publication, the tapes were eventually printed in book form as *John Lennon: For The Record* in late 1984. The conversation

was most interesting for its insights into Lennon's difficult relationship with Messrs Harrison and McCartney, and for exposing one of Lennon's periodic, short-lived vendettas against a friend—the unfortunate victim this time being Derek Taylor, former Beatles and Apple press officer.

• **FEBRUARY 14 TO 18, 1972:** As noted elsewhere, the Lennons spent this week co-hosting *The Mike Douglas Show* on American TV. Between musical segments, they engaged in generally fruitless conversation with Douglas and a variety of guests, the most entertaining of whom included activists Bobby Seale and Jerry Rubin, comedian George Carlin, and consumer affairs monitor Ralph Nader.

• **APRIL 16, 1973:** In one of their final interviews together before their 18-month separation, the Lennons spoke to DJ Elliott Mintz about their idealistic hopes for the future. "1973 is our year," John announced. "The whole ball game changes now. Yoko is becoming herself again." Little did he realise that becoming herself would also entail kicking him out.

• **LATE OCTOBER 1973:** Throughout the mid-seventies, Lennon remained on better terms with the British rock paper *Melody Maker* than with any other publication. In early November, they published an interview carried out in Los Angeles by Chris Charlesworth in which Lennon discussed his new 'Mind Games' album, his relationship with the other Beatles and the possibilities of a reunion, and hinted at a few difficulties in his present relationship with Yoko. *Melody Maker* subsequently published informative Lennon interviews, by Ray Coleman and Charlesworth respectively, to mark the release of 'Walls And Bridges' in 1974 and 'Rock 'n' Roll' in 1975.

• **SEPTEMBER 27, 1974:** Listeners to the breakfast show on radio station KHJ in Southern California were on this day treated to a rather manic John Lennon as their guest DJ. Lennon cued up a succession of tracks from his new 'Walls And Bridges' album, took requests for Beatles songs, and engaged in surreal conversations with teenage phone-in callers.

• **SEPTEMBER 28, 1974:** The following day, at the other end of America, a considerably more relaxed Lennon was the guest of Dennis Elsas on the afternoon show at WNEW in New York. This was John's most enjoyable radio appearance, showing him at his most witty and urbane—reading adverts, satirising the weather forecasts, and talking humorously about the prospects for that Beatles reunion and the making of his new album. Lennon also took along some of his favourite singles to play on the air—among them Bobby Parker's 'Watch Your Step' and Derek Martin's 'Daddy Rolling Stone'—and once again previewed the 'Walls And Bridges' album.

• **EARLY OCTOBER 1974:** Back in California the following week, Lennon guested on KSAN-FM in San Francisco with the king of American DJs, the late Tom Donahue. Another warm and witty dialogue ensued, with John comparing the use of tape echo on Carl Perkins' 'Blue Suede Shoes' and Ike And Tina Turner's 'River Deep Mountain High;' admitting how much work he had put into splicing together Harry Nilsson's 'Subterranean Homesick Blues;' and playing obscure oldies like Rosie And The Originals' 'Angel Baby' and The Move's 'Brontosaurus'. Along the way, he gave still more exposure to 'Walls And Bridges', and unveiled 'Too Many Cooks', a track he had produced for Mick Jagger earlier in the year, for its one and only official public airing.

• **FEBRUARY 1975:** A few days after moving back in with Yoko at the Dakota, Lennon gave a major interview to Pete Hamill for *Rolling Stone*—which allowed him to announce the couple's reunion, plug the 'Rock 'n' Roll' album, and update America on the current state of his immigration case.

• **LATE MARCH 1975:** On April 18, 1975, BBC TV broadcast an interview with Lennon carried out by the show's host, Bob Harris, in New York a few weeks earlier. In a country starved of Lennon TV appearances, the show was a godsend—especially as it included the performances of 'Stand By Me' and 'Slippin' And Slidin'' discussed elsewhere in this book. Lennon merely repeated familiar stories about his reunion with Yoko and his problems with Phil Spector during the 'Rock 'n' Roll' sessions, however, and the interview is more interesting for its demonstration of Lennon's good health and humour than anything else.

• **APRIL 28, 1975:** Likewise this live TV interview, carried out by the deadpan Tom Synder for the *Tomorrow* chat show. Synder's prurient, lethargic questioning was constantly outshone by the wit of his guest, who yet managed to remain polite and good-humoured throughout. The couple were joined for the second half of this programme by Lennon's immigration lawyer, Leon Wildes.

• **JANUARY 1, 1976:** Less than three months after the birth of their son, Sean, John and Yoko were interviewed at the Dakota by their friend, Elliott Mintz, for the Earth News service. Most of the conversation revolved around Yoko's difficulties with the birth, and the couple's delight at having finally succeeded in bringing a child to term.

• **OCTOBER 4, 1977:** At the end of several months' vacation in Japan, the Lennons held a press conference in Tokyo, at which they confirmed their plan of remaining out of the public eye until their son was five-years-old. Surprisingly, the event went unremarked in the British press, and this final media contact for almost three years passed almost unnoticed outside Japan.

• **SEPTEMBER 9 TO 28, 1980:** When John and Yoko finally broke media silence during the recording sessions for 'Double Fantasy,' they chose the men's magazine *Playboy* as their vehicle rather than the rock press. Interviewer David Sheff spent three weeks with the Lennons, attending sessions and video shoots as well as sharing time at home in the Dakota. The result was the longest and most detailed conversation since the *Lennon Remembers* encounter of 1970—and in its way every bit as revealing as that epochal confessional. The *Playboy* interview, which appeared in the January 1981 issue of the magazine just days before Lennon's death, and was subsequently printed in book form in a fuller version, captured Lennon the publicity man, selling the story of the miraculous artistic comeback after five years' silence, and presenting the front of a cleansed, refreshed artist and human being. The text represents the strongest case for the defence in the dispute about Lennon's true state of mind in 1980; among many highlights it includes a detailed breakdown of who-wrote-what among the Lennon/McCartney songs.

• **MID-SEPTEMBER 1980:** During the *Playboy* interviews, Lennon also gave time to Barbara Graustark of *Newsweek*, who with their shorter deadlines were able to rush a heavily edited version of the conversation into their September 29 issue. The interview was superseded by the *Playboy* text, even in the longer form published in the book *Strawberry Fields Forever*.

• **DECEMBER 5, 1980:** Jonathan Cott completed a circle by carrying out both the first and last *Rolling Stone* interviews with John Lennon. He found a man of short temper with no time for fools, and the tapes of the conversation display an entirely different persona to the man on the *Playboy* tapes. Not surprisingly, the story Lennon was selling was the same: Cott merely sought to question it more closely than Sheff had done.

• **DECEMBER 6, 1980:** The following day, it was the charming and humorous Lennon who surfaced in a four-hour interview with Andy Peebles of BBC Radio One. Peebles chose to take the Lennons through a survey of their solo career, keeping strictly to his

script and apparently missing many of Lennon's asides. The painstaking questioning did keep the dialogue at a low ebb, but some of John and Yoko's comments on their early artistic collaborations showed that not all of their avant-garde spirit had departed them.

• **DECEMBER 8, 1980:** On the final afternoon of his life, Lennon went through the tale of his artistic rebirth one more time, for RKO Radio. Completing a triptych of personalities in four days, this Lennon sounded as if he was speeding, babbling his way through lengthy avowals of his spiritual faith and his belief in life after death, and impatiently knocking aside most of the interviewer's attempts to interrupt. That conversation and a final photo session for *Rolling Stone* complete, Lennon went downstairs to the Dakota entrance, signed a copy of 'Double Fantasy' for Mark Chapman, and proceeded with Yoko to a mixing session at the Hit Factory Studios downtown.

Appendix 2

L E T T E R S

. . . .

As with the interviews, researching every letter John Lennon ever wrote is a job for a bored academic with endless funds. Various items of family correspondence and replies to letters from fans have been auctioned at rock memorabilia sales in Britain and America over the last decade, but with few exceptions they offer little insight into the man who wrote them.

The same can't be said for the extract from a letter to ex-Beatle Stu Sutcliffe which was reprinted in Hunter Davies' authorised biography, *The Beatles*. Explicit in its language and self-pity, it reveals the empathy the pair of former Liverpool Art College students shared; there's little hint here, as elsewhere in Lennon's early prose, that he has anything to hide from his correspondent.

Throughout the sixties, The Beatles made a point of sending postcards—usually in Lennon's hand—to the editors of the London music papers when the group were on tour. Friendship aside, and there's no doubt that The Beatles did consider some journalists as their friends, the exercise had the effect of making the group seem more approachable and human in the eyes of the public, as the correspondence was guaranteed a prominent position in the next available issue. The postcards that Lennon wrote reveal some of his simple word-play, but nothing that would surprise readers of *In His Own Write*.

It was only in the late sixties and early seventies that Lennon began to use the letter columns of the music press—primarily *Melody Maker* in London and *Rolling Stone* in San Francisco—as a vehicle for his own arguments. His open letter to Paul McCartney, following Paul's interview in *Melody Maker* on November 20, 1971, was a classic of its kind. Lennon's comments had to be censored 'in deference to the laws of libel:' he blasted McCartney for his middle-brow views and lack of political commitment, accused him of doing his best to obstruct a legal settlement of The Beatles' court battle, and ended up advising his former partner to 'Join the Rock Liberation Front before it gets you!'

Lennon employed similar tactics against Todd Rundgren in 1974, again in response to a *Melody Maker* interview. Rundgren had accused Lennon of irrelevance in the modern age; Lennon replied that most of Rundgren's music was heavily influenced by The Beatles, and that Todd was simply miffed because Lennon hadn't recognised him in a Los Angeles club.

Another *Melody Maker* letter from the Lennons, in October 1971, replied to accusations from two readers in the *Mailbag* column that John and Yoko were simply spouting revolutionary rhetoric from the safety of their capitalist enclave, Apple. 'Apple was/is a capitalist concern', Lennon wrote. 'We brought in a capitalist to prevent it sinking...I personally have had enough of Apple/Ascot and all other properties which tie me down, mentally and physically–I intend to cash in my chips as soon as I can–and be FREE.'

Similar defences of their lifestyle and beliefs can be found in the pages of *International Times* and the other British underground press; and in early seventies issues of *Rolling Stone*. But the most valuable source of Lennon correspondence, and the most poignant, was unveiled by Derek Taylor in his limited edition autobiography, *Fifty Years Adrift*. An inveterate keeper of correspondence, cuttings and the trivia which makes up everyday life, Taylor had preserved postcards and letters from Lennon, mostly written from New York between 1973 and 1975. They show little difference between the prose style of the public and private Lennon; the letters are full of word-play, involved puns, private jokes and *non sequiturs*, broken only by the occasional item of news: 'I meself have decided to be or not to be for a coupla years? Boredom set in...how many back beats are there? I ask meself. Am thinking of becoming a magician', Lennon wrote early in 1975.

And later that same year, as the couple awaited the birth of their son, Lennon wrote to Taylor: 'I ain't in a hurry to sign with anyone...or do anything...am enjoying my pregnancy...thinking time...what's it all about time too. I'll outlive the bastards in more ways than one (whatever their age)...My head and body are as clear as a bell...some nice window pane... and some incredibly LEGAL MUSHROOMS.' Writing, at last, for private not public consumption, to a friend who had shared the mayhem and magic of Apple and Beatlemania, Lennon had no need to disguise the truth. Like his home demos, Lennon's personal correspondence cuts through the fog of image and public expectation, and allows us close to the man behind the art.

Appendix 3

D I S C O G R A P H Y

. . . .

Only original UK and US releases are contained in this discography. Reissues, repackaging of previously released material and releases in different formats (e.g. cassettes, CDs) are not included. Also omitted are the many unauthorised albums and singles of interview material which have been issued since 1964.

• THE BEATLES: UK SINGLES

MY BONNIE/THE SAINTS (both sides by Tony Sheridan and The Beatles)
(Polydor NH 66-833) January 1962

LOVE ME DO/P.S. I LOVE YOU
(Parlophone R 4949) October 1962

PLEASE PLEASE ME/ASK ME WHY
(Parlophone R 4983) January 1963

FROM ME TO YOU/THANK YOU GIRL
(Parlophone R 5015) April 1963

SHE LOVES YOU/I'LL GET YOU
(Parlophone R 5055) August 1963

I WANT TO HOLD YOUR HAND/THIS BOY
(Parlophone R 5084) November 1963

SWEET GEORGIA BROWN/NOBODY'S CHILD
(both sides with Tony Sheridan)
(Polydor NH 52-906) January 1964

WHY/CRY FOR A SHADOW (A-side with Tony Sheridan)
(Polydor NH 52-275) February 1964

CAN'T BUY ME LOVE/YOU CAN'T DO THAT
(Parlophone R 5114) March 1964

AIN'T SHE SWEET/IF YOU LOVE ME BABY (B-side with Tony Sheridan)
(Polydor NH 52-317) May 1964

A HARD DAY'S NIGHT/THINGS WE SAID TODAY
(Parlophone R 5160) July 1964

I FEEL FINE/SHE'S A WOMAN
(Parlophone R 5200) November 1964

TICKET TO RIDE/YES IT IS
(Parlophone R 5265) April 1965

HELP!/I'M DOWN
(Parlophone R 5305) July 1965

DAY TRIPPER/WE CAN WORK IT OUT
(Parlophone R 5389) December 1965

PAPERBACK WRITER/RAIN
(Parlophone R 5452) June 1966

YELLOW SUBMARINE/ELEANOR RIGBY
(Parlophone R 5493) August 1966

PENNY LANE/STRAWBERRY FIELDS FOREVER
(Parlophone R 5570) February 1967

ALL YOU NEED IS LOVE/BABY YOU'RE A RICH MAN
(Parlophone R 5620) July 1967

HELLO GOODBYE/I AM THE WALRUS
(Parlophone R 5655) November 1967

LADY MADONNA/THE INNER LIGHT
(Parlophone R5675) March 1968

HEY JUDE/REVOLUTION
(Apple R5722) August 1968

GET BACK/DON'T LET ME DOWN
(Apple R5777) April 1969

THE BALLAD OF JOHN AND YOKO/OLD BROWN SHOE
(Apple R5786) May 1969

SOMETHING/COME TOGETHER
(Apple R5814) October 1969

LET IT BE/YOU KNOW MY NAME (LOOK UP THE NUMBER)
(Apple R5833) March 1970

TWIST AND SHOUT (live)/FALLING IN LOVE AGAIN (live)
(Lingasong NB 1) June 1977

SEARCHIN'/MONEY/TILL THERE WAS YOU
(Audiofidelity AFS 1) October 1982

• **THE BEATLES: UK EPs**

MY BONNIE (with Tony Sheridan)
My Bonnie/Why/Cry For A Shadow/The Saints
(Polydor H 21-610) July 1963

TWIST AND SHOUT
Twist And Shout/A Taste Of Honey/Do You Want To
Know A Secret/There's A Place
(Parlophone GEP 8882) July 1963

THE BEATLES' HITS
From Me To You/Thank You Girl/Please Please Me/
Love Me Do
(Parlophone GEP 8880) September 1963

THE BEATLES NO. 1
I Saw Her Standing There/Misery/Anna/Chains
(Parlophone GEP 8883) November 1963

ALL MY LOVING
All My Loving/Ask Me Why/Money/P.S. I Love You
(Parlophone GEP 8891) February 1964

LONG TALL SALLY
Long Tall Sally/I Call Your Name/Slow Down/
Matchbox
(Parlophone GEP 8913) June 1964

EXCERPTS FROM THE FILM *A HARD DAY'S NIGHT*
I Should Have Known Better/If I Fell/Tell Me Why/
And I Love Her
(Parlophone GEP 8920) November 1964

EXCERPTS FROM THE ALBUM 'A HARD DAY'S NIGHT'
Anytime At All/I'll Cry Instead/Things We Said
Today/When I Get Home
(Parlophone GEP 8924) December 1964

BEATLES FOR SALE (NO. 1)
No Reply/I'm A Loser/Rock And Roll Music/Eight
Days A Week
(Parlophone GEP 8931) April 1965

BEATLES FOR SALE (NO. 2)
I'll Follow The Sun/Baby's In Black/Words Of Love/I
Don't Want To Spoil The Party
(Parlophone GEP 8938) June 1965

THE BEATLES' MILLION SELLERS
She Loves You/I Want To Hold Your Hand/Can't Buy
Me Love/I Feel Fine
(Parlophone GEP 8946) December 1965

YESTERDAY
Yesterday/Act Naturally/You Like Me Too Much/It's
Only Love
(Parlophone GEP 8948) March 1966

NOWHERE MAN
Nowhere Man/Drive My Car/Michelle/You Won't See
Me (Parlophone GEP 8952) July 1966

MAGICAL MYSTERY TOUR (double EP set)
Magical Mystery Tour/Your Mother Should Know/I
Am The Walrus/The Fool On The Hill/Flying/Blue
Jay Way

(Parlophone MMT 1, mono; SMMT 1, stereo)
December 1967

• **THE BEATLES: UK LPs**

PLEASE PLEASE ME
I Saw Her Standing There/Misery/Anna/Chains/
Boys/Ask Me Why/Please Please Me/Love Me Do/P.S.
I Love You/Baby It's You/Do You Want To Know A
Secret/A Taste Of Honey/There's A Place/Twist And
Shout
(Parlophone PMC 1202, mono; PCS 3042, stereo)
March 1963

WITH THE BEATLES
It Won't Be Long/All I've Got To Do/All My Loving/
Don't Bother Me/Little Child/Till There Was You/
Please Mr Postman/Roll Over Beethoven/Hold Me
Tight/You Really Got A Hold On Me/I Wanna Be Your
Man/Devil In Her Heart/Not A Second Time/Money
(Parlophone PMC 1206, mono; PCS 3045, stereo)
November 1963

THE BEATLES' FIRST (with Tony Sheridan)
Ain't She Sweet/Cry For A Shadow/My Bonnie/If You
Love Me Baby/Sweet Georgia Brown/The Saints/
Why/Nobody's Child (plus 4 tracks not by The
Beatles)
(Polydor 236 201) June 1964

A HARD DAY'S NIGHT
A Hard Day's Night/I Should Have Known Better/If I
Fell/I'm Happy Just To Dance With You/And I Love
Her/Tell Me Why/Can't Buy Me Love/Any Time At
All/I'll Cry Instead/Things We Said Today/When I
Get Home/You Can't Do That/I'll Be Back
(Parlophone PMC 1230, mono; PCS 3058, stereo)
July 1964

BEATLES FOR SALE
No Reply/I'm A Loser/Baby's In Black/Rock And Roll
Music/I'll Follow The Sun/Mr Moonlight/Kansas
City; Hey Hey Hey Hey/Eight Days A Week/Words Of
Love/Honey Don't/Every Little Thing/I Don't Want
To Spoil The Party/What You're Doing/Everybody's
Trying To Be My Baby
(Parlophone PMC 1240, mono; PCS 3062, stereo)
December 1964

HELP
Help!/The Night Before/You've Got To Hide Your
Love Away/I Need You/Another Girl/You're Gonna
Lose That Girl/Ticket To Ride/Act Naturally/It's
Only Love/You Like Me Too Much/Tell Me What You
See/Yesterday/Dizzy Miss Lizzy
(Parlophone PMC 1255, mono; PCS 3071, stereo)
August 1965

RUBBER SOUL
Drive My Car/Norwegian Wood/You Won't See Me/
Nowhere Man/Think For Yourself/The Word/
Michelle/What Goes On/Girl/I'm Looking Through
You/In My Life/Wait/If I Needed Someone/Run For
Your Life
(Parlophone PMC 1267, mono; PCS 3075, stereo)
December 1965

REVOLVER
Taxman/Eleanor Rigby/I'm Only Sleeping/Love You
To/Here There And Everywhere/Yellow Submarine/
She Said She Said/Good Day Sunshine/And Your Bird
Can Sing/For No One/Dr Robert/I Want To Tell You/
Got To Get You Into My Life/Tomorrow Never Knows
(Parlophone PMC 7009, mono; PCS 7009, stereo)
August 1966

A COLLECTION OF BEATLES OLDIES
She Loves You/From Me To You/We Can Work It Out/
Help!/Michelle/Yesterday/I Feel Fine/Yellow
Submarine/Can't Buy Me Love/Bad Boy/Day
Tripper/A Hard Day's Night/Ticket To Ride/
Paperback Writer/Eleanor Rigby/I Want To Hold
Your Hand
(Parlophone PMC 7016, mono; PCS 7016, stereo)
December 1966

SGT. PEPPER'S LONELY HEARTS CLUB BAND
Sgt. Pepper's Lonely Hearts Club Band/With A Little
Help From My Friends/Lucy In The Sky With
Diamonds/It's Getting Better/Fixing A Hole/She's

Leaving Home/Being For The Benefit Of Mr Kite/
Within You Without You/When I'm 64/Lovely Rita/
Good Morning Good Morning/Sgt. Pepper's Lonely
Hearts Club Band (reprise)/A Day In The Life
(Parlophone PMC 7027, mono: PCS 7027, stereo)
June 1967

THE BEATLES (double album)
Back In The USSR/Dear Prudence/Glass Onion/Ob-
La-Di, Ob-La-Da/Wild Honey Pie/The Continuing
Story Of Bungalow Bill/While My Guitar Gently
Weeps/Happiness Is A Warm Gun/Martha My Dear/
I'm So Tired/Blackbird/Piggies/Rocky Raccoon/
Don't Pass Me By/Why Don't We Do It In The Road/I
Will/Julia/Birthday/Yer Blues/Mother Nature's Son/
Everybody's Got Something To Hide Except For Me
And My Monkey/Sexy Sadie/Helter Skelter/Long
Long Long/Revolution 1/Honey Pie/Savoy Truffle/
Cry Baby Cry/Revolution 9/Goodnight
(Apple PMC 7067/8, mono; PCS 7067/8, stereo)
November 1968

YELLOW SUBMARINE
Yellow Submarine/Only A Northern Song/All
Together Now/Hey Bulldog/It's All Too Much/All You
Need Is Love (plus six tracks by George Martin and
his Orchestra)
(Apple PMC 7070, mono; PCS 7070, stereo) January
1969

ABBEY ROAD
Come Together/Something/Maxwell's Silver
Hammer/Oh Darling/Octopus's Garden/I Want You
(She's So Heavy)/Here Comes The Sun/Because/You
Never Give Me Your Money/Sun King/Mean Mr
Mustard/Polythene Pam/She Came In Through The
Bathroom Window/Golden Slumbers/Carry That
Weight/The End/Her Majesty
(Apple PCS 7088) September 1969

LET IT BE (boxed set with book)
Two Of Us/Dig A Pony/Across The Universe/I Me
Mine/Dig It/Let It Be/Maggie Mae/I've Got A
Feeling/The One After 909/The Long And Winding
Road/For You Blue/Get Back
(Apple PXS 1) May 1970

THE BEATLES AT THE HOLLYWOOD BOWL
Twist And Shout/She's A Woman/Dizzy Miss Lizzy/
Ticket To Ride/Can't Buy Me Love/Things We Said
Today/Roll Over Beethoven/Boys/A Hard Day's
Night/Help!/All My Loving/She Loves You/Long Tall
Sally
(EMI EMTV 4) May 1977

**LIVE AT THE STAR CLUB, HAMBURG, GERMANY,
1962 (double LP)**
I Saw Her Standing There/Roll Over Beethoven/
Hippy Hippy Shake/Sweet Little Sixteen/Lend Me
Your Comb/Your Feet's Too Big/Twist And Shout/Mr
Moonlight/A Taste Of Honey/Besame Mucho/
Reminiscing/Kansas City/Hey Hey Hey/Nothin'
Shakin'/To Know Her Is To Love Her/Little Queenie/
Falling In Love Again/Ask Me Why/Be-Bop-A-Lula/
Hallelujah I Love Her So/Red Sails In The Sunset/
Everybody's Trying To Be My Baby/Matchbox/I'm
Talkin' 'Bout You/I Wish I Could Shimmy Like My
Sister Kate/Long Tall Sally/I Remember You
(Lingasong LNL 1) May 1977

THE COMPLETE SILVER BEATLES
Three Cool Cats/Crying Waiting Hoping/Besame
Mucho/Searchin'/The Sheik Of Araby/Money/To
Know Her Is To Love Her/Take Good Care Of My
Baby/Memphis Tennessee/Sure To Fall/Till There
Was You/September In The Rain
(Audiofidelity AFELP 1047) September 1982

JOHN LENNON: UK SINGLES

**GIVE PEACE A CHANCE/REMEMBER LOVE (by
The Plastic Ono Band)**
(Apple 13) July 1969

**COLD TURKEY/DON'T WORRY KYOKO
(MUMMY'S ONLY LOOKING FOR HER HAND IN
THE SNOW (by The Plastic Ono Band)**
(Apple 1001) October 1969

INSTANT KARMA!/WHO HAS SEEN THE WIND
(Apple 1003) February 1970

POWER TO THE PEOPLE/OPEN YOUR BOX
(Apple R 5892) March 1971

**HAPPY XMAS (WAR IS OVER)/LISTEN THE SNOW
IS FALLING**
(Apple R 5970) November 1972

MIND GAMES/MEAT CITY
(Apple R 5994) November 1973

**WHATEVER GETS YOU THROUGH THE NIGHT/
BEEF JERKY**
(Apple R 5998) October 1974

NO.9 DREAM/WHAT YOU GOT
(Apple R 6003) January 1975

STAND BY ME/MOVE OVER MS L
(Apple R 6005) April 1975

IMAGINE/WORKING CLASS HERO
(Apple R 6009) October 1975

(JUST LIKE) STARTING OVER/KISS KISS KISS
(Geffen K 79186) October 1980

WOMAN/BEAUTIFUL BOYS
(Geffen K 79195) January 1981

**I SAW HER STANDING THERE/WHATEVER GETS
YOU THROUGH THE NIGHT/LUCY IN THE SKY
WITH DIAMONDS (all with Elton John)**
(DJM DJS 10965) March 1981

WATCHING THE WHEELS/I'M YOUR ANGEL
(Geffen K 79207) March 1981

NOBODY TOLD ME/O SANITY
(Polydor POSP 700) January 1984

BORROWED TIME/YOUR HANDS
(Polydor POSP 701) March 1984

**BORROWED TIME/YOUR HANDS/NEVER SAY
GOODBYE**
(Polydor POSPX 701, 12-inch) March 1984

I'M STEPPING OUT/SLEEPLESS NIGHTS
(Polydor POSP 702) July 1984

**I'M STEPPING OUT/SLEEPLESS NIGHTS/
LONELINESS**
(Polydor POSPX 702, 12-inch) July 1984

**EVERY MAN HAS A WOMAN WHO LOVES HIM/
IT'S ALRIGHT (B-side by Sean Lennon)**
(Polydor POSP 712) November 1984

· JOHN LENNON: UK LPs

**UNFINISHED MUSIC NO. 1: TWO VIRGINS (with
Yoko Ono)** No tracks listed
(Apple APCOR 2, mono: SAPCOR 2, stereo)
November 1968

**UNFINISHED MUSIC NO. 2: LIFE WITH THE
LIONS (with Yoko Ono)**
Cambridge 1969/No Bed For Beatle John/Baby's
Heartbeat/Two Minutes Silence/Radio Play
(Zapple 01) May 1969

WEDDING ALBUM (with Yoko Ono)
John And Yoko/Amsterdam
(Apple SAPCOR 11) November 1969

**LIVE PEACE IN TORONTO 1969 (by The Plastic Ono
Band)**
Blue Suede Shoes/Money/Dizzy Miss Lizzy/Yer
Blues/Cold Turkey/Give Peace A Chance/Don't
Worry Kyoko (Mummy's Only Looking For Her Hand
In The Snow)/John John (Let's Hope For Peace)
(Apple CORE 2001) December 1969

JOHN LENNON: PLASTIC ONO BAND
Mother/Hold On/I Found Out/Working Class Hero/
Isolation/Remember/Love/Well Well Well/Look At
Me/God/My Mummy's Dead
(Apple PCS 7124) December 1970

IMAGINE
Imagine/Crippled Inside/Jealous Guy/It's So Hard/I
Don't Want To Be A Soldier, Mama, I Don't Want To
Die/Gimme Some Truth/Oh My Love/How Do You
Sleep/How/Oh Yoko
(Apple SAPCOR 10004) October 1971

**SOME TIME IN NEW YORK CITY (double album,
with Yoko Ono)**

Woman Is The Nigger Of The World/Sisters O
Sisters/Attica State/Born In A Prison/New York
City/Sunday Bloody Sunday/Luck Of The Irish/John
Sinclair/Angela/We're All Water/Cold Turkey/Don't
Worry Kyoko/Well (Baby Please Don't Go)/Jamrag/
Scumbag/Au
(Apple PCSP 716) September 1972
MIND GAMES
Mind Games/Tight A$/Aisumasen/One Day At A
Time/Bring On The Lucie/Nutopian International
Anthem/Intuition/Out The Blue/Only People/I Know
(I Know)/You Are Here/Meat City
(Apple PCS 7165) November 1973
WALLS AND BRIDGES
Going Down On Love/Whatever Gets You Through
The Night/Old Dirt Road/What You Got/Bless You/
Scared/No. 9 Dream/Surprise Surprise/Steel And
Glass/Beef Jerky/Nobody Loves You When You're
Down And Out/Ya Ya
(Apple PCTC 254) October 1974
ROCK 'N' ROLL
Be-Bop-A-Lula/Stand By Me/Rip It Up/Ready Teddy/
You Can't Catch Me/Ain't That A Shame/Do You
Wanna Dance/Sweet Little Sixteen/Slippin' And
Slidin'/Peggy Sue/Bring It On Home To Me/Send Me
Some Lovin'/Bony Moronie/Ya Ya/Just Because
(Apple PCS 7169) February 1975
SHAVED FISH
Give Peace A Chance/Cold Turkey/Instant Karma!/
Power To The People/Mother/Woman Is The Nigger
Of The World/Imagine/Whatever Gets You Through
The Night/Mind Games/No.9 Dream/Happy Xmas
(War Is Over)/Give Peace A Chance (live)
(Apple PCS 7173) October 1975
DOUBLE FANTASY (with Yoko Ono)
(Just Like) Starting Over/Kiss Kiss Kiss/Clean-Up
Time/Give Me Something/I'm Losing You/I'm
Moving On/Beautiful Boy (Darling Boy)/Watching
The Wheels/I'm Your Angel/Woman/Beautiful Boys/
Dear Yoko/Every Man Has A Woman Who Loves
Him/Hard Times Are Over
(Geffen K 99131) November 1980
**HEART PLAY (AN UNFINISHED DIALOGUE) (with
Yoko Ono)**
Interview material
(Polydor 817 238-1) December 1983
MILK AND HONEY: A HEART PLAY (with Yoko Ono)
I'm Stepping Out/Sleepless Night/Don't Wanna Face
It/Don't Be Scared/Nobody Told Me/O Sanity/
Borrowed Time/Your Hands/Forgive Me, My Little
Flower Princess/Let Me Count The Ways/Grow Old
With Me/You're The One
(Polydor POLH 5) January 1984
LIVE IN NEW YORK CITY
New York City/It's So Hard/Woman Is The Nigger Of
The World/Well, Well, Well/Instant Karma/Mother/
Come Together/Imagine/Cold Turkey/Hound Dog/
Give Peace A Chance
(Polydor PCS 7301) February 1986
MENLOVE AVENUE
Here We Go Again/Rock And Roll People/Angel
Baby/My Baby Left Me/To Know Her Is To Love Her/
Steel And Glass/Scared/Old Dirt Road/Nobody Loves
You When You're Down And Out/Bless You
(Polydor PCS 7308) October 1986

• **RELATED UK RELEASES:**

**BAD TO ME/I CALL YOUR NAME by Billy J. Kramer
with The Dakotas**
Both sides written by Lennon.
(Parlophone R 5049) July 1963
HELLO LITTLE GIRL by The Fourmost
A-side written by Lennon.
(Parlophone R 5056) August 1963
I'M IN LOVE by The Fourmost
A-side written by Lennon.
(Parlophone R 5078) November 1963
**YOU'VE GOT TO HIDE YOUR LOVE AWAY by The
Silkie**

A-side written and produced by Lennon and
McCartney.
(Fontana TF 1525) September 1965
WE LOVE YOU by The Rolling Stones
A-side featuring Lennon's backing vocals.
(Decca F 12654) August 1967
**HOW I WON THE WAR by Musketeer Gripweed And
The Third Troop**
A-side featuring vocal contribution by Lennon.
(United Artists UP 1196) October 1967
DEAR DELILAH by Grapefruit
A-side produced by Lennon and McCartney with
Terry Melcher.
(RCA 1615) January 1968
YOKO ONO: PLASTIC ONO BAND by Yoko Ono
Album produced by Lennon, who also plays guitar
throughout. Why/Why Not/Greenfield Morning I
Pushed An Empty Baby Carriage All Over The City/
Aos/Touch Me/Paper Shoes
(Apple SAPCOR 17) December 1970
**GOD SAVE US/DO THE OZ by Bill Elliott And The
Elastic Oz Band**
Both sides produced and written by Lennon, who
also sings lead on the B-side.
(Apple 36) July 1971
**MRS LENNON/MIDSUMMER NEW YORK by Yoko
Ono**
Both sides produced by Lennon.
(Apple 38) October 1971
FLY (double album) by Yoko Ono
Album produced by Lennon, who also plays guitar on
some tracks. Midsummer New York/Mind Train/
Mind Holes/Don't Worry Kyoko/Mrs Lennon/
Hirake/Toilet Piece/O Wind/Airmale/Don't Count
The Waves/You/Fly/Telephone Piece
(Apple SAPTU 101/2) December 1971
**MIND TRAIN/LISTEN THE SNOW IS FALLING by
Yoko Ono**
Both sides produced by Lennon.
(Apple 41) January 1972
ELEPHANT'S MEMORY by Elephant's Memory
Album produced by Lennon, who also appears on
several tracks. Liberation Special/Baddest Of The
Mean/Cryin' Blacksheep Blues/Chuck And Bo/
Gypsy Wolf/Madness/Life/Wind Ridge/Power
Boogie/Local Plastic Ono Band
(Apple SAPCOR 22) November 1972
**POWER BOOGIE/LIBERATION SPECIAL by
Elephant's Memory**
Both sides produced by Lennon.
(Apple 45) December 1972
**APPROXIMATELY INFINITE UNIVERSE by Yoko
Ono**
Album produced by Lennon, who also appears on two
tracks. Yang Yang/Death Of Samantha/I Want My
Love To Rest Tonight/What Did I Do/Have You Seen A
Horizon Lately/Approximately Infinite Universe/
Peter The Dealer/Song For John/Catman/What A
Bastard The World Is/Waiting For The Sunrise/I Felt
Like Smashing My Face In A Clear Glass Window/
Winter Song/Kite Song/What A Mess/Shirankatta/
Air Talk/I Have A Woman Inside My Soul/Move On
Fast/Now Or Never/Is Winter Here To Stay/Looking
Over From My Hotel Window
(Apple SAPDO 1001) February 1973
DEATH OF SAMANTHA/YANG YANG by Yoko Ono
Both sides produced by Lennon.
(Apple 47) May 1973
RINGO by Ringo Starr
Lennon wrote and appears on one track, I'm The
Greatest.
(Apple PCTC 252) November 1973
FEELING THE SPACE by Yoko Ono
Lennon appears on three tracks, She Hits Back,
Woman Power, Men Men Men.
(Apple SAPCOR 26) November 1973
MEN MEN MEN by Yoko Ono
B-side features Lennon.

(Apple 48) December 1973
PUSSY CATS by Harry Nilsson
Lennon produced the album, and co-wrote Mucho
Mungo; Mt. Elba. Many Rivers To Cross/
Subterranean Homesick Blues/Don't Forget Me/All
My Life/Old Forgotten Soldier/Save The Last Dance
For Me/Mucho Mungo; Mt. Elba/Loop De Loop/Black
Sails/Rock Around The Clock
(RCA APL 1-0570) August 1974

**MANY RIVERS TO CROSS/DON'T FORGET ME by
Harry Nilsson**
Both sides produced by Lennon.
(RCA 2459) September 1974

ONLY YOU by Ringo Starr
A-side features Lennon.
(Apple R 6000) November 1974

GOODNIGHT VIENNA by Ringo Starr
Album features title track composed by Lennon, who
also appears on Only You.
(Apple PCS 7168) November 1974

**LUCY IN THE SKY WITH DIAMONDS/ONE DAY AT
A TIME by Elton John**
Both sides written by Lennon, who also appears on
both tracks.
(DJM DJS 340) November 1974

**SAVE THE LAST DANCE FOR ME/ALL MY LIFE by
Harry Nilsson**
Both sides produced by Lennon.
(RCA 2504) January 1975

JOHN DAWSON WINTER III by Johnny Winter
Lennon wrote Rock And Roll People.
(Blue Sky 80586) February 1975

I SAW HER STANDING THERE by Elton John Band
B-side features Lennon on vocal and guitar.
(DJM DJS 354) February 1975

YOUNG AMERICANS by David Bowie
Lennon appears on two tracks, Across The Universe
and Fame, both of which he either wrote or co-wrote.
(RCA RS 1006) March 1975

FAME by David Bowie
Lennon co-wrote and appears on A-side.
(RCA 2579) July 1975

RINGO'S ROTOGRAVURE by Ringo Starr
Lennon wrote and appears on Cookin'.
(Polydor 2382 040) September 1976

WALKING ON THIN ICE by Yoko Ono
·Lennon produced and appeared on both sides.
(Geffen K 79202) February 1981

IT'S ALRIGHT by Yoko Ono
Never Say Goodbye includes recording of Lennon's
voice.
(Polydor POLD 5073) December 1982

• **THE BEATLES: US SINGLES**

MY BONNIE/THE SAINTS (with Tony Sheridan)
(Decca 31382) April 1962

PLEASE PLEASE ME/ASK ME WHY
(Vee Jay VJ 498) February 1963

FROM ME TO YOU/THANK YOU GIRL
(Vee Jay VJ 522) May 1963

SHE LOVES YOU/I'LL GET YOU
(Swan 4152) September 1963

**I WANT TO HOLD YOUR HAND/I SAW HER
STANDING THERE**
(Capitol 5112) January 1964

MY BONNIE/THE SAINTS (with Tony Sheridan)
(MGM K 13213) January 1964

PLEASE PLEASE ME/FROM ME TO YOU
(Vee Jay VJ 581) January 1964

TWIST AND SHOUT/THERE'S A PLACE
(Tollie 9001) March 1964

CAN'T BUY ME LOVE/YOU CAN'T DO THAT
(Capitol 5150) March 1964

**DO YOU WANT TO KNOW A SECRET/THANK YOU
GIRL**
(Vee Jay VJ 587) March 1964

**WHY/CRY FOR A SHADOW (A-side with Tony
Sheridan)**
(MGM K 13227) March 1964

LOVE ME DO/P.S. I LOVE YOU
(Tollie 9008) April 1964

SIE LIEBT DICH/I'LL GET YOU
(Swan 4182) May 1964

**SWEET GEORGIA BROWN/IF YOU LOVE ME BABY
(with Tony Sheridan)**
(Atco 6302) June 1964

**AIN'T SHE SWEET/NOBODY'S CHILD (B-side with
Tony Sheridan)**
(Atco 6308) July 1964

**A HARD DAY'S NIGHT/I SHOULD HAVE KNOWN
BETTER**
(Capitol 5222) July 1964

**I'LL CRY INSTEAD/I'M HAPPY JUST TO DANCE
WITH YOU**
(Capitol 5234) July 1964

AND I LOVE HER/IF I FELL
(Capitol 5235) July 1964

SLOW DOWN/MATCHBOX
(Capitol 5255) August 1964

I FEEL FINE/SHE'S A WOMAN
(Capitol 5327) November 1964

**EIGHT DAYS A WEEK/I DON'T WANT TO SPOIL
THE PARTY**
(Capitol 5371) February 1965

TICKET TO RIDE/YES IT IS
(Capitol 5407) April 1965

HELP!/I'M DOWN
(Capitol 5476) July 1965

YESTERDAY/ACT NATURALLY
(Capitol 5498) September 1965

DAY TRIPPER/WE CAN WORK IT OUT
(Capitol 5555) December 1965

NOWHERE MAN/WHAT GOES ON
(Capitol 5587) February 1966

PAPERBACK WRITER/RAIN
(Capitol 5651) May 1966

YELLOW SUBMARINE/ELEANOR RIGBY
(Capitol 5715) August 1966

PENNY LANE/STRAWBERRY FIELDS FOREVER
(Capitol 5810) February 1967

**ALL YOU NEED IS LOVE/BABY YOU'RE A RICH
MAN**
(Capitol 5964) July 1967

HELLO GOODBYE/I AM THE WALRUS
(Capitol 2056) November 1967

LADY MADONNA/THE INNER LIGHT
(Capitol 2138) March 1968

HEY JUDE/REVOLUTION
(Apple 2276) August 1968

GET BACK/DON'T LET ME DOWN
(Apple 2490) May 1969

**THE BALLAD OF JOHN AND YOKO/OLD BROWN
SHOE**
(Apple 2531) June 1969

SOMETHING/COME TOGETHER
(Apple 2654) October 1969

**LET IT BE/YOU KNOW MY NAME (LOOK UP THE
NUMBER)**
(Apple 2764) March 1970

THE LONG AND WINDING ROAD/FOR YOU BLUE
(Apple 2832) May 1970

• **THE BEATLES: US EPs**

THE BEATLES
Misery/Ask Me Why/A Taste Of Honey/Anna

(Vee Jay VJEP 1-903) March 1964

FOUR BY THE BEATLES
Roll Over Beethoven/All My Loving/This Boy/Please
Mr Postman
(Capitol EAP 2121) May 1964

FOUR BY THE BEATLES Honey Don't/I'm A Loser/
Mr Moonlight/Everybody's Trying To Be My Baby
(Capitol R 5365) February 1965

• **THE BEATLES: US LPs**

INTRODUCING THE BEATLES
I Saw Her Standing There/Misery/Anna/Chains/
Boys/Love Me Do/P.S. I Love You/Baby It's You/Do
You Want To Know A Secret/A Taste Of Honey/
There's A Place/Twist And Shout
(Vee Jay VJLP 1062) July 1963

MEET THE BEATLES
I Want To Hold Your Hand/I Saw Her Standing
There/This Boy/It Won't Be Long/All I've Got To Do/
All My Loving/Don't Bother Me/Little Child/Till
There Was You/Hold Me Tight/I Wanna Be Your Man/
Not A Second Time
(Capitol T 2047, mono; ST 2047, stereo) January
1964

INTRODUCING THE BEATLES
Reissue of earlier album of same title, with Ask Me
Why and Please Please Me replacing Love Me Do and
P.S. I Love You
(Vee Jay VJLP 1062) January 1964

**THE BEATLES WITH TONY SHERIDAN AND
THEIR GUESTS**
My Bonnie/Cry For A Shadow/The Saints/Why (plus
eight tracks not by The Beatles)
(MGM SE 4215) February 1964

**JOLLY WHAT! THE BEATLES AND FRANK
IFIELD ON STAGE**
Please Please Me/From Me To You/Ask Me Why/
Thank You Girl (plus eight tracks by Frank Ifield)
(Vee Jay VJLP 1085) February 1964

THE BEATLES' SECOND ALBUM
Roll Over Beethoven/Thank You Girl/You Really Got
A Hold On Me/Devil In Her Heart/Money/You Can't
Do That/Long Tall Sally/I Call Your Name/Please Mr
Postman/I'll Get You/She Loves You
(Capitol T 2080, mono; ST 2080, stereo) April 1964

A HARD DAY'S NIGHT
A Hard Day's Night/Tell Me Why/I'll Cry Instead/I'm
Happy Just To Dance With You/I Should Have Known
Better/If I Fell/And I Love Her/Can't Buy Me Love
(plus four tracks by George Martin and his
Orchestra)
(United Artists UAS 6366) June 1964

SOMETHING NEW
I'll Cry Instead/Things We Said Today/Anytime At
All/When I Get Home/Slow Down/Matchbox/Tell Me
Why/And I Love Her/I'm Happy Just To Dance With
You/If I Fell/Komm Gib Mir Deine Hand
(Capitol T 2108. mono; ST 2108, stereo) July 1964

**THE BEATLES VS. THE FOUR SEASONS (double
album)**
Contains one album with same tracks as the second
issue of INTRODUCING THE BEATLES, plus one
album by The Four Seasons
(Vee Jay VJDX 30) October 1964

AIN'T SHE SWEET
Ain't She Sweet/Sweet Georgia Brown/Take Out
Some Insurance On Me Baby/Nobody's Child (plus
eight tracks by The Swallows)
(Atco SD 33-169) October 1964

**SONGS, PICTURES AND STORIES OF THE
FABULOUS BEATLES**
Same tracks as second issue of INTRODUCING THE
BEATLES (Vee Jay VJLP 1092) October 1964

**THE BEATLES' STORY (double album;
documentary)**
On Stage With The Beatles/How Beatlemania
Began/Beatlemania In Action/Man Behind The
Beatles: Brian Epstein/John Lennon/Who's A
Millionaire?/Beatles Will Be Beatles/Man Behind

The Music: George Martin/George Harrison/A Hard
Day's Night–Their First Movie/Paul McCartney/
Sneaky Haircuts And More About Paul/Twist And
Shout (live)/The Beatles Look At Life/Victims Of
Beatlemania/Beatle Medley/Ringo Starr/Liverpool
And All The World!
(Capitol STBO 2222) November 1964

BEATLES '65
No Reply/I'm A Loser/Baby's In Black/Rock And Roll
Music/I'll Follow The Sun/Mr Moonlight/Honey
Don't/I'll Be Back/She's A Woman/I Feel Fine/
Everybody's Trying To Be My Baby
(Capitol T 2228, mono; ST 2228, stereo) December
1964

THE EARLY BEATLES
Love Me Do/Twist And Shout/Anna/Chains/Boys/
Ask Me Why/Please Please Me/P.S. I Love You/Baby
It's You/A Taste Of Honey/Do You Want To Know A
Secret
(Capitol T 2309, mono; ST 2309, stereo) March 1965

BEATLES VI
Kansas City; Hey Hey Hey Hey/Eight Days A Week/
You Like Me Too Much/Bad Boy/I Don't Want To Spoil
The Party/Words Of Love/What You're Doing/Yes It
Is/Dizzy Miss Lizzy/Tell Me What You See/Every
Little Thing
(Capitol T 2358, mono; ST 2358, stereo) June 1965

HELP!
Help!/The Night Before/You've Got To Hide Your
Love Away/I Need You/Another Girl/Ticket To Ride/
You're Gonna Lose That Girl (plus six tracks of
incidental music)
(Capitol MAS 2386, mono; SMAS 2386, stereo)
August 1965

RUBBER SOUL
I've Just Seen A Face/Norwegian Wood/You Won't
See Me/Think For Yourself/The Word/Michelle/It's
Only Love/Girl/I'm Looking Through You/In My
Life/Wait/Run For Your Life
(Capitol T 2442, mono; ST 2442, stereo) December
1965

YESTERDAY AND TODAY
Drive My Car/I'm Only Sleeping/Nowhere Man/Dr
Robert/Yesterday/Act Naturally/And Your Bird Can
Sing/If I Needed Someone/We Can Work It Out/What
Goes On/Day Tripper
(Capitol T 2553, mono; ST 2553, stereo) June 1966

REVOLVER
Taxman/Eleanor Rigby/Love You To/Here, There
And Everywhere/Yellow Submarine/She Said She
Said/Good Day Sunshine/For No One/I Want To Tell
You/Got To Get You Into My Life/Tomorrow Never
Knows
(Capitol T 2576, mono; ST 2576, stereo) August 1966

THIS IS WHERE IT STARTED
My Bonnie/Cry For A Shadow/The Saints/Why (plus
six tracks not by The Beatles)
(Metro MS 563) August 1966

**THE AMAZING BEATLES AND OTHER GREAT
ENGLISH GROUP SOUNDS**
Ain't She Sweet/Take Out Some Insurance On Me
Baby/Nobody's Child/Sweet Georgia Brown (plus six
tracks not by The Beatles)
(Clarion 601) October 1966

SGT. PEPPER'S LONELY HEARTS CLUB BAND
Same tracks as UK release
(Capitol MAS 2653, mono; SMAS 2653, stereo) June
1967

MAGICAL MYSTERY TOUR
Magical Mystery Tour/The Fool On The Hill/Flying/
Blue Jay Way/Your Mother Should Know/I Am The
Walrus/Hello Goodbye/Strawberry Fields Forever/
Penny Lane/Baby You're A Rich Man/All You Need Is
Love
(Capitol MAL 2835, mono; SMAL 2835, stereo)
November 1967

THE BEATLES
Same tracks as UK release
(Apple SWBO 101) November 1968

YELLOW SUBMARINE

Same tracks as UK release
(Apple SW 153) January 1969

ABBEY ROAD
Same tracks as UK release
(Apple SO 383) October 1969

HEY JUDE (also pressed as THE BEATLES AGAIN)
Can't Buy Me Love/I Should Have Known Better/
Paperback Writer/Rain/Lady Madonna/Revolution/
Hey Jude/Old Brown Shoe/Don't Let Me Down/The
Ballad Of John And Yoko
(Apple SW 385) February 1970

IN THE BEGINNING–CIRCA 1960
Same tracks as UK THE BEATLES' FIRST album
(Polydor 24-4504) May 1970

LET IT BE
Same tracks as UK release
(Apple AR 34001) May 1970

THE BEATLES AT THE HOLLYWOOD BOWL
Same tracks as UK release
(Capitol SMAS 11638) May 1977

**THE BEATLES LIVE AT THE STAR CLUB,
HAMBURG, GERMANY, 1962 (double album)**
I'm Gonna Sit Right Down And Cry/Roll Over
Beethoven/Hippy Hippy Shake/Sweet Little Sixteen/
Lend Me Your Comb/Your Feet's Too Big/Where Have
You Been All My Life/Mr Moonlight/A Taste Of
Honey/Besame Mucho/Till There Was You/Kansas
City; Hey Hey Hey Hey/Nothin' Shakin'/To Know Her
Is To Love Her/Little Queenie/Falling In Love Again/
Sheila/Be-Bop-A-Lula/Hallelujah I Love Her So/Red
Sails In The Sunset/Everybody's Trying To Be My
Baby/ Matchbox/I'm Talking About You/Shimmy
Shake/Long Tall Sally/ I Remember You
(Lingasong LS2 7001) June 1977

THE COMPLETE SILVER BEATLES
Same tracks as UK release
(Audio Rarities AR 2452) September 1982

THE SILVER BEATLES VOL. 1
Three Cool Cats (extended)/Memphis Tennessee
(extended)/Besame Mucho/The Sheik Of Araby/Till
There Was You/Searching (extended)/Sure To Fall
(extended) (extended tracks were edited versions of
originals)
(Phoenix-10 PHX 352) September 1982

THE SILVER BEATLES VOL. 2
Searching (extended)/Take Good Care Of My Baby
(extended)/Money (extended)/To Know Her Is To
Love Her/Three Cool Cats (extended)/September In
The Rain (extended)/Crying, Waiting, Hoping
(extended tracks were edited versions of originals)
(Phoenix-10 PHX 353) September 1982

- **MISCELLANEOUS BEATLES
RECORDINGS**

MY BONNIE/THE SAINTS
Germany only; Beatles' first appearance on record,
with Tony Sheridan
(Polydor 24 673) June 1961

THE BEATLES' CHRISTMAS RECORD UK; Fan
Club flexi-disc December 1963

KOMM GIB MIR DEINE HAND/SIE LIEBT DICH
Germany only; German-language versions of I Want
To Hold Your Hand and She Loves You (Odeon 22671)
March 1964

ANOTHER BEATLES CHRISTMAS RECORD
UK; Fan Club flexi-disc December 1964

THE BEATLES' THIRD CHRISTMAS RECORD
UK; Fan Club flexi-disc December 1965

THE BEATLES' FOURTH CHRISTMAS RECORD
UK; Fan Club flexi-disc December 1966

CHRISTMAS TIME IS HERE AGAIN!
UK; Fan Club flexi-disc December 1967

THE BEATLES 1968 CHRISTMAS RECORD
UK; Fan Club flexi-disc December 1968

**NO ONE'S GONNA CHANGE OUR WORLD (various
artists LP)**
UK; includes original version of Across The

Universe
(Regal Starline SRS 5013) December 1969

THE BEATLES SEVENTH CHRISTMAS RECORD
UK; Fan Club flexi-disc December 1969

FROM THEM TO US
UK LP; Fan Club record including previous
Christmas flexi material (Apple LYN 2154)
December 1970

THE BEATLES' CHRISTMAS RECORD
US LP; Fan Club record including previous
Christmas flexi material (Apple SBC 100) December
1970

- **SESSIONS** Come And Get It/Leave My Kitten
Alone/Not Guilty/I'm Looking Through You/What's
The New Mary Jane/How Do You Do It/Besame
Mucho/The One After 909/If You've Got Trouble /
That Means A Lot/While My Guitar Gently Weeps/
Mailman Bring Me No More Blues/Christmas Time
Is Here Again
Slated for release early in 1985, this album of
unissued and alternate Beatles tracks was
withdrawn at the request of Apple and the group.
Also postponed was a single, which would have
coupled Leave My Kitten Alone with an alternate
take of Ob-La-Di, Ob-La-Da.

- **JOHN LENNON: US SINGLES**

**GIVE PEACE A CHANCE/REMEMBER LOVE (by
the Plastic Ono Band)**
(Apple 1809) July 1969

**COLD TURKEY/DON'T WORRY KYOKO
(MUMMY'S ONLY LOOKING FOR HER HAND IN
THE SNOW) (by The Plastic Ono Band)**
(Apple 1813) October 1969

**INSTANT KARMA!/WHO HAS SEEN THE WIND
(with Yoko Ono)**
(Apple 1818) February 1970

MOTHER/WHY (B-side by Yoko Ono)
(Apple 1827) December 1970

**POWER TO THE PEOPLE/TOUCH ME (B-side by
Yoko Ono)**
(Apple 1830) March 1971

IMAGINE/IT'S SO HARD
(Apple 1840) October 1971

**HAPPY XMAS (WAR IS OVER)/LISTEN THE SNOW
IS FALLING (with Yoko Ono)**
(Apple 1842) December 1971

**WOMAN IS THE NIGGER OF THE WORLD/
SISTERS O SISTERS (with Yoko Ono)**
(Apple 1848) April 1972

MIND GAMES/MEAT CITY
(Apple 1868) October 1973

**WHATEVER GETS YOU THROUGH THE NIGHT/
BEEF JERKY**
(Apple 1874) September 1974

NO. 9 DREAM/WHAT YOU GOT
(Apple 1878) December 1974

STAND BY ME/MOVE OVER MS L
(Apple 1881) March 1975

SLIPPIN' AND SLIDIN'/AIN'T THAT A SHAME
(Apple 1883, release cancelled) June 1975

(JUST LIKE) STARTING OVER/KISS KISS KISS
(Geffen GEF 49604) October 1980

WOMAN/BEAUTIFUL BOYS
(Geffen GEF 49644) January 1981

WATCHING THE WHEELS/I'M YOUR ANGEL
(Geffen GEF 49695) March 1981

NOBODY TOLD ME/O SANITY
(Polydor 817 254-7) January 1984

I'M SETTING OUT/SLEEPLESS NIGHT
(Polydor 821 107-7) March 1984

BORROWED TIME/YOUR HANDS
(Polydor 821 204-7) May 1984

EVERY MAN HAS A WOMAN WHO LOVES HIM/

IT'S ALRIGHT (B-side by Sean Lennon)
(Polydor 881 378-7) October 1984

· JOHN LENNON: US LPs

UNFINISHED MUSIC NO. 1: TWO VIRGINS (with Yoko Ono)
Same tracks as UK album, but retitled Two Virgins Nos. 1 to 10. Together/Hushabye Hushabye
(Apple T 5001) November 1968

UNFINISHED MUSIC NO. 2: LIFE WITH THE LIONS (with Yoko Ono)
Same tracks as UK release
(Apple ST 3357) May 1969

WEDDING ALBUM (with Yoko Ono)
Same tracks as UK release
(Apple SMAX 3361) October 1969

LIVE PEACE IN TORONTO 1969 (with the Plastic Ono Band)
Same tracks as UK release
(Apple SW 3362) December 1969

JOHN LENNON: PLASTIC ONO BAND
Same tracks as UK release
December 1970 (Apple SW 3372)

IMAGINE
Same tracks as UK release
(Apple SW 3379) September 1971

SOME TIME IN NEW YORK CITY (double album, with Yoko Ono)
Same tracks as UK release
(Apple SVBB 3392) June 1972

MIND GAMES
Same tracks as UK release
(Apple SW 3414) November 1973

WALLS AND BRIDGES
Same tracks as UK release
(Apple SW 3416) September 1974

ROOTS
Be-Bop-A-Lula/Ain't That A Shame/Stand By Me/
Sweet Little Sixteen/Rip It Up/Ready Teddy/Angel
Baby/Do You Want To Dance/You Can't Catch Me/
Bony Maronie/Peggy Sue/Bring It On Home To Me/
Send Me Some Lovin'/Slippin' And Slidin'/Be My
Baby/Ya Ya/Just Because
(Adam VIII A 8018, release withdrawn) January 1975

ROCK 'N' ROLL
Same tracks as UK release
(Apple SK 3419) February 1975

SHAVED FISH
Same tracks as UK release
(Apple SW 3421) October 1975

DOUBLE FANTASY (with Yoko Ono)
Same tracks as UK release
(Geffen GHS 2001) November 1980

HEARTPLAY (AN UNFINISHED DIALOGUE) (with Yoko Ono)
Same material as UK release
(Polydor 817 238-1) December 1983

MILK AND HONEY: A HEART PLAY (with Yoko Ono)
Same tracks as UK release
(Polydor 817-160-1 Y-1) January 1984

LIVE IN NEW YORK CITY
Same tracks as UK release
(Capitol 746196-1) February 1986

MENLOVE AVENUE
Same tracks as UK release
(Capitol 746576-1) October 1986

· RELATED US RELEASES:

BAD TO ME/I CALL YOUR NAME by Billy J. Kramer with The Dakotas
Both sides composed by Lennon.
(Liberty 55626) September 1963

HELLO LITTLE GIRL by The Fourmost
A-side written by Lennon.
(Atco 6280) November 1963

I'M IN LOVE by The Fourmost
A-side written by Lennon.
(Atco 6285) February 1964

YOU'VE GOT TO HIDE YOUR LOVE AWAY by The Silkie
A-side written and produced by Lennon and McCartney.
(Fontana 1525) September 1965

WE LOVE YOU by The Rolling Stones
A-side features Lennon's backing vocals.
(London 905) August 1967

YOKO ONO: PLASTIC ONO BAND by Yoko Ono
Album produced by Lennon, who also plays guitar throughout. Same tracks as UK release.
(Apple SW 3373) December 1970

GOD SAVE US/DO THE OZ by Bill Elliott And The Elastic Oz Band
Both sides written and produced by Lennon, who also sings lead on the B-side.
(Apple 1835) July 1971

FLY by Yoko Ono
Album produced by Lennon, who also appears on several tracks. Same tracks as UK release.
(Apple SVBB 3380) September 1971

MRS LENNON/MIDSUMMER NEW YORK by Yoko Ono
Both sides produced by Lennon.
(Apple 1839) September 1971

THE POPE SMOKES DOPE by David Peel and The Lower East Side
Album produced by Lennon, who also appears on several tracks. I'm A Runaway/Everybody's Smoking Marijuana/F Is Not A Dirty Word/The Hippie From New York City/McDonald's Farm/The Ballad Of New York City–John Lennon Yoko Ono/The Ballad Of Bob Dylan/The Chicago Conspiracy/The Hip Generation/I'm Gonna Start Another Riot/The Birth Control Blues/The Pope Smokes Dope
(Apple SW 3391) April 1972

ELEPHANT'S MEMORY by Elephant's Memory
Album produced by Lennon, who also appears on several tracks. Same tracks as UK release.
(Apple SMAS 3389) September 1972

LIBERATION SPECIAL/MADNESS by Elephant's Memory
Both sides produced by Lennon.
(Apple 1854) November 1972

NOW OR NEVER/MOVE ON FAST by Yoko Ono
Both sides produced by Lennon.
(Apple 1853) November 1972

LIBERATION SPECIAL/POWER BOOGIE by Elephant's Memory
Both sides produced by Lennon.
(Apple 1854) December 1972

APPROXIMATELY INFINITE UNIVERSE by Yoko Ono
Album produced by Lennon, who also appears on two tracks. Same tracks as UK release.
(Apple SVBB 3399) January 1973

DEATH OF SAMANTHA/YANG YANG by Yoko Ono
Both sides produced by Lennon.
(Apple 1859) February 1973

WOMAN POWER/MEN MEN MEN by Yoko Ono
Lennon appears on both sides.
(Apple 1865) September 1973

FEELING THE SPACE by Yoko Ono
Lennon appears on three tracks, as on UK release.
(Apple SW 3412) November 1973

RINGO by Ringo Starr
Lennon wrote and appears on I'm The Greatest.
(Apple SWAL 3413) November 1973

MANY RIVERS TO CROSS/DON'T FORGET ME by Harry Nilsson
Both sides produced by Lennon.
(RCA PB 10001) July 1974

PUSSY CATS by Harry Nilsson
Album produced by Lennon. Same tracks as UK release.

(RCA CPL 1-0570) August 1974

SUBTERRANEAN HOMESICK BLUES/MUCHO MUNGO; MT. ELBA by Harry Nilsson
Both sides produced by Lennon, who also co-wrote B- side.
(RCA PB 10078) October 1974

ONLY YOU by Ringo Starr
Lennon appears on A-side.
(Apple 1876) November 1974

GOODNIGHT VIENNA by Ringo Starr
Lennon appears on Only You and title track, co-writing the latter.
(Apple SW 3417) November 1974

LUCY IN THE SKY WITH DIAMONDS/ONE DAY AT A TIME by Elton John
Lennon wrote and appears on both sides.
(MCA 40344) November 1974

JOHN DAWSON WINTER III by Johnny Winter
Lennon wrote Rock And Roll People.
(Blue Sky PZ 33292) November 1974

LOOP DE LOOP/DON'T FORGET ME by Harry Nilsson
Both sides produced by Lennon.
(RCA PB 10139) December 1974

I SAW HER STANDING THERE by Elton John Band

B-side features Lennon.
(MCA 40364) February 1975

YOUNG AMERICANS by David Bowie
Lennon appears on Across The Universe and Fame, both of which he wrote or co-wrote.
(RCA APL 1-0998) March 1975

GOODNIGHT VIENNA by Ringo Starr
Lennon wrote and appears on A-side.
(Apple 1882) June 1975

FAME by David Bowie
Lennon co-wrote and appears on A-side.
(RCA JB 10320) June 1975

RINGO'S ROTOGRAVURE by Ringo Starr
Lennon wrote and appears on Cookin'.
(Atlantic SD 18193) September 1976

WALKING ON THIN ICE/IT HAPPENED by Yoko Ono
Lennon produced and appeared on both sides.
(Geffen GEF 49683) February 1981

IT'S ALRIGHT by Yoko Ono
Never Say Goodbye features Lennon vocal.
(Polydor PD-1-6364) November 1982

NEVER SAY GOODBYE by Yoko Ono
A-side features Lennon vocal.
(Polydor 810 556-7) January 1983

INDEX

INDEX